The Experts' Book of the Shooting Sports

Edited by DAVID E. PETZAL

AMERICA'S FOREMOST
SHOOTING AND HUNTING EXPERTS
DISCLOSE THE SECRETS OF
THEIR SPECIALTIES

A CORD COMMUNICATIONS BOOK □
SIMON AND SCHUSTER
NEW YORK   1972

First printing
SBN 671-21328-8
Library of Congress Catalog Card Number: 72-83904
Designed by Jack Jaget
Manufactured in the United States of America
By H. Wolff Book Mfg. Co., Inc., New York, N.Y.

ACKNOWLEDGMENTS

I would like to extend my thanks to the following people for their help in the creation of this book: Mel Bookstein, for much hard work in its planning and editing; Warren Page, for his excellent advice; Arlene Taylor, who handled the voluminous correspondence necessary and, on more than one occasion, corrected my grammar for me—and Griffin & Howe, who insist on being paid for their work and provided me with the incentive to undertake the job. The photographs, unless specifically credited, are the property of the various authors.

To my fellow shooters—with whom I have shivered in duck blinds and on deer stands, cursed departing (and unbroken) clay targets and been scared witless by the booming flight of uncooperative grouse—this book is dedicated.

CONTENTS

HANDGUN SHOOTING

SHOTGUN SHOOTING

HELPFUL HINTS AND INTERESTING MISCELLANY

     BY PETE BROWN   251
15   Custom Guns
     BY JOHN AMBER   267
16   Care, Cleaning and Repair
     BY DAVID E. PETZAL   280

     About the Authors   293

     Index   297

THE TERM "shooting sports" encompasses a range of activities so diverse that their only common denominator is the involvement of firearms. These sports are as unlike one another as are American professional football, basketball and baseball—all of which employ a ball. Each of the shooting sports requires specialized equipment and, what is more important, specialized knowledge. The waterfowl hunters who take up competitive rifle shooting or the trapshooters who want to hunt big game will have a hard time of it unless they have someone to guide them as they take their first steps.

Some of the men who have contributed to this volume are highly proficient in many aspects of shooting. Each, however, is especially skilled in one particular phase. Warren Page, for instance, holds many bench-rest championships, but his expertise as a hunter of big game is second to none. Dick Baldwin, in his turn, is an upland hunter of no mean accomplishment, but a list of the honors he has won at trapshooting would fill several of these pages. Each contributor to this book has excelled in one particular field above all others and has here distilled his experience for the benefit of those who wish to follow.

As this is written, the subjects of gun control and hunting are— no pun intended—explosive issues to many people. Hunters in particular have come in for a large share of the brickbats. The collection of antihunting hate letters received by the shooting editor of one major outdoor magazine is a study in ignorance, hysteria, viciousness and, one suspects from some of them, mental illness.

The question then arises, why take up a sport that requires a gun? The answer is simple: a challenge is involved. This challenge can come in two forms: it can be that of outscoring one's competitors on a target range or that of outwitting a bird or animal. Let's look at each in turn, starting with man versus target.

Those who would bring home trophies won with a rifle, pistol or shotgun should know that they have a hard road ahead of them. The demands on a competitor are prodigious. It is not enough to spend an occasional weekend in practice; devoting hours every day, every week, every month is more realistic. Techniques must be honed to perfection, and kept there. If you can't concentrate, or can't withstand tremendous pressure, or can't stay unrattled when things go wrong, you are whipped before you start. For example, at one running of the National Skeet Championships, two men broke 1,050 targets apiece without a miss before they were declared co-champions. To help you gauge the magnitude of this feat, an average good shotgunner is more than happy to break 25 straight.

It is worth noting that many of those who pursue target shooting most seriously are not hunters. Their particular pastime leaves room for no other. This leads to some peculiar attitudes. I know of clay-target shooters who look askance at hunters, and many hunters look with disdain at those whose "birds" are made of pitch.

It is also worth noting that competitive shooting in all its forms is among the safest of sports. By comparison, taking a spin in your car is suicidal. There have been possibly a billion shots fired in clay-bird competition without a single fatality. Football costs lives every season; racing drivers are incinerated yearly; swimmers drown; the catalogue of tragedies that started as sport could go on. Shooting, which uses deadly weapons as its basis—but which observes safety procedures with a vengeance—is about as dangerous as croquet.

The challenge offered to a hunter is different. He must pit himself against nature and against the superior senses (and, some say, intelligence) of an animal. There is a popular notion among those who have never hunted that a man who walks into the fields or woods with a gun is automatically assured of a full bag, by virtue of simple technological superiority. These uninformed souls have never beheld the spectacle of modern man attempting to outwit a wild creature in its own element. The statistics tell the story: in most states, a hunter-success ratio of 25 per cent is considered excellent. To put it more graphically, imagine how a deer would fare if turned loose in the middle of New York City. This gives you some idea of what the average urban man faces when he takes up the hunter's calling.

Lack of success is not the only potentially discouraging factor for the nimrod. It is guaranteed that he will be cold, hot, exhausted or all three in turn. Sometimes these hardships are minor; sometimes they are not. A world-renowned California big-game hunter recently went on an expedition to Mongolia. The object of the hunt was a rare wild sheep. He collected his trophy, but at the cost of $50,000 in expenses, plus two weeks in the hospital spent recuperating from malnutrition, exhaustion and exposure. Some hunters follow their sport to the death. There are graveyards in Alaska and Kenya where the bones of hunters lie, victims of carelessness or bad luck.

Yet men continue to hunt—more than 15 million in the United States alone. If you seek one single answer why, you will not find it here. There are probably nearly as many answers as there are men who go afield in search of game. I am sure that one reason they do not go is to kill something for the sake of watching it die; they do not enjoy death as such. However, they recognize that what is to be eaten must first be deprived of life, be it a barnyard chicken or a beef steer or a whitetail buck. Killing something is the logical end of the sport; it is not the object—at least for the person worthy of the title "sportsman."

It is one of the ironies of our time that the staunchest ally of wildlife—the hunter—is labeled as the exterminator of species, the layer-to-waste of the world's fauna. The truth is that without the time, energy, interest and money invested by hunters, there would be far fewer wild animals and birds than there are today. A case in point is an organization of sportsmen—hunters, if you will—known as Ducks Unlimited. This group was formed in the 1930s, when a succession of terrible droughts dried up the marshlands of the Canadian plains where most of North America's wildfowl breed. Without water, the ducks and geese perished by the millions. American and Canadian sportsmen—hunters, if you will—contributed the money to create the wetlands that saved the birds and that continue to foster their proliferation. No one else cared enough.

Any damage done to wildlife by sport hunting pales beside the havoc wrought by pollution and the loss of wild land to the bulldozer. We do not have the will to stop the fouling of our own environment. It would cost the taxpayer money—too much money, and heaven knows he is burdened enough. Were we to stop hunting—stop the flow of money that proceeds from hunting-license sales into the work of foresters, biologists and wildlife departments—who would foot the bill to keep the deer and pheasant alive? The animal-loving public-at-large? Don't kid yourself. That would take money, and what politician would dare ask a tax increase to ensure the welfare of a bunch of animals? Hunters pursue and kill living things, but they also preserve and protect them. No one else cares enough.

I said earlier that there was no simple answer to the question of why men hunt, but perhaps I was wrong. There is a passage from a book called *Killers in Africa*, written by a white hunter, Alexander Lake, that states the answer very well. Speaking of Nicobar Jones, an expatriate American hunter who was his tutor, Lake wrote:

He saw beauty everywhere. I've seen him stand watching a flowing arc of leaping springbok [impala], muttering "Purty! Purty!" until the last of the herd had disappeared, then plod back to camp, meatless and hungry. Everything in Africa was "purty" to Jones—the sky, the veld, the forest, morning and night, noonday and sunset, rain and wind, a loping lion, a galloping giraffe—everything.

That says it pretty well, and I think most hunters would agree with Nicobar Jones.

DAVID E. PETZAL

New York City
April, 1972

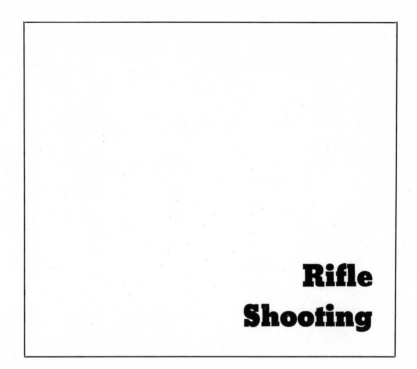

Rifle
Shooting

1

RIFLE
TARGET SHOOTING

BY GARY ANDERSON

MANY OF TODAY's sports trace their ancestry to a survival or combat skill. Probably the first reason man wanted to run fast was in order to catch something to eat—or in order to escape something that wanted to eat him. Man threw the javelin or spear to kill his prey or help him fight his battles. Wrestling and boxing began as ancient combat skills. Fencing was first of all a martial skill. Even team sports like soccer and football probably had their origins in military battle tactics.

Most sports we know today did not begin as games—their original purpose was deadly serious. But slowly, as man gained control of his environment and had more leisure time, he sublimated these survival and combat skills into sports, which serve an entirely different purpose. Now he participates in sports because he wants an interesting and relaxing recreation or because he enjoys competition and the thrill of trying to be best at something.

The only difference between target shooting and any other sport is that target shooting is much less removed from its ancestry. Many men all over the world still vividly remember how their own military training emphasized skill with their individual rifle or pistol. A few even remember how their ability to use that weapon kept them alive. And the day is not too long past when a man's skill with a rifle or shotgun decided whether his family would have meat on the table.

The sport of target shooting is still so close to its heritage that many target competitors began because they wanted to improve their hunting proficiency or because the scarcity of game and the pressures of urbanization did not give them enough satisfying opportunities to use their shooting skills. Target shooting is also an important part of today's military training. Many of the best target shooters are military men who chose target competition because this was the best way to improve their ability to use their combat rifle or pistol. Many junior rifle clubs in the United States receive .22-caliber rifles and ammunition from the government through the training program of the National Board for the Promotion of Rifle Practice because small-bore-target-rifle training has been proved an invaluable way of preparing young people for the probability of military service that lies ahead of them.

Shooting does have much closer ties to the survival and combat skills that created it, but the real reasons people engage in target shooting are the same reasons people participate in any sport. It offers relaxation and enjoyment. It offers everything from friendly competition to prestigious Olympic and international championships. The first thing that must be said about target shooting, then, is that it is not primarily military training or hunting practice. It is, first of all, a recreational and competitive sport.

Target shooting is one of the safest of all sports. Records kept by the National Rifle Association, the governing body of target rifle shooting in the United States, show that accidents in properly supervised target-shooting activities are practically nonexistent. The reason for this enviable safety record is the strict safety discipline practiced on all ranges. The first phase of training for a marksman is always safety training. The rules of the range are strict and rigidly enforced. Among these, the cardinal rule of all target ranges is always to keep the rifle action open except when the shooter is actually on the firing line and the range officer has given the command to load and start firing. Violation of this rule is the worst sin a shooter can commit.

Not only is target shooting one of the safest sports; it is also

Gary Anderson is shown here holding a target air rifle, used for 10-meter competition in the standing position. This is a highly sophisticated arm, capable of great accuracy.

one of the world's most popular sports. Ninety-two nations belong to the International Shooting Union, the governing body of target shooting in the world. In the Olympic Games, only track and boxing attract more participating nations than shooting. The 50-meter prone rifle match traditionally has more participants than any other Olympic event. There are an estimated 25.5 million target shooters in the world. Basketball, volleyball and soccer are probably the only sports that can claim more adherents than that on a worldwide scale.

Here in the United States, shooting has not yet achieved mass popularity as it has in Switzerland, Germany, the Soviet Union and Scandinavia, but the U.S.A. does have approximately 75,000 rifle shooters. Target shooting, moreover, appears destined for rapid growth here because of the changes brought about in our country by increasing population, urbanization and a declining supply of game.

One of the special advantages of target shooting as a competitive or recreational sport is that, unlike many sports that require great speed, strength or size for success, shooting is open to practically anyone. All that is required is a strong interest. Great physical strength is not needed. Women have often been quite successful in shooting because of this. One of the greatest rifle

shooters of all time has been Margaret Thomson Murdock, a
young American. Keen eyesight is not important either, and many
of the best shooters wear glasses. But to rise to the top ranks of
competitive marksmen, good physical condition, a high degree
of muscular and nervous control and tremendous motivation are
required.

The objective of target shooting is to hit the center of a paper
target as many times as possible during a particular event, or
course of fire. With the exception of the 1,000-yard high-power
target, all rifle targets now allow a maximum of 10 points for
each shot. The target's scoring rings decrease in value as they
become larger, down to 5 points on some targets and as low as
1 point on the ISU (International Shooting Union) targets.
Shots outside the scoring rings are scored as misses. In scoring,
when any portion of the bullet hole touches or breaks a scoring
ring it is given the higher value. The size of the scoring rings depends on the distance and the kind of event being fired. For example, the 10 ring on the 10-meter air-rifle target is only a 1-mm
dot, while the smallest ring on the 1,000-yard high-power-rifle
target is 36 inches in diameter. The most difficult targets are
those used in international matches. Their 10 rings cover just
over one minute of angle, which is smaller than the accuracy potential of all but the best rifles.

In addition to different targets and distances, the various competitive rifle events can also be described by the kind of rifle
used, its caliber, the position, the aiming equipment employed
and whether the firing is slow or rapid. Rifle events range from
purely recreational or fun shooting to the intensely competitive
ISU events. There are so many different kinds of rifle events that
practically anyone can find a form of shooting that appeals to
him. But before this choice can be made, it is necessary to have a
basic understanding of the competition positions and fundamental techniques of rifle shooting.

TARGET RIFLE POSITIONS

There are four competition positions: prone, kneeling, standing
and sitting. Of these, prone, kneeling and standing are interna-
tionally recognized and are used by all shooting nations. The

sitting position is uniquely American and is now commonly used in our country only for military- and high-power-rifle shooting.

Of the four positions, prone is the steadiest. A good prone position is so solid that the competitor must use an extremely accurate, highly tuned rifle with carefully selected ammunition to be a consistent prone-match winner. When a good prone shooter puts a telescope on his rifle, he will often be able to hold the cross hairs on a bullet hole at 50 or 100 yards. The important features of the prone position are:

The body lies straight, almost directly behind the rifle, with only a 10-to-20-degree angle between the body and the direction of fire.

The body is rolled slightly onto the left side with the left heel pointing up and the right toe out to the right. Sometimes the right knee is also bent and drawn up.

The right shoulder is higher than the left shoulder.

The weight of the rifle and upper torso is supported by both elbows, with about 80 per cent of this weight on the left elbow.

The left arm should be a straight-line extension of the left leg and

The prone position, as demonstrated by a junior marksman with the standard ISU rifle. Note that the right hand grips the rifle as in a firm handshake, and that both eyes are open.

The low kneeling position, in which the shooter sits on the side of his foot, is slowly gaining popularity.

left side of the body. The left elbow is positioned 1 to 1½ inches left of a point directly underneath the rifle.

The rifle is high enough to keep the back of the left hand 6 to 8 inches off the ground.

The sling, and not the muscles of the left arm, supports all the weight of the rifle.

The right wrist is kept straight. The right hand grips the rifle as in a firm handshake.

The head drops naturally and comfortably to the stock without any strain to force it forward, backward or to the side.

Kneeling is probably the hardest position to learn because the best position for any shooter is so dependent on the proportions of his arm, leg and torso lengths. Many shooters do no better kneeling than standing because of their difficulty in finding the proper position. On the other hand, a good kneeling position is often as steady as prone.

There are two basic kneeling positions. One is called the high kneeling position. Here, the shooter sits on the back of his right heel. He provides support for his foot by placing a kneeling roll 4 to 6 inches in diameter under his ankle. In the low kneeling position, the shooter sits on the inside of his right foot. The choice between the two depends on each particular shooter's body proportions. If his torso is long or his arms and legs are short, the low kneeling is better. If his legs and arms are long or his torso is short, the high position is better. Some shooters may be forced to use the high position simply because they cannot turn their right foot in far enough to be able to sit comfortably on the side of it. Once the choice between the high and low positions is made, the fundamentals of the kneeling position apply equally to both:

The shooter sits with as much body weight as possible resting on the right heel or foot.

The shoulders are rolled forward and the back is bowed out in an attempt to let the body weight slump down.

The position is turned so that the right knee points approximately 45 degrees away from the target.

The left knee is placed in front of the body so that it points toward the target.

In the high position, the left lower leg is perpendicular to the ground. In the low position, the foot is farther forward and the lower leg forms a 45-degree angle with the ground.

This is Victor Konyakhin of the U.S.S.R., world small-bore kneeling champion in 1966, in the high position, using a kneeling roll.

After the left leg is placed and the body is slumped into position, the left elbow is allowed to rest on the left knee wherever it falls. This may be ahead of, behind or on top of the knee.

The height of the rifle is determined by where on the forearm the left hand supports the rifle.

The sling, and not the muscles of the left arm, supports the rifle.

The head drops down only slightly as it contacts the cheekpiece. The head position is comfortable and unstrained.

The right arm is held out away from the body at about a 45-degree angle.

The standing position is the most important in rifle shooting because it is the most difficult position in which to shoot high scores. Most top shooters spend as much time training in standing as in all the other positions combined. The important standing-position features are:

The feet are placed approximately shoulder width apart and are pointed 90 degrees away from the target. The toes may be spread out slightly.

The weight of the body and rifle is distributed equally on both feet. Both knees are kept straight.

The standing position, posed with a scoped small-bore gallery rifle. The left wrist is kept straight and the left arm is rested on the side of the body. Ideally, the right elbow should be higher to form more of a pocket for the butt of the gun.

The body is not erect. The upper body and shoulders are bent back and to the right, away from the weight of the rifle and target.

The left arm supports the weight of the rifle. The elbow or upper arm is rested on the left hip or side with the elbow directly under the rifle.

The left arm and shoulder are totally relaxed.

The right elbow extends horizontally (as far as is comfortable) from the body. The right arm pulls the rifle back into the shoulder slightly.

The rifle is placed high enough on the shoulder so that the shooter need tip his head down only slightly to see through the sights.

The left hand supports the rifle just ahead of the trigger guard.

In standing, the elevation of the muzzle needed to point at the target is controlled by the left-hand position or, in the case of a free rifle, by the use of a palm rest. If a palm rest is used, its grip rests on the ball of the left thumb or the heel of the hand. This grip is usually placed behind the balance point of the rifle to make it muzzle-heavy. Muzzle elevation is controlled by upward or downward adjustment of the palm rest until holding the rifle places no strain on the back.

When a palm rest is not used and the forearm of the rifle rests directly on the left hand, the height of the rifle is controlled by the hand position. The best hand positions are listed here in order of increasing height. If the lowest position does not raise the rifle to target height, the next-higher position is tried. The wrist is always kept straight in these hand positions. These are the left-hand positions for standing:

The rifle rests in the V formed by the thumb and hand.

The rifle rests on top of the closed fist.

The rifle is supported between the thumb and first knuckle.

The rifle is supported by the thumb and a V formed by the first two or second and third fingers.

The rifle is supported on the thumb and second knuckle.

Military- or high-power-rifle shooters and small-bore position shooters living in some areas of the country also compete in the sitting position. Sitting is an awkward position for a short-armed junior, but for the adult it is relatively easy to learn. As in kneel-

The cross-ankled and cross-legged (shown here) sitting positions are extremely steady. You can see the relaxed position of the shooter's left hand; the rifle's forearm is supported by the palm.

ing, finding the proper position is the key. Three variations of the sitting position are commonly taught. These are the open-legged sitting, with the shooter's feet spread and extending forward; the cross-legged sitting, with the ankles crossed and drawn back close to the shooter's body; and the cross-ankled sitting, with the ankles crossed and legs extended forward. In the cross-legged sitting, the two elbows are rested in Vs formed by the folded legs. In the other two sitting positions, the elbows are rested on the legs ahead of the knees.

Of the three sitting positions, open-legged sitting is the least stable and is used only as a last resort. The choice between the cross-legged and cross-ankled positions depends on body proportions. Shooters with a long torso or short arms generally use the cross-ankled position. Shooters with a short torso or long arms do best with the cross-legged sitting.

In sitting, the body is turned 30 to 60 degrees away from the target. The torso leans quite far forward, and the legs are allowed to relax; they are not lifted to support the body and rifle. The left hand must be placed farther back on the forearm of the rifle than in either prone or kneeling. The sling is also adjusted shorter in sitting. It is important to find a sitting position in which the eye can look through the sights with only a slight downward tilt to the head. If the head must be tipped down too far, it is best to raise the rifle by pulling the left hand back and shortening the sling or by trying a different variation of the position.

TARGET RIFLE TECHNIQUES

In addition to knowing the shooting positions, every target rifle shooter must also master the fundamental techniques of rifle marksmanship. Applying each one of them is essential for good scores in any target rifle event. Some of these techniques are used to build better, more stable positions. They include:

Bone Support. One of the paramount rules for developing any position is that whenever possible, bones and ligaments instead of muscles should be used to support the body and rifle in position. For example, the left elbow, in each of the positions, is located so that the weight of the rifle falls directly on the elbow. In kneeling, the left lower leg is placed so that the weight of the rifle falls along a plane that coincides with the bone of the lower leg. The advantage of bone support over muscle support explains why it is so much better to rest the left arm on the hip or side than to hold the arm away from the body and support the rifle with muscles.

In some cases bone support is not possible, but ligaments are still used to avoid having muscles do the work of supporting the rifle or body. This is why, for example, the back is bent rearward and to the right in standing and the shoulders are bowed forward in kneeling. In an erect position the muscles of the back must keep the spine rigid, but if the spine is allowed to bend, the ligaments of the back will hold it in its curved position and minimize the muscle activity that makes the position so unsteady.

Sling Support. The sling is not very useful in standing, but it is always used by target shooters in prone, kneeling and sitting. It is adjusted so that it, and not the muscles of the left arm, does all the work of supporting the rifle. The sling is placed either high or low on the arm, but not in the middle of the arm. The sling must be fastened so that it does not slip down during firing. Most shooters try to have the main pull of the sling be from the outside of the arm.

The best way to adjust the sling initially is first to get into position without it. Once the body is in the correct position and the left hand is so placed on the forearm that it holds the rifle at the proper height, the sling can be fastened to the arm and tightened until it takes over the work of holding up the rifle.

Muscle Control. Even with perfect bone, ligament and sling support, no position can support itself without the help of muscles. While the muscles should not do any direct supporting, they do perform important tasks in controlling the work of the bones and ligaments as they support the body and rifle. A few muscles are completely relaxed. A conscious effort must be made to relax the muscles of the left shoulder, arm and hand, in particular. Other muscles—such as the leg muscles in standing, the back and stomach muscles in kneeling and the muscles of the right arm in each position—should be lightly tensed in order to control the movements of the body and rifle. Great muscular strength is never necessary for shooting, but precise muscular control is always needed.

Balance. Balance is one of the keys to building a steady position. In determining whether a position is balanced, the body and rifle are thought of as one unit. The center of gravity of this unit—the downward force of its weight—should be directly over the support surfaces of the position. The support surfaces for prone are both elbows and the lower body; for sitting, both feet and the buttocks; for kneeling, the left foot, right knee and right foot (with or without kneeling roll); and for standing, the two feet. If the weight of the body/rifle unit is not balanced above these support surfaces, then muscles must be used to compensate for the unbalanced position and the rifle movements are much greater. The reason shooters bend back away from the rifle in standing, for example, is to counterbalance the weight of the rifle over the feet.

There are other basic techniques involved when a shooter fires a shot. It is best to think of these actions or techniques in the sequence in which they occur. They include:

Breathing. Practically every shooter knows he must hold his breath while attempting to fire a shot. If he continued to breathe while aiming at the target, the rifle would never stop moving. Most target shooters control their breathing by continuing to breathe naturally until just before starting to aim at the bull. At this point, the breath is allowed to exhale normally. At the end of normal exhalation, the breath is held. Even in this relaxed condition, the lungs still hold ample oxygen for the six to ten seconds it takes to fire a shot.

Aiming. In aiming, the shooter attempts to align his sights with the aiming bull so that, if they are properly adjusted, the bullet will hit the 10 ring. There are two basic phases to aiming, sight alignment and sight picture.

Sight alignment refers to centering the front sight in the middle of the rear peephole or aperture. Most target rifles have a hooded front sight. To align the sights, the shooter centers the entire front sight in the rear one. If there is no front-sight hood, as is the case with the service rifle and some junior-grade rifles, the top of the front-sight post is centered. When a telescope is used, no sight alignment is necessary, of course, since slight misalignments of the eye behind the scope do not move the cross hairs.

The second phase of aiming, sight picture, refers to the proper relationship between the aligned sights and the aiming bull, or target. With iron sights, there are two types of front sight or front-sight inserts suitable for target shooting. They are the ring, or aperture, and the square-topped post. For the proper sight picture with the ring, the bull is simply centered in the middle of the ring. The square-topped post is held at the very bottom of the bull. The proper sight picture with the post looks like a ball sitting on a fence post. Advanced shooters always try to maintain a small gap, or "line of white," between the top of the post and the bottom of the bull. The proper sight picture for a telescope sight is the cross hairs or dot intersecting the center of the 10 or X ring.

Hold Concentration. Shooters often want to know, "What should I think about when I fire a shot?" The answer is that the shooter should think about holding the rifle steady. As he aims, he sees how the rifle is moving. The most important factor in firing a good shot is concentrating on these movements, consciously trying to make them smaller and keeping them centered on the bull.

Trigger Control. More bad shots in rifle shooting stem from poor trigger control than from any other cause. The worst trigger-control mistakes occur when the shooter tries to make a perfect shot but is not holding the rifle steady enough. When he does not hold steady enough to fire perfect shots, he tries to jerk the trigger very quickly at the instant a perfect sight picture occurs. When he jerks the trigger, the rifle has already started to move away from the 10 ring, and the violent motion of the trigger finger makes things worse by pushing the rifle farther away from its aim.

A shooter applies proper trigger control by concentrating on the hold and slowly squeezing the trigger all the time the hold is centered. As long as the hold or wobble area is centered, small hold movements will be much less costly than jerking the trigger in an attempt to "grab" a perfect shot. The trigger squeeze may last from two to six seconds, depending on how steady the position is and how difficult it is to keep the wobble area centered. As skill in trigger control is improved, squeezing the trigger should become a semi- or subconscious action while primary attention always remains on hold concentration.

Calling the Shot and *Follow-Through.* At the instant the shot is fired, a visual photo of the sight picture is taken. This visual image, or "call," tells the shooter almost exactly how far off center and in what direction his bullet should strike. If the shot does not go where it is called, it means the rifle was not sighted in or that a mistake in wind doping or trigger control was made.

Because there is a delay between the release of the trigger and the exit of the bullet from the barrel, the shooter has to follow through. That is, he must continue to concentrate on holding the rifle steady until the shot leaves the barrel and the recoil jump begins.

The final rifle marksmanship techniques affect those things a shooter does to make sure his shots go where he calls them. The most important of these techniques are:

Sight Adjustment. The sights on any rifle must always be adjusted so that the shots go exactly where they are aimed or called.

Except under rapidly changing wind conditions when a telescope is used, a shooter never compensates for the off-call shots by holding over; he does so by moving the sights. All good target sights have elevation and windage knobs that are marked according to the direction in which the strike of the bullet will be moved on the target. Even good target shooters must pay careful attention to where their groups are forming to make sure the sights are perfectly centered.

Wind Doping. Small changes in wind velocity or direction are enough to move a shot that would be a 10 into the 9 or even 8 ring on most rifle targets. Each shooter has to learn to "read" the wind by observing the flags on the range, mirage movements in his spotting scope and other clues like tree and grass movements or dust blowing behind the target. Through experience he learns how much these wind changes are worth. To compensate for wind, the shooter may either adjust the windage on the sight to the degree he estimates as necessary or wait until the wind changes back to a preselected average condition.

Weather Control. Other external elements like temperature, mirage, light and altitude also affect the strike of the bullet or how the shooter aims. Higher temperatures make the bullet go higher. Mirage optically displaces the target in the direction in which it is moving. Light affects the way a shooter sees his aiming bull and often its clarity. A shooter traveling to take part in a match at a higher altitude would find his sight adjustments from his home range too high. Most of these effects are small, but becoming a good shooter depends on applying techniques that improve every small detail that affects the score.

TARGET RIFLE EVENTS

A dozen different rifle-competition events are available to shooters in the United States. They are designed to appeal to the wide variety of shooting interests American marksmen have. These different events are categorized as international, national/recreational and military competitions, according to their purposes and objectives. International shooting events are governed by rules of the International Shooting Union. They include Olympic Games shooting events, World Shooting Championships, Pan-

American Games shooting events, matches between the national teams of different countries and, in the United States, national, regional, state and local championships. These are the most serious and demanding of all shooting events. International competitors have to spend thousands of hours in serious, dedicated training and live the life of a totally committed athlete. But the tremendous effort required of these competitors pays handsome dividends. Victories won in international events are the most important of all shooting awards. International rifle events include:

50-Meter Three-Position. This is the so-called small-bore free-rifle match. It is fired at 50 meters on a target with a 10 ring only .48 inch in diameter. The 50-meter ISU target has now been proportionately reduced for indoor firing at 50 feet in American competition as well. This reduced international target is the basis for all of our intercollegiate competition as well as major segments of our junior and open indoor championships. The standard course of fire in 50-meter three-position shooting is 40 shots each in prone, standing and kneeling. Time limits are liberal, and a wide variety of equipment is permitted. The rifle may weigh as much as 17.6 pounds and can have such special accessories as a hook butt plate, thumbhole stock, set trigger and palm rest. Telescopic sights are not permitted in international events.

50-Meter Standard-Rifle. This event is identical to the 50-meter three-position event except for limitations placed on the rifle, and a 60- instead of a 120-shot course of fire. The standard rifle cannot weigh more than 11 pounds and cannot have any free-rifle accessories like the hook butt plate, thumbhole stock, set trigger or palm rest.

50-Meter Prone. The course of fire in this event is 60 shots prone. Target and equipment rules are identical to 50-meter three-position rules.

300-Meter Free-Rifle. This is the oldest and most prestigious of all shooting events. It has been a world championship and Olympic event since the start of the World Shooting Championships at Lyon, France, in 1897. At the 300-meter distance, the 10 ring is 3.9 inches in diameter, or just over one minute of angle. The course of fire is the same as in the 50-meter three-position event. The rifles are also the same, except, of course, that they are centerfire rather than rimfire. Any caliber up to 8 mm may be used, but the two most popular are the 7.62 NATO or .308 Winchester and the 7.62-mm Russian.

Air-Rifle. Air-rifle is a new event in international competition. It traces its development to restrictions against manufacture of powder-burning firearms in postwar Germany and to its booming popularity in Western Europe. Air rifles are identical in weight, balance and design to standard rifles. They are highly accurate and capable of minute-of-angle accuracy at short ranges when match rifles and pellets are used. Air-rifle competition is conducted only in the standing position at 10 meters. The target has a tiny 1-mm dot for a 10 ring.

The rifle-shooting events conducted exclusively in the United States can be categorized as national/recreational events. They are designed to provide exciting and fulfilling recreational opportunities to large numbers of shooters who participate primarily for fun. In contrast to the international rifle shooter, who must be a highly dedicated athlete, the national/recreational participant is typically a weekend shooter who regards his competition as a hobby. Many of these events require less training time for championship proficiency. Many also place a higher emphasis on equipment and ammunition quality than on marksmanship. These events include:

Small-Bore Gallery. This is the most popular rifle event in the United States. It involves either three- or four-position shooting, indoors at 50 feet, on a target somewhat easier than the reduced international target. Most gallery shooting is done with 15-to-20-power telescopic sights. Either the .22 free rifle or a standard rifle may be used. This event forms the basis of our highly popular indoor winter league matches.

Small-Bore Outdoor Position. This is the same as small-bore 50-foot shooting except that it is done outdoors at 50 yards. It has not achieved wide popularity because of its conflict with 50-meter three-position shooting.

Small-Bore Outdoor Prone. This is a perfectionists' game that places great emphasis on the scientific efforts of its adherents to achieve maximum accuracy from small-bore rimfire rifles and ammunition. Small-bore prone is fired at distances of 50 yards, 50 meters and 100 yards. A 2-minute-of-angle 10 ring and 1-minute-of-angle X ring are used at 50 and 100 yards, while the 50-meter target is proportionately somewhat smaller. Prone-position matches usually have four 40-shot sessions with iron sights one day and four 40-shot sessions with scope sights the next day.

High-Power-Match-Rifle. This event traces its history to the National Match Course developed for military-rifle training, qualification and competition. High-power shooting has more variety than any other shooting event, with firing in prone, sitting and standing positions; rapid-fire and slow-fire shooting and short-range and long-range firing. The course of fire includes slow-fire standing at 200 yards, rapid-fire sitting at 200 yards, rapid-fire prone at 300 yards and slow-fire prone at 600 yards. The high-power target has a 7-inch 10 ring at 200 and 300 yards and a 12-inch 10 ring at 600 yards. Standard bolt-action rifles in .308 or .30/06 are used. The rifles must have a 3-pound trigger pull and cannot have special accessories like palm rests or hook butt plates. High-power-match-rifle shooters also must become highly skilled handloaders in order to produce the quality ammunition needed for this event.

High-Power Long-Range. This event is fired at 1,000 yards on the old military "C" target with its 36-inch bull. Thirty-caliber or 7-mm Magnum cartridges are generally used in order to moderate the great effect of wind at such extreme ranges. Firing is done in the prone position with either iron or telescopic sights. Although highly spectacular, this event has never attained great popularity because of the limited availability of 1,000-yard ranges and the high cost of the special magnum rifles.

Air-Rifle. The national air-rifle program in the United States is identical to the ISU air-rifle event except that American rules do not allow the use of a shooting jacket or glove. These restrictions were made to keep the cost of competitive air-rifle shooting as low as possible.

The third category of target rifle events is military competitions. These events were created for training and qualification purposes. Underlying the continued existence of target-shooting competitions for military rifles is the assumption that a highly trained rifle marksman is a more competent combat soldier.

Military-rifle shooting in the United States is done with M-1 and M-14 service rifles over the same courses of fire and at the same targets as high-power-match-rifle shooting. Service rifles and high-power match rifles are often found shooting side by side in the same match. Service-rifle shooting has been quite popular with many civilian shooters and clubs because of their interest in improving the general level of civilian military preparedness. One of the most prized of all American shooting honors, the Distinguished Rifleman's Badge, is awarded for outstanding competitive proficiency with the service rifle.

After a shooter develops an interest in a particular event, he needs to find a way to get started. The first step to take is to join a shooting club. Most shooting clubs in the United States have a program that covers most of our popular rifle events. Club membership offers access to a range and also instruction from accomplished match shooters. (If a local club cannot be found, the National Rifle Association should be contacted for a list of the nearest clubs and their officers.)

Most active target shooters are willing to lend a rifle and shooting jacket to a prospective competitor to give him a chance to find out if he likes the game. If interest is kindled, one of the important first steps in getting started is to obtain the right equipment. The items listed here are broken down into two categories. Equipment in the first category includes those things that are necessary for any target shooting. The second category includes those items that are not absolutely necessary and can be acquired as skill and interest continue to develop. The mandatory items of target-rifle equipment include:

Rifle. The kind of rifle selected depends on the event it is intended for as well as the level of proficiency the shooter hopes to attain. The various target rifles commercially available in the United States that are suitable for competition events are listed in the rifle chart on pages 42-43. These arms are grouped according to whether they are top-grade competition rifles or are intended for beginners and juniors. Since many of the best competitors use custom-made rifles, some features of custom target arms for events in which they are often used are also listed.

Rear Sight. A good click-adjustable aperture rear sight is a necessity for any kind of target shooting. Rifles manufactured in

Europe are always available with excellent factory sights, while American target rifles are available with Redfield sights which are also excellent. Target sights should have ¼- or ⅙-minute click adjustments for both elevation and windage. They should be fitted with an aperture disk with a .044- or .048-inch opening.

Front Sight. Except on service rifles and junior-grade target rifles, a hooded front sight with interchangeable inserts is used. A variety of both post and ring inserts come with the sight. The proper post size is one that appears to be the same width as or just slightly wider than the bull when it is in the front sight. Ring sizes can appear to be anywhere from 25 per cent to three times larger than the bull when they are used in aiming. Generally, the post is better when the hold is not as steady, while the ring is better for steady positions like prone.

Sling. A good leather sling is a must for shooting in the three lower positions. A simple leather strap 1¼ or 1½ inches wide with several adjustment holes is best. The sling should have a keeper or fastener to hold it in position on the arm. More expensive sling cuffs are available, but they offer no advantage over the simple strap.

Spotting Telescope. Ranges in Europe have the targets mounted on motorized carriers so that the target can be brought back to the firing line after every shot. In the United States, the targets are almost always left in position and shooters use a 20-to-30-power spotting scope to locate their bullet holes. Suitable spotting scopes range from $50 to $150 in price. The most expensive scopes are variable-power models. If indoor or outdoor high-power shooting is done, a less expensive 20-power glass will serve adequately. For small-bore prone and international shooting, a 25-to-30-power scope with excellent resolution is usually chosen. The spotting scope is an indispensable tool for reading mirage and wind changes as well as for spotting bullet holes.

Spotting-Scope Stand. A tripod or bipod stand is necessary to support the scope in such a way that the shooter can look at his target without moving out of his position. The stand should be one that can be dismantled for easy carrying. Position shooters will need a stand with extensions that permit the scope to be raised to kneeling- and standing-position heights.

Shooting Glove. A leather mitten or glove is worn to protect the left hand from the sling or to make the hand more comfortable when it is holding the rifle in standing. Commercial shooting gloves are available, but many shooters use ordinary leather mittens or gloves bought in work-clothing stores.

Shooting Jacket. The shooting jacket provides padding for the elbows and shoulder and protects the left arm from sling pressure. Fully acceptable cloth shooting jackets with rubber or leather pads are commercially available for about $25. The most serious national and international marksmen use special leather shooting jackets that cost about $100.

Ear Protectors. One of the minor disadvantages of shooting is that it is a noisy sport. Ear muffs or ear plugs are essential to protect the marksman from loss of hearing and should be worn during all shooting—including small-bore firing.

Cleaning Equipment. The only way the shooter can maintain the accuracy of a precision match-rifle barrel is to clean it after each day's firing. A one-piece plastic-covered cleaning rod, bristle brush, cleaning solvent and patches or cotton are the items needed to complete this task.

Ammunition. In most cases, ordinary hunting or plinking ammunition is not accurate enough for any kind of target shooting except informal practice. High-power-rifle competitors almost always use their own handloads in order to get the kind of quality ammunition they need, as well as to lower the cost of shooting. Small-bore shooters use standard-velocity .22 rimfire ammunition, while the top competitors use .22 match-grade cartridges. A target-rifle ammunition chart appears on page 43 to show the types of ammunition ordinarily used by competitors.

A rifle, ammunition, sights, sling, glove, jacket, spotting scope and stand, ear protectors and cleaning equipment are the necessary items for target-rifle shooting. There are many other pieces of gear, however, that are quite useful in the various rifle events. Many of these items are gradually accumulated by every serious rifle competitor. Optional items of target-rifle equipment include a kneeling roll, a shooting mat, shooting glasses, a cartridge block (small-bore), a rifle case, an adjustable rear-sight iris, a mirage band (centerfire), an equipment kit or shooting stool, a shooting cap, rear-sight filters, a scoring gauge, a scorebook or shooting diary and a target telescope.

Once a target-rifle shooter has obtained the necessary items of equipment and has mastered the shooting positions and fundamental techniques of rifle marksmanship, he is able to start enjoying his sport and developing his skill. The personal satisfaction that rifle shooting affords comes from both practice and competition.

A rifle shooter's practice may vary from the recreational shooter's Saturday-afternoon trip to the range to the three or four hours of daily training by the serious international marksman. But even the recreational shooter with limited time for practice has learned that there are certain practice rules that apply to all kinds of target-rifle training:

Regular short periods of practice are better than a few days with long practice sessions.

A greater percentage of time should be spent in the more difficult positions.

Good physical condition is a definite asset.

A careful record should be kept of all shooting, including informal practice. The bad scores are the most important to note.

Practice is more productive when done with a friend or fellow club members.

Some time should always be devoted to analyzing training or match results and to maintaining equipment.

The top shooters in the world have demonstrated how dedicated and involved marksmanship training can become when these simple training rules are applied to the objective of winning a world championship or Olympic gold medal. These shooters average four or five hours of rigorous training a day, six days a week, forty-eight to fifty weeks a year. Most of their training time is spent working on the more difficult standing and kneeling positions. They usually keep a detailed shooting diary of all their experiments and training experiences. Mental attitude is extremely important to them, and much of their training is spent trying to control their thinking and nervousness, which has such a tremendous effect on match scores. Physical condition is also very important to them. Most international champions run several miles a day to maintain top condition, and they also carefully control their diet. They do all this because they know rifle shooting is a sport in which the dedication and effort they apply in training is the one thing that determines how far they can go.

The ultimate test for any target shooter is his performance in competition. The recreational shooter has available to him matches that begin with club, local league and local championships and culminate in state, regional and national championships. The international shooter starts with local and regional championships and, if he does well enough to qualify, can try out for the United States team that will participate in an Olympic, world or Pan-American championship through our national championships for international-type shooting. To become a member of the team that represents this country in international competition is an honor reserved for only a few of our best marksmen.

Whether a target-rifle shooter succeeds in winning an Olympic gold medal or in merely improving his last score, he can still leave the range a winner, for he knows that as one of the world's great sports, shooting has given him a chance to enjoy his life more, as well as to experience the personal growth and development that comes from all sports participation.

TARGET-RIFLE SELECTION CHART

Event	Intermediate/Junior	Top-Grade Competition	Custom Features
50-meter three-position	none	Savage/Anschutz M1413 Finnish Lion Champion Hammerli M 506 Remington 40XB International Walther KKM Match Winchester 52 International	Custom thumb-hole stock, modified palm rest, glass bedding

50-meter standard-rifle	Savage/Anschutz Mk10
	Savage/Anschutz M64
	Remington M540-X
	Remington M513T (used)
	Winchester M75 (used)
	Mossberg M144-LS
		Savage/Anschutz 1407
		BSA International
		Remington 40XB
		  (standard barrel)
		Walther UIT
		Winchester 52D
		  (standard barrel)	

50-meter prone	see standard-rifle list
	  above
		Anschutz M1411
		BSA Mk III
		Remington 40XB
		  (heavy barrel)
		Winchester 52D
		  (heavy barrel)
			Custom stock, stainless-steel barrel, custom trigger

300-meter free-rifle	none	Hammerli-Tanner Lienhard-Anschutz Remington 40XB International Schultz-Larsen	Custom rifle on Remington 40X action, stainless barrel with 1–12 or 1–14 twist, fitted to take accessories from 50-meter free rifle

300-meter Army-rifle	none	Hammerli-Tanner
		Lienhard-Anschutz UIT
		  Standard
		Carl Gustaf M63
		Winchester M70
		  International Army	

Air-rifle	Savage/Anschutz M335 Winchester/Diana M435 Weirauch HW 50	Savage/Anschutz M250 Daisy/Feinwerkbau M300 Walther LGV Winchester/Diana M333 Weirauch HW 55	
Gallery-rifle Small-bore outdoor position	see 50-meter three-position and standard-rifle lists above		
Small-bore prone	see 50-meter prone list above		

Event	Intermediate/Junior	Top-Grade Competition	Custom Features
High-power-match-rifle	Springfield and Mauser service rifles and M722 Remington sporters modified for target use	Remington 40XB Winchester M70 Target	Custom rifle on M70 action (pre-1964 preferred), with 1–10 or 1–12 barrel twist
Service-rifle	none	M-1 National Match M-14 National Match (M-14 National Match not sold)	Glass bedding, accurization

AMMUNITION SELECTION CHART

Event	Training/Intermediate-Grade Ammunition	Match-Grade Ammunition
Small-bore	Peters Standard Velocity Remington Standard Velocity Western Xpert Winchester Leader Eley Rifle Club	Western Mark III Winchester EZXS Remington Match Peters Match Eley Tenex Eley Match RWS R50
300-meter international	none	Handloads with 168-grain Sierra or Hornady or 185-grain Lapua bullets
High-power-match 200 and 300 yards		Handloads with 168-grain Sierra or Hornady bullets
High-power-match 600 yards		Handloads with 185-grain Lapua or 190-grain Sierra or Hornady bullets
Service-rifle	government ball ammunition	Lake City National Match or handloads with 168-grain bullets
Air-rifle	Bimoco Match National Pellets	N & N Match (imported by Daisy) RWS Match (imported by Savage)

2

BENCH-REST
SHOOTING

BY JIM GILMORE

WAY BACK in the early 1930s, some long-forgotten gun nut envisioned a new approach to rifle competition. "Bench-rest," he dubbed it. And while he probably never intended it so, his efforts set into motion a snowballing series of technical triumphs which even today are shaping the shooting fortunes of sophisticated riflemen.

They call it the "pinnacle of precision," this crazy bench-rest game, and not without reason. It's a sport unlike any other, with a history of achievement that can hardly be ignored.

Competitive bench-rest shooters have historically been front-runners in the search for technological improvements. Their discoveries have predated the gun industry's by years, and have, in fact, been directly responsible for the development of better factory rifles, new and improved reloading tools and techniques and a more knowledgeable group of shooters in general.

But such successes are only spin-offs from the bench-rest game. Its real forte is promoting excellence in competition among riflemen from Maine to California.

Operating under sanction of the National Bench Rest Shooters Association, this dedicated group observes a detailed system of

regulations defining different classes of match rifles, standards for
match conduct and a universal system for recognizing world records.

Bench-rest marksmen shoot for group size, rather than score,
and matches are frequently won and lost by scant thousandths,
sometimes even ten-thousandths, of an inch.

The NBRSA approves competition for four classes of rifles:
Bench Rest rifles (sometimes called "unrestricted" guns), Heavy
Varmint rifles, Light Varmint rifles and Sporter rifles.

The Bench Rest "big guns" are by far the most impressive of
the lot, featuring just about all the inventiveness their shooters
can muster. As defined by NBRSA specs, a Bench Rest rifle is
simply: "Any rifle having a barrel 18 or more inches long, measured from the face of the (closed) bolt to the muzzle, and having
a safely operated firing mechanism." There are no limits on barrel
dimensions, scope power or supporting rests.

A typical Bench Rest rifle weighs 35 pounds, has a heavy custom action, sports a 28-inch "bull" barrel measuring a straight
1.350 inches in diameter and is mounted on precision mechanical
rests designed to return the rifle to the original point of aim after
each shot is fired.

Bench Rest-rifle specialists are generally considered the elite
of the game, but they also comprise its smallest segment. By far
the most popular class in NBRSA goings-on is the Heavy Varmint
division.

A Heavy Varmint rifle, the NBRSA says, is: "Any rifle having a
safe manually and mechanically operated firing mechanism,
weighing not more than 13½ pounds inclusive of sight."

The stock must have a flat or convex forearm with a total width
of not more than 3 inches. Barrels must be not less than 18 inches
long, with a maximum diameter of 1.250 inches 5 inches forward
of the face of the closed bolt. Diameter must not be greater at
any point than would be defined by a straight taper from a 1.250-
inch diameter 5 inches forward of the bolt face to a diameter of
.900 inch at the muzzle of a 29-inch barrel.

The barrel may be attached to the receiver, bedding blocks or
sleeve (or combination) for a distance of no more than 4 inches,
measured from the face of the closed bolt. Overall length of the
receiver, bedding blocks or sleeve (or combination) may not ex-

This rifle was built on an aluminum I-beam. It utilizes a Shilen barreled action and a 2-inch-objective Unertl scope. The barrel is gripped in a split steel block.

ceed 14 inches. (Maximum dimensions do not include scope blocks and sight bases.)

A Light Varmint rifle is any rifle weighing not more than 10½ pounds including sights, and otherwise meeting requirements of the Heavy Varmint class.

Sporter rifles must be not less than .23 caliber (6 mm, for all practical purposes) and otherwise meet requirements of the Light Varmint class. No scope limit is placed on any of the four classes.

Varmint rifles are fired from atop a pedestal rest on the front and a sandbag on the rear. The supports may not be attached to the bench, and each must be movable independently of the other.

The usual course of fire for Varmint-class rifles calls for five 5-shot groups at 100 yards and five 5-shot groups at 200 yards, with a warm-up match at the beginning of the tournament and usually before each successive range change. Groups are measured to the nearest thousandth of an inch by a modified vernier dial caliper with a magnifier and bullet-hole reticle. Aggregates (average of five record groups at each range) are scored in ten-thousandths of an inch. The 100-yard aggregate is the average of actual five-group measurements, while the 200-yard aggregate is divided by 2 so that the score may be expressed in minutes of angle. Grand aggregates (combination of aggregates at both 100 and 200 yards) are also scored in ten-thousandths of an inch and expressed in MOA.

In addition to the standard course of fire, NBRSA also sanctions 300-yard events and combination 200-yard/300-meter aggregates in all classes. Three-hundred-yard matches, however, are relatively few, simply because most clubs have facilities only for 100- and 200-yard events.

Each competitor's target card contains two targets—one sighter, at which he may fire as many shots as he wishes, and a record target, at which the official group is fired.

Bench Rest rifles use the same target as Varmint- and Sporter-class rifles, but follow a different course of fire. Matches through the regional level specify five 10-shot groups at each range (100 and 200 yards), while the National Match course calls for ten 10-shot groups at each range.

Varmint and Sporter riflemen are allotted seven minutes in which to complete their 5-shot record groups, while "big gun" shooters get an extra five minutes.

Since one-hole groups only slightly larger than the diameter of a bullet are commonplace in all classes of NBRSA competition, it's often impossible to determine simply by looking at a record target that a competitor did, in fact, fire the required number of shots.

To ensure against inadvertent 4-shot (or 9-shot) groups, a moving paper backing strip runs behind each competitor's record target. Powered by an electric motor and take-up reel, the strip moves about 1½ inches per minute, "widening" groups to ensure that all shots will be counted.

Failure to fire the required number of rounds results in disqualification. A shooter can also disqualify if he fires a shot outside the border of his record target. (The border on the official 100-yard target measures 3½ by 4¾ inches. The border on the 200-yard target is twice that size.)

The possibility of disqualification is only one of many potential nemeses a bench-rest shooter must contend with. Long before he begins to worry about missing the target, he must face what sometimes seem equally frustrating problems: deciding in which classes he wants to compete, and then selecting his equipment.

Since almost nobody begins in the Bench Rest-rifle class (newcomers generally consider it rather exotic), that option may be eliminated at once, leaving only three remaining choices. Among those, happily, there's only one logical category: Heavy Varmint.

Why? For several reasons. To begin with, the Heavy Varmint rifle is far and away the easiest to master. It's very forgiving when novice shooters make mistakes in their hold (by varying the amount of body contact with the rifle from shot to shot), it has the highest accuracy potential of all three classes because of the nature of its design (as a rule of thumb, more weight allowance means bigger barrels, better groups) and it's also the most popular in the organization, which in turn means there are more matches for Heavy Varmint rifles than for any other bracket. Match frequency is vital to the newcomer, because he needs all the practice he can get in actual competition.

Okay, so what about equipment?

The first question a potential new shooter usually asks is: "Can I buy a factory rifle that will be competitive with all the custom rifles in use?" The answer is yes . . . probably.

Remington's Model 40XB-BR (the BR stands for "bench rest") has proved highly competitive, but it's absolutely the *only* factory-built gun that deserves even a hint of consideration. Despite its success, most new shooters still seem to favor custom equipment. They reason that if they buy the same kind of goodies the winning shooters use, they're probably going to be ahead of the game in the long run, and that logic is difficult to refute.

If you don't care to plunk down the cash for the best equipment money can buy, however, there's a compromise between the all-custom rigs and those turned out on factory production lines. Ed Shilen of Shilen Rifles, Inc., Irving, Texas, several years ago perfected a technique for attaching an aluminum sleeve to Remington bolt-actions. The sleeve increases rigidity and bedding area, both of which are important considerations when pinpoint accuracy is the aim. Following Shilen's introduction of a stand-

A fluted barrel retains its stiffness, but weighs less than an unfluted one of the same diameter.

ardized sleeve, other expert bench-rest riflesmiths such as Pat B. McMillan, Phoenix, Ariz., and Clyde Hart, Lafayette, N. Y., have followed suit, experiencing similar success. In fact, even the most ardent fanciers of precision custom guns concede that the little sleeved Remingtons are every bit as good as their rifles.

If you want to go the distance, however, proven custom actions are available from many sources. Hart, McMillan, Charles A. Williams of Garland, Texas, Tom Gillman of Hot Springs, Ark., or any of several others will be happy to accommodate you. Shilen also markets a slick new action which sells for $175 complete with trigger. Expect to pay around $200 for any of the others, including trigger. (The most frequently used triggers are the 2-ounce Remington, the Model 700 Remington converted to 2-ounce type and the Canjar.)

Barrels are equally important, and there are only a few custom tubes to choose from: Shilen, Hart, Garrott (7544 East 27th Street, Tulsa, Okla. 74124), A&M (Box 173, Prescott, Ariz. 86301) and Douglas (5504 Big Tyler Road, Charleston, W. Va. 25312). Shilen and Hart account for well over 90 per cent of all barrels used on competitive bench-rest guns. Made of stainless steel, their match-grade barrels are button-rifled, hand-lapped, bore-scoped, air-gauged and built to almost unbelievable tolerances.

Inside the bore, no eccentricity or variation in size greater than
.0001 inch is acceptable.

Garrott and A&M tubes have also produced excellent results.
Their rifling is broached with a cutter, rather than "ironed" in
with a button.

Stock patterns by Shilen and Hart are popular, but McMillan,
Gillman and others build excellent custom "handles" of their own
design.

Starting from scratch, a new shooter would probably do well to
order a complete rifle from a top bench-rest riflesmith rather than
order a boxful of components and have his local gunsmith put
them together. The first way, there's almost a lead-pipe guarantee
the gun will work when the shooter gets it. If it doesn't, the man
it was bought from will make it work; his reputation depends
on it.

Choosing a scope is the next task, and it can be somewhat difficult, since several excellent models are available. While Unertl
still holds a slight popularity edge with its 1½-inch and 2-inch
models (and to a lesser extent the BV-20), Redfield's revolution-
ary 3200 with internal adjustments and rigid mounts (which
don't allow the scope to recoil) appears to be accounting for more
current sales than any other model. Lyman's Super Targetspot is
also a fine product but, like the Unertl, is dependent on conventional target-type mounts which allow the scope to recoil after
each shot and necessitate the use of external adjustments.

Many shooters shun conventional target-type mounts because
the clearance necessary between the raised rib on the tube and
the mated front mount can cause misalignment from shot to shot.
And there's also the possibility of misalignment due to grains
of sand becoming trapped under the contact points.

Weight is no consideration in choosing a scope for 13½-pound
rifles, but subtract 3 pounds from the allowable weight and it
becomes very much a factor in the Light Varmint and Sporter
classes.

While many of the country's most accomplished shooters simply reduce barrel dimensions and use the same type of scope on
their 10½-pound guns as on their Heavy Varminters, others prefer a lighter-weight scope which permits the use of a larger
barrel. Among the lightweights, Remington's 20XBR scope
(companion for the 40XB-BR) and Unertl's BV-20 scope have

been the undisputed leaders, followed by a scattering of Lyman and Weaver hunting scopes converted to a magnification of 20X. The latter two scopes are both designed for mounting entirely on the receiver, and they weigh less than 20 ounces, while full-size Lymans, Unertls and Redfields average 25 to 30 ounces.

Although it's still perhaps a bit early to speculate, a glass introduced in 1970 may well solve the lightweight-scope problem for good. Lyman finally heeded bench shooters' pleas for a target-quality 20X scope with internal adjustments and rigid hunting-type mounts, and this scope just might prove to be the biggest thing to hit the market since Redfield's 3200.

Having decided on the type of rifle he wants and the components from which it will be assembled, the freshman bench shooter's next dilemma is caliber.

Experienced competitors have tested all factory cartridges and just about every wildcat imaginable, and in the Heavy Varmint and Light Varmint classes the .224 family of cartridges is still tops. Many wildcat versions of the .222, .222 Magnum and .223 have produced excellent results, but after taking a second look, even those who formerly shunned the standard .222 in favor of larger-capacity cases are beginning to doubt whether the wildcat hotshots offer any significant advantages.

All things considered, the standard .222 Remington is the *only* totally practical choice for a new shooter. He's going to be plenty busy learning a whole new spectrum of techniques without having to worry about building wildcat brass and all that.

In the Sporter class, where 6 mm is the legal minimum, the 6x47 (.222 Magnum necked up to .243) is the hands-down favorite, followed by wildcats such as the 6x225 (.225 Winchester necked up to 6 mm) and the 6x224 (necked-up .224 Weatherby).

An alternative choice is the standard .308, but think long and hard before ordering one. Some shooters—most, in fact—simply can't tolerate the constant beating the .30s administer. Remember, you'll be firing something like 100 rounds (including sighters) in a single match, so an individual's tolerance to recoil becomes an important factor.

Don't be misled, either, by field experience, even if you've been hunting with a .338 for years and blapping jackrabbits with a .30/06. Shooting from the bench is altogether different from shooting in the field, and 100 to 110 rounds per session is lots of shooting.

It should be noted, however, that the few experts who *can* make the .30s perform fare very well, and in fact hold a decided advantage over users of .224s and 6 mms when shooting in a high wind—which is still another problem the bench-rest competitor must learn to cope with.

Wind. It's something you can't even see. Can it really make much difference in where the bullet hits? You'd better believe it can! In fact, wind and mirage (which we'll discuss later) are what bench-rest shooting's all about.

Wind does curious things, things you'd never notice if you weren't trying to outfigure it on the rifle range. For example, if you feel a brisk breeze blowing against the left side of your face while you're sitting at the bench, it's reasonable to assume that the bullet should strike somewhere to the right of where it would in a calm condition, isn't it? It is, but only if the downrange wind is blowing in the same direction as the wind at your bench, which frequently isn't the case.

Bench-rest shooters build all kinds of gadgets to help in figuring wind effects. Streamers, flags, even miniature cardboard tetrahedrons—anything to warn of sudden wind shifts or changes in velocity—adorn ranges throughout the country.

Visit a bench-rest match and look downrange, especially during a 200-yard stage. Quite commonly you'll notice a left-hand wind at your bench, while the flags at 100 yards will be dangling straight down (no wind) and at 200 yards, streamers beneath the target board are whipping briskly in a right-hand direction.

Winds from 90 degrees left and right, blowing in different directions at various points downrange, are plenty challenging for even seasoned experts. But the breeze can also come from directly in front, or from behind you. Or it can "fishtail," swinging rapidly 30 to 40 degrees on either side of the line between you and the target.

But head winds and tail winds shouldn't affect a bullet much, should they? They shouldn't, perhaps, but the fact is that they do, and unless you learn how to handle them you'll be a fair-weather shooter the rest of your days.

It seems there's no irrefutable rule for predicting effects of head winds and tail winds. It's been my experience that in *most* cases, on *most* ranges, head winds cause the bullet to strike higher on the target while tail winds make it hit lower. But the effect can be—and often is—exactly the opposite. Why? I don't have the answer, and furthermore, I don't know anybody who does. Fortunately, you can shoot very respectable groups without knowing the "why" of it, because the effect is almost always consistent throughout a given day at a given range, and you have a sighter target on which to experiment. That's all you need. Proficiency will come with experience if you stay with the endeavor long enough to learn.

Having learned, however, you've still solved only a fraction of your problem, because there's another condition which usually accounts for at least 6o per cent of your total group dispersion. Bench shooters call it "mirage."

As used in shooting terminology, mirage refers simply to the shimmering heat waves generated by sunlight refracting through air layers of different densities and radiating off the ground. Even though many noncompetitive riflemen aren't even aware of its existence, the phenomenon is by far the most treacherous condition a shooter must deal with.

Must deal with, that is, if he expects to shoot winning groups any time other than early morning, late evening or night. (At these hours mirage is usually very mild, and sometimes nonexistent.)

Ignore mirage on the 100-yard range and it'll make your custom bench-rest gun shoot like a featherweight factory Sporter. Overlook it at 200 yards and your groups can easily average *four times* the size they should be were you a competent "doper."

The shooter's problem with mirage stems from the fact that it optically displaces the target, whether it's a paper card, a tiny varmint or a bull elephant. It's like looking at a fish that's underwater. He's not really where he appears to be. This fact alone would cause little difficulty if only mirage followed a constant, unchanging pattern. We'd simply change our point of impact to compensate for it and blaze away. But that's not how it works.

Mirage can seldom be considered as a single entity, because in practical application it's a slave of the wind, constantly changing its pattern with every gust that whips across the range. On

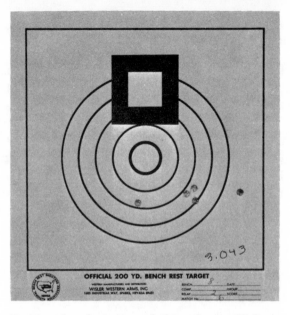

Here's what happens when a shooter fails to compensate for mirage effects. This 200-yard Heavy Varmint group measured over 3 inches.

those rare occasions when no wind is present, mirage is said to "boil." Its undulating waves flow upward, displacing the target image in the same direction. Add a moderate wind from the left and the waves (they look a little like ripples on a lake) assume a more horizontal path, skittering briskly to the right. A right-hand wind produces the opposite effect, while head winds, tail winds and quartering winds further compound the problem.

Whenever mirage is present, you may be sure it's optically displacing the target image, and always in the direction of flow. If it's boiling, the target appears to be higher than it actually is. If it's running from 9 o'clock (left to right) your target will appear to the right of where it would be in a no-mirage condition, and a right-to-left flow optically moves your target to the left.

Knowing the *direction* of flow, however, solves only part of your problem, because *intensity* is equally important. Intensity determines how far in a given direction your bullet will be displaced. The intensity of the overall condition is directly proportional to the density of the mirage (the denser and soupier it appears, the greater the optical displacement) and the intensity of the wind propelling it.

Suppose you're shooting at 200 yards. In a zero-wind, zero-mirage condition, your Heavy Varmint rifle is sighted to place shots in the center of the 1-inch X ring. Then introduce mirage, without wind. It boils, and your bull appears to go up. Next add a slight breeze from the left—just enough to barely break up the boil. Instead of flowing parallel to the ground, the heat waves may now assume an angled path, canting 30 to 45 degrees from vertical. Shoot now, and your bullet will still strike above the X ring but lower than the previous shot and farther to the right. (Remember, we've eliminated most of the boil and introduced a slight lateral displacement.) Reversing the condition produces an opposite effect.

The most serious error a bench shooter can make is to fire at least two of his shots on the record target in opposite conditions. If he fires in extremes of a constant left-to-right or right-to-left condition, his group certainly won't win any awards, but it'll still be only *half* as big as if he fired in a "reverse," or two completely opposite conditions.

How much is mirage worth? That, as I've said, depends entirely on its intensity. In severe conditions I've found it necessary to vary my aiming point as much as 3 to 4 inches when shooting one group in two extremes of the *same* condition (say, mirage running from right to left, then reversing) in order to keep all shots in the same general area. And if the condition reverses, you might well have to correct as much as half a foot to keep from disqualifying at 200 yards.

Veterans in the bench-rest game maintain that a new shooter *really* gets a taste of what the sport is all about the first time he realizes he must hold all the way to the edge of the target card in order to hit the center. And be assured that to deliberately aim several inches outside the disqualifying border and trigger a shot requires more than a little faith in your ability.

To make matters worse, it's usually difficult (and sometimes impossible) to spot your bullet holes when mirage is doing its worst. This means that even though you may have plenty of time and ammunition, experimenting on the sighter target may prove of little value.

Contrary to what many newcomers to the game believe, quality of equipment is no factor at all in a bench-rest shooter's suc-

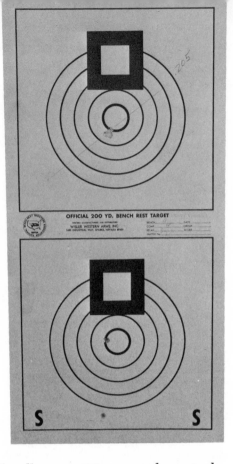

This is how it should be done. In this 200-yard Heavy Varmint group, the upper target shows five shots in a hole that measures .205 inch. (The lower target is a sighter.)

cess, simply because virtually all competitive guns have to be superb just to stay in the running.

Any good Heavy Varmint rifle will *consistently* average well under .300 inch for five 5-shot groups at 100 yards. The best Light Varmint and Sporter guns are nearly as good, only they're somewhat more difficult to shoot because variations in hold have a catastrophic effect on group size.

So what's the secret to making these "super rifles" shoot? Actually, there is none. Fate has nothing to do with rifle accuracy; it's all a matter of tolerances. Given a top-quality custom barrel, a good action, a superb bedding job and well-made handloads, there's no reason why a varmint rifle shouldn't easily approach the .300 standard, and likely surpass it. The bench-rest riflesmith clears most of the hurdles involving tolerances, leaving only the reloading aspect to the shooter.

Reloading ammunition for bench-rest competition is an altogether different matter from assembling hunting loads. Bench

shooters use a unique array of specialized loading tools designed
for accuracy and portability. With only a handful of exceptions,
they load all their ammunition at the range, and in fact, few own
more than 20 cases for a given rifle.

The most common specialty tool in the bench-rest game is the
straight-line bullet seater such as the one produced by L. E.
"Sam" Wilson, P. O. Box 324, Cashmere, Wash. 98815. Reamed
with a chambering reamer, straight-line seaters support a case
along its entire length. A short, closely fitted steel rod with a
concave tip seats the bullet accurately, producing a finished cartridge of nearly perfect concentricity. The seating punch screws
into a knob atop the seater and is adjustable for different seating
depths. A small aluminum or steel base plate supports the case
and seater at the bottom during the seating operation. Seating
force is applied by a gentle push with the hand, or with a small
arbor press.

Equally necessary to precision reloads are straight-line "knock-

*Here, shooters load their ammo in the back of a pickup truck prior
to a match. Portable reloading equipment is a must for bench-rest competition.*

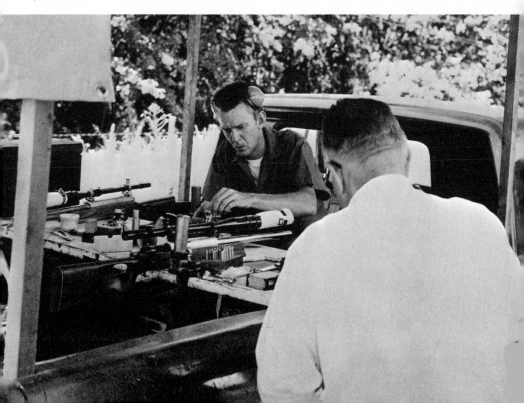

out" dies for resizing and depriming. (They are called knock-out dies because a plastic hammer is used to "knock" the cases into the die and "knock" them out again.) Also built with a chambering reamer, these dies ensure perfect support along the entire case while resizing only the neck. And since bench shooters use only high-quality bolt-action rifles which keep the brass from stretching, full-length resizing is never necessary. In fact, it's woefully detrimental to both accuracy and case life.

Custom knock-out dies are designed to squeeze case necks only enough to hold the bullet snugly. Press-type dies, which may or may not be concentric and which are used in presses that may or may not be concentric, usually squeeze the necks to a diameter much smaller than necessary. The cases are then pulled back across an expander button to stretch the brass to "proper" size. (As a rule, such dies produce a finished inside diameter much smaller than optimum, causing bullets to be squeezed far too tightly.)

Unnecessary stresses imposed by conventional dies work-harden the brass, making it brittle and greatly shortening the useful life of a case. Reloaded with proper tools, a .222 case should function perfectly through 50 reloads (not squib loads, either). Mine are usually good for 75, and I've fired one lot, for experimental purposes, close to 100 times each.

Cases should be discarded whenever necks begin to split or when primer pockets become so loose that gas leaks occur (they'll erode the face of your bolt), whichever happens first.

Then there's the matter of powder charges. While a few "old school" hangers-on still meticulously weigh each load, at least 95 per cent of today's bench-resters throw every charge from a measure. What about those stories you've read insisting that every third, fifth or tenth charge should be weighed? Nonsense! As long as you're using small-kernel powders common to bench-rest shooting (Ball-C #2, Reloder 7, Reloder 11, H-380, 748-BR, 4198, etc.) you're wasting time and effort with a scale. Any good measure, precalibrated with a scale, will throw charges adequate for bench-rest competition, and certainly there's no higher forum for evaluating reload quality.

If you want to change charges or load different types of powders, however, better pick either the Belding & Mull measure or the new Spencer measure produced by the Plano Gun Shop, Plano, Texas. Both use a B&M micrometer drop tube which can be set, changed and reset with amazing accuracy. (You must first use a scale, of course, to record correct settings for the tube.)

Along with the straight-line seater, knock-out dies and powder measure you'll also need a priming tool. Lee Custom Engineering markets an inexpensive (less than $5) model that'll do a perfectly acceptable job. Contrary to what you may have read, there's no "technique" to seating primers. Just push 'em in until they stop and then don't push any more.

To get the best out of your reloads, you should also turn your case necks; they're not necessarily concentric when they come from the factory. Neck-wall thickness shouldn't vary by more than .0005 inch. Neck-turning tools are available from Forster-Appelt, Lanark, Ill., and Ferris Pindell, Connersville, Ind. Lee Custom Engineering is also marketing an inside neck reamer (which you can get from your local dealer) designed to do the same job. Unlike the Forster-Appelt and Pindell tools, however, it isn't adjustable.

Having turned and trimmed your cases, selected several powders with which to experiment and assembled all your loading paraphernalia in a portable tool box, you've only to select your bullet.

Four factory match bullets are available to .224-caliber shooters. Sierra's 53-grain hollow-point has long led sales ratings, followed by the Sierra 52-grain boattail hollow-point, Speer's 52-grain Silver Match and Hornady's 53-grain hollow-point. Most 6 mm shooters using factory bullets favor Sierra hollow-points in 75- and 60-grain weights, and .30-caliber specialists go all out for the popular Sierra 168-grain International.

Or, if you really want to go first class, there are several commercial sources of custom-made bullets. But be prepared to pay at least $6 per 100 for .224s and a dollar more for .243s.

Once you've finished your rifle, tuned it to perfection in good conditions and practiced a bit in wind and mirage, you should then visit an NBRSA match just to get an idea what's going on. (You can write NBRSA Secretary Bernice McMullen, 607 West Line Street, Minerva, Ohio 44657, for a complete list of NBRSA clubs in your area.) You'll see how matches are conducted, meet

some of the shooters and get a close-up look at the sport and
those who take part in it.

Perhaps you'll even be surprised to learn that some of the
country's most formidable competitors aren't just veterans from
the gun industry who've spent their entire lives on the rifle range.
They're engineers, factory laborers, printers, attorneys, ranchers,
teachers, stockbrokers, machinists, businessmen, you name it.
And many, including some of the best, have shot only half a
dozen years or so—which says a lot about the sport and the reason it's growing.

Not that they're the biggest battery of competitive shooters in
the country, or even *one* of the biggest. Indeed, they're among
the smallest. But despite that handicap (if it is a handicap), these
dedicated bench-rest specialists have advanced the state of their
art to a phenomenal level, at the same time preserving a relaxed
spirit of camaraderie completely inconsistent with the times.

Since the earliest days of the organization, NBRSA members
have pushed a national program of friendly competition in an informal atmosphere—a program that places a premium on individual achievement. That's the way it's always been, that's the way
the shooters want to keep it—and that's the reason I know it isn't
likely to change.

3

SMALL-GAME
HUNTING

BY CHARLES F. WATERMAN

SMALL-GAME hunting is simultaneously one of our most popular and one of our most ignored sports. I'd be willing to bet that more rabbits are taken each year than animals of all the big-game species put together—but many otherwise avid and experienced hunters tend to ignore the smaller critters once they acquire their first centerfire rifle and bag something with antlers.

This is a shame, since stalking small game with a rifle or shotgun takes a back seat to no other aspect of hunting as far as skill, marksmanship and the ability to outthink your quarry are concerned. Any rifleman who can pick off a gray squirrel running and jumping through the oak tops shouldn't have much trouble with deer or moose. And most successful squirrel hunters know their way around the woods pretty well.

Early-season squirrels or those living in unhunted country can be bagged by almost anyone stomping through the timber with a gun, but after a few shots and a few squirrel casualties, the picture changes. And some of the best gray squirrel hunting is done on a small scale; there are experts who do all of their shooting in a single wood lot—and a small one at that. These guys can turn into stumps for long periods, breathe very little and waste very little ammunition.

I know a fellow who shoots his squirrels with a .410 shotgun and another who uses nothing but a .300 Weatherby Magnum. The magnum wielder goes to great lengths to handload short-range stuff that will be deadly but not too destructive. He believes firmly in the phrase "Beware of the man with one gun," and uses the same rifle for elk, for coyotes and for deer in between. Using one gun is part of his pleasure.

There are three kinds of squirrel "shots" if you want to be practical. There's the running, jumping, falling, swinging situation when the squirrel is bent on leaving the area fast. There's the stationary target, often pretty small, when the squirrel is hiding, having already seen you and possibly showing only one eye and part of his head—or less. There is the wide-open shot in which the squirrel walks out in plain sight when you are sitting with your back to a tree or a log, moving only your eyeballs. This last one would be dead easy except that the target always shows up where you didn't expect him and is likely to leave while you are squirming around to let him have it. Anybody knows that these several situations require several guns—but since more than one is inconvenient to carry, you'll have to compromise.

Probably the ideal squirrel rifle would be a semiautomatic .22 with a *low-power* scope. Since I don't like to let logic get in the way of fun, I have something quite different. Being partial to bolt-actions and feeling it would be good practice for larger game, I found an ancient Winchester 52 target gun, had the barrel cut off to 24 inches and mounted a 2½X Bushnell scope on it. It's rough on squirrels, although the rapid fire of an auto would be better during treetop evacuations.

Ranges are short, usually 100 feet or less. There are exceptions, when you spot a squirrel completely outside what you consider your shooting area. It doesn't happen too often, because when he's that far away he's usually hidden by brush if he's on the ground or by branches if he's in a tree. When it does happen, the steady-holding weight of the old 52 feels pretty good.

Figuring clean kills are more important than the loss of a little meat, I believe in hollow-points. A squirrel is seldom far from a hollow tree or a nest, and quick kills are important. For those who confine themselves to head shots the hollow-point isn't necessary, of course, but it does no harm. Most centerfire rifles are unnecessarily powerful. At the other extreme is the air rifle, which is okay for careful shooting at close range. The last squirrel I killed was with a Sheridan, but it was a head shot and I had plenty of time. Trouble is that the hunter most likely to have an air rifle will be a youngster, who is likely to take a wild shot occasionally, and that cripples game.

I have done considerable squirrel hunting with pistols, but it's a hard way to go if they're wild. Most of my pistol hunting has been on fox squirrels, usually easier marks than the intellectual grays. If you want to shoot at them on the move, a .22 auto is best because we're back in the spray-and-pray category now, but I've always liked revolvers for hunting and have shot very few moving squirrels with pistols. The handguns I've used most on squirrels are a Smith & Wesson K-22 and an Officers Model .38 Colt.

The .38 was handloaded with 2.5 grains of Bullseye and wadcutters, a very quiet combination that has long been used by target shooters. It is a very-short-range proposition and excellent for settled communities. (Remember that most squirrel shots are taken at a high angle.) The flat-nosed wadcutter punches a good-sized hole, but it's going pretty slowly and isn't overly destructive. The handgun has some advantages for the hunter who operates from a stand, in that it's easy to cover oddball angles—as long as you shoot with one hand only. If you use both hands, as most handgun hunters prefer to, you'll make more fuss in getting lined up than you would with a rifle or shotgun. Incidentally, a handgun really steadies down when you point it upward with one hand. Most of those wiggles you get when aiming horizontally disappear when the gun's weight pushes right back against your shoulder.

I started my squirrel hunting on midwestern fox squirrels in an area where shooting pressure was very light. It was no great feat to pop one out of a 30-foot Osage orange tree with a pistol—and much easier with a rifle. At the time, I figured shotgunning squirrels was on a par with ground-sluicing quail. I still don't care much for scatterguns on squirrels, but I have seen spots where they were excusable, and even absolutely necessary. In many cases, not only was a shotgun needed, but a special kind of shooting was required. It was a poking, stabbing business, and you might as well forget the smooth swing you'd cultivated all those years.

This goofy shooting takes place in some of the big oak ham-
mocks of the South, where a target may be traveling the tree
crowns some 80 feet up, jumping from branch to branch, airborne part of the time and then stopping dead to gather himself
for another take-off. Forget your shotgun training and start over.
(Of course, there are other shots that are dead easy—too easy to
be anything more than collecting meat. Real hogs sometimes fire
shotguns into squirrel nests. I guess there's not a law against it,
but there should be.)

Most shotgun users go for fairly large shot, from No. 6s to 4s, in
light loads. The range is usually short enough so that a sufficient
number of pellets will strike, many of which will go through the
animal. Small shot makes a mess of the cleaning operation. Choke?
Well, improved-cylinder should do it in larger gauges. If you go
for a .410 it should be full choke. For most game the little .410 is
either a stunt or a mistake, but there may be a place for it with
the meat hunter who confines it to close shots on squirrels. Let's
be fair about this: Many squirrel hunters consider the shooting a
minor part of this kind of hunt. They get their fun from locating
the game and working it into shooting position, and the actual kill
is something of an anticlimax.

*Two gray squirrel hunters use sign language—not voices—to point out
likely spots.*

The gray squirrel is one of the most popular game animals in the United States. He's smart, makes a tough target and tastes great.

You can take a .22 target rifle with a high-power scope and be deadly on motionless targets, but moving ones are hard to find. Open sights are not as good as peep sights, but they work pretty well on moving game. As my eyes got older I found the peeps a big help, and the scope best of all. You're looking upward even more than a wildfowler, which is hard on necks and eyes. Much of the time you'll find dark glasses a really important assist, since you'll be looking into a bright background. It's a perfect situation for eyestrain—picking out a dark object against a dark tree trunk with the whole works backlighted by a bright sky.

You can sometimes find squirrels by walking briskly along without paying much attention to your noise in the hope that they'll be surprised and show themselves when they leave their feeding spots, which may have been on the ground. You can still-hunt very slowly and quietly, watching both ground and trees. You can find a known squirrel area and take a stand. You can use a dog that will trail them on the ground and locate the trees they have gone up. Almost any breed or mixture of breeds can become a squirrel dog with a little experience, as long as he can trail a little. A cold nose may be a handicap: if your dog trails to a tree that a squirrel climbed several hours ago, your quarry has probably long since gone to sleep in a hollow limb or strolled through the tops to another part of the forest. It's better to know that the trail is fresh.

Squirrel hunting is most popular in the East, though the gray squirrel, primarily a resident of true forests, is found as far west

as Kansas and the fox squirrel is found as far west as Colorado.
The fox squirrel, which may weigh 3 pounds to the gray's pound
and a half, lives more in marginal areas and frequently in small
patches of woods. The grays stay much closer to the heavy timber,
but a fox squirrel is often caught well off base. Because he adapts
to areas of less timber, the fox is getting along well with land development. There's no shortage of gray squirrels, but our current
population probably doesn't compare to the swarms of them
hunted by the first settlers. Marginal areas may have helped deer
and quail, but the gray squirrel likes mature forest.

The red squirrel is much smaller than the gray and is seldom
hunted. Appearing in a variety of color schemes, the red lives
over much of the continent and is quite capable of whipping a
fox or a gray whenever he feels like it. The reds have a variety of
local names. There's also a tassel-eared squirrel in the Southwest,
and an Arizona gray squirrel is found there and in New Mexico
and Mexico.

In much of its range the fox squirrel is reddish-gray, but in the
South it appears with nearly white and black markings. The gray
sometimes has whitish ear trimmings, and there are black squirrels
that belong to the gray classification.

An ideal gray squirrel residence is tall oaks or hickories with
some dead trees for dens. The grays use hollow trees for bulky
nests built from leaves and sticks both for resting and for rearing
young. Squirrels may change residence now and then, and they
often repair old nests that are beginning to fall apart. Squirrels
will also enlarge woodpecker holes to suit residential requirements. The destruction of an old den tree may cause the hunting
to fade out in that immediate vicinity, because many generations
of grays—or fox squirrels too, for that matter—may occupy the
same hollow tree.

Finding squirrel habitat is simple if there are numerous nests.
Well-used den trees can be spotted pretty easily. Squirrels go to
water frequently, and a nearby creek is a good indication. You
can often find tracks in muddy spots. Most squirrels do their nut
eating on fairly high limbs, and if you watch the ground closely
you can find the shell cuttings. If you're planning to take a stand,
the cuttings are a big help, for a given squirrel often uses the
same perch repeatedly. If you find several patches of cuttings

This is typical squirrel country in a southern oak hammock.

close enough together to be seen from one stand, you're in a good place.

Real eager beavers sometimes take up a stand before dawn, but that's not necessary. Just move into position quietly and stay put for a while. Such a procedure is too much for a squirrel's curiosity, and you'll frequently find one peeking around to see what you're doing, even though he hid when you first arrived. Generally, he appears as a bump on a limb or trunk or as a shapeless ball in a crotch. If there has been no hunting at all he may start barking at you, but don't count on that.

There are several squirrel calls that work. Although I can't start any squirrel convention with one, I can often get an animal to show himself, even if he doesn't answer. Some of the calls produce barks when tapped against something. There are striker calls that you actuate by hitting a piece of wood against the call proper, and there are some squeeze-bulb rigs. Squirrels have a variety of vocal expressions, and you can sometimes get results by an exaggerated kissing sound made by pressing your lips against your wrist and inhaling. Two small stones knocked together can sound a little like a squirrel bark.

Many a gray has been collected when he became curious about an intermittent rustling sound on the ground. You can make that "call" by swishing a branch around in the leaves. It sounds like a

These are different kinds of squirrel calls. At left is a Lohman striker call, at center are two tapping calls by Olt and at right is a Faulk bulb call.

Rustling a palmetto frond can sometimes attract game.

squirrel hunting, burying or exhuming nuts and is reassuring to a bushytail who has been lying low in a tree and doesn't know what became of you. After all, a squirrel can be surprisingly noisy on the ground.

Once you're settled in a good spot, you may be agreeably surprised at how well you can hear squirrel operations. You can hear a squirrel grinding up a nut at a surprising distance. You can even hear him walking around on the limbs, and you may hear the tiny patter of particles of bark that he knocks loose as he travels. If there's movement in the tree crowns, you can hear the leaves rustle. If there's ground activity, you can hear it for a considerable distance, as squirrels apparently make no effort at caution once they've left a tree.

You just can't tell what will happen after you've been completely quiet for a while. On several occasions I have rolled my eyes until they hurt trying to locate a squirrel within a few yards but out of my field of fire. Once I turned my head very slowly to find a fox squirrel inspecting me from a distance of 2 feet, having come down the trunk of the tree against which I was leaning. Needless to say, that one got away when I tried to put my gun on him. I have had nut cuttings sprinkle down on my camouflage shirt and have gone through painful contortions in vain efforts to locate the culprit.

Unobtrusive clothing is good. When you're in heavily hunted country it might be wise to use red camouflage clothing, as squirrels, like deer, are color-blind by our standards. As in the case of a deer stand, you can hide yourself too well—so well that you can't get into shooting position without shaking the whole forest. It's safe to expect a squirrel to appear where you least expect him, no matter how many nut cuttings, nut burials and den trees you have scouted.

Some of the best of the stand hunters try to have several animals working within range before firing the first shot. The idea is that the gunner will bag one squirrel and then mark the spots where the others disappear. For, shy as they may be about other sounds and movements, spooky gray squirrels that have been hunted frequently sometimes pay little attention to gunfire. A 12-gauge-shotgun blast sometimes stops feeding activities for only a minute or two as long as the shooter holds his position. If he makes a clean kill and doesn't gallop out to pick up his game, he may have other chances within a few minutes.

But sooner or later you end up with a treed squirrel you can't see. You know what tree he went into, and you know he hasn't jumped to another one. If it's a big old den tree with holes all over it, you might as well move on, but if it appears to have no dens or nests, you may be able to locate him. Probably the most likely giveaway will be light from the sky shining through the fringe of his tail. Tails are mighty important to squirrels, but they sometimes don't hide them very well. If your game is lying atop a limb and you can make out his head, you have it made. But if you can't spot a vulnerable place to aim at, things get complicated.

A common situation is for the quarry to choose a near-vertical limb or a spot on the main trunk and then keep moving around so that there's always tree between you and him. This can turn into a sort of manual-of-arms with waltzing overtones. You walk around the tree and he circles ahead of you. You stop and reverse the field and he does the same. You hurry and he hurries. Stalemate.

So you can keep circling at the same speed for a little while until he accepts the pattern, and then you simply stop. He may circle on around and come into plain sight—or he may not. You can throw a stick to the other side of the tree in the hope he'll think that's you and will pop into the target area. You can hang your coat on something and sneak around in the hope he'll keep watching it. If you have a dog, you can send him to one side and be ready on the other side—but many squirrels know dogs can't climb trees and won't fall for that one.

If none of these tactics works, you can walk off for some distance as if you're giving up the whole thing, but take up a firing position while still within range in the hope the squirrel will decide you've left and will come out into the open. It may help to say, "He's too smart for me; I'm going to give up!" in a loud voice, but I doubt it.

You can say all you want to about bobwhite quail, ruffed grouse or white-tailed deer, but the most popular game in the United States is still the cottontail rabbit, which has been gunned, trapped and dogged in dozens of ways and shows no sign of suffering from hunting pressure. The ups and downs of the bunny population are the result of rabbit problems, the mysterious thing called "cycle," and man and his hunting schemes have very little to do with it.

Cottontails are usually done in with shotguns, although .22 rifles come a close second. No. 6 shot is a pretty good size: not because you need anything that big for the killing, but because a rabbit full of No. 8s becomes a culinary problem. A fairly open choke is best. Here again, the rabbit shooter may have to do some snap shooting at short range in the brush, a bad place for the smooth swing.

Out in the open I can't see much excuse for missing very many cottontails, but when the target is nothing but a white dab of cotton popping through the brambles and is visible only half the time, you'll need to make quick decisions. Fortunately, a crippled rabbit isn't nearly as likely to escape as is a poorly hit squirrel; but cottontails will dive into any kind of hole or hollow that's available, and the bunny is irritatingly familiar with his territory.

His Majesty the cottontail is the most popular game animal, large or small, in North America.

It's the cottontails' small range that leads to the belief that beagles deliberately turn them back toward the guns. I won't deny that some little pooches have that in mind, but the bunny has a limited area in which he wants to run, and he eventually comes back to near where he started unless he has a real fortress somewhere along the route. Of course, many beaglers and basset lovers just want to hear the music and aren't interested in shooting. Anyway, only a small percentage of the annual rabbit bag is made in the classic manner.

Almost any mutt can be some sort of rabbit dog, rooting out bunnies the unaided shooter wouldn't see and making some sort of announcement about what brush piles contain game. Once you start stomping on a real brush pile, the dog may be more harm than help, chasing the rabbit right back to security every time you get him headed out. Bouncing a brush pile should be done carefully, as it's a good place to sit down suddenly and find your gun pointed where it shouldn't be.

Cottontails like to make their forms near creeks, seeming to prefer damp ground for reasons no one has satisfactorily explained to me. If you can find a farm creek with a fringe of willows and some sedge it may be good rabbit habitat, even if nearby fields are closely harvested, plowed or pastured. That little strip of weeds and brush narrows things down until you stand an excellent chance without dogs.

When there's fresh snow, things become remarkably simplified. In a few night hours, a dozen rabbits can beat down paths enough to make you believe they're taking over the whole country. They do a lot of racing and playing, especially in fresh snow, and their ranges overlap, so that the skein of rabbit trails is continuous. The forms are usually a little off to one side of the trail, and it's pretty hard for a cottontail to hide in snow. If fresh snow stops late enough at night to prevent the rabbits from building a complete highway system, you can follow individual trails straight to their originators. This kind of shooting is generally at very close range, for bunnies hold pretty tight. If you prefer to kick them up and shoot them on the run with a rifle, you generally find it isn't as easy as it looks. Better use a fast repeater and don't count the empties.

There is another kind of rabbit hunting that isn't practiced much these days. Cottontails come out to feed early in the evening, often well before dusk, and you can use a scope-sighted .22 to good advantage if you watch the edges of the briar patches and the weedy fence rows. Such rabbits are apt to be pretty close to the thick stuff they spent the day in, so you may not have much luck getting them to run for your shotgun. As you approach they'll just hop back into the rough.

I have seen spots where a tight-shooting shotgun was called for—a matter of rabbits being put out by dogs or other hunters working tight cover surrounded by open fields. In those few instances I might well have used the full-choked Model 12 Winchester I insisted was what I needed when I was a youngster. But for the most part I'll pick something more open for rabbits, probably a modified or an improved-cylinder. A double with those two borings is difficult to beat. Most rabbit hunters aren't gun nuts. Rusty single-barrels with undistinguished names have done in a lot of bunnies, and rabbit stew tastes just as good whether the makings were gathered with an engraved sidelock or with a pitted bolt-action.

The snowshoe, found over much of the North Woods, has been served in many big-game-hunting camps—collected with handguns, sometimes with light shotguns and not infrequently with big-game rifles when hunters figured the noise wouldn't scare more important quarry. It's a big rabbit and probably less proficient as a hider than the cottontail, but I have seen snowshoes sift into some pretty small holes in the rocks. Snowshoe rabbits change color with the seasons and occasionally turn white before the snows arrive, thus becoming visible at great distances. In high country they are sometimes quite tame, but in areas where they have been hunted they work about like cottontails ahead of dogs.

The jackrabbits (there are several varieties) are often considered pests, aren't usually eaten and provide perfect training for the big-game hunter. On jacks, you can do almost any kind of shooting you want. Along toward evening they're likely to show up on the western sage flats or in open grassland, and if you want to shoot at 200 or 300 yards with your big-game rifle, you can have at it with either moving or stationary targets. After you've sighted at a jackrabbit a few times, an antelope buck seems easy.

The jackrabbit will make you a good shot at running game and do it pretty quickly. Many years ago I got my first taste of that with Wells Erving, a competitive big-bore shooter. We'd go into some California desert country and walk through the sage until a jack got up, whereupon Wells would go to work in classic offhand stance, working the bolt of his scope-sighted .30/06, rapid-fire. There might be a few puffs of dust in the wrong place, but the rabbit was in big trouble as long as the country was open enough to keep him running in a fairly straight line. After watching it a few times, I decided that was for me.

I went about it a little differently, figuring that since I do most of my big-game shooting sitting down, that would be the way to shoot jackrabbits. It was perfect practice. I'd jump a jack, make sure there were no rattlesnakes in the immediate area and then sit down in a hurry and go to work. The puffs of dust were a big help, but after a couple of misses the jack was likely to speed up.

I'd say that most freshly jumped jacks leave at around 20 or 25 miles an hour, carrying their ears up. From chasing them with automobiles, I've found that they flap an ear back now and then at about 30 miles an hour. Somewhere around 40 miles an hour they put both ears back and buckle down to some serious traveling. They seldom get into that gear unless something is actually chasing them and getting pretty close.

SMALL-GAME HUNTING 75

If you want numbers, I suppose a scope-sighted .22 semiauto would be your best answer; but if it's big-game practice you're after, the kick of a heavier cartridge is an important factor. (I have even hunted jacks with a handgun, trying to find them sitting at modest range. Moving jacks are rough duty for a pistol.) Jacks should be shot with something fairly destructive, as their build will let a slow-moving solid bullet go through from the side without much damage, leaving a cripple.

Jack concentrations move from month to month, and there are migrations across the plains country. You'll find droves of them in a section several miles across, and then find practically none in adjoining country that looks just the same. If you plan to hunt them somewhere near a main highway, look for dead jacks that have been killed by cars. A batch of fresh highway kills indicates you're in good jackrabbit country, however temporary the situation may be.

If you plan to hunt where there's very little road traffic, you can find jack concentrations by a little night driving with a car or truck. Jackrabbits are quite active after dark, and you keep cruising until you see rabbits in your lights. If you spot several, the chances are they'll be right there the following day. Daylight driving, on the other hand, tells you nothing.

Jackrabbits, we'll say, are practice game. The other rabbits and most of the squirrels are good to eat, often happy additions to camp meat in big-game country. Some big-game hunters go to considerable trouble along this line, working up very light loads that will shoot well in their big-game rifles. With some jockeying they can come up with squib charges that zero correctly at very short range without a need for adjusting the scope sight originally set for long-range shooting. That makes for camp meat without much noise and without the necessity for a second gun. In addition to rabbits or squirrels, the reduced loads can be used for grouse in areas where it's legal.

The small-game animals may be with us after more exotic trophies are gone. In the meantime, they give many a youngster his first chance at real hunting, they afford practice for experienced sportsmen and they are the objectives of many hunters who can't manage trips for more glamorous game. A lot of shooters aren't even interested in anything else.

4

VARMINT HUNTING

BY JOHN LACHUK

IN TERMS of rounds fired and men in the field, *Marmota monax*, the portly woodchuck, is still undisputed king of varmints. Approximately 500 million of his kind inhabit open forests and clearings from the Atlantic to the Plains States, south to Alabama and Arkansas, along the lower reaches of Canada and up into Alaska.

Apparently all he adds to the scheme of nature is his regal stature—all 14 to 18 inches of him, squatted on his haunches, imperiously surveying his kingdom of hayfield or meadow. This rotund monarch's troubles begin when he disputes land rights with the farmer who tills his domain and raises the corn, wheat, alfalfa, beans, peas, barley, etc., upon which King Chuck dines. Then too, his main castle of underground burrows with multiple entrances, supplemented by as many as a dozen vacation villas, all with numerous holes and high-rise mounds, presents the farmer and his stock with the constant prospect of a broken leg.

All of which leads to a more or less constant state of war, with the chuck pursuing a scorched-earth policy, trying to eat the farmer out of land and livelihood, and the farmer countering with chemical warfare. The farmer usually welcomes allies armed with small-bore high-velocity rifles and the good sense to direct their fire away from livestock and outbuildings. To join this army, just apply at the nearest farmhouse.

When nature lays a cold white blanket over his domain, the king retires to slumber away one-third of his life. Legend has it that this would-be weather prognosticator emerges from his den on February 2. If his imperial shadow graces the earth, he scurries back to the arms of Morpheus—a prophecy of another six weeks of winter ravages.

From March through May, woodchuck boars indulge in romantic pursuit of woodchuck sows. The product is four to six pups . . . which are soon out digging more holes in loamy hillsides, under tree stumps, at the base of rock piles, along fence rows, etc. —all within easy walking distance of lush greenery. One ecological merit of the woodchuck is his penchant for leaving numberless underground burrows deserted, to be sublet by rabbits and other small fur bearers who gain protection thereby from predators and the elements.

During the "dog days" of late summer and early autumn, stocky ground hogs seek out their coolest dens for a summer siesta that lasts until the balmy Indian summer, during which they reappear briefly to gorge for the four-month fast to follow and to gather dry grasses for softening their winter pads.

Learned varmint hunters practice voluntary conservation by waiting until July to hunt woodchucks. By then the young are able to fend for themselves, and taking adults won't endanger the entire family. Also, knowledgeable nimrods don't completely shoot out a given area, instead leaving a "seed crop" for the next year.

To locate good woodchuck territory, search the sunny, rocky hillsides and the perimeters of tilled fields for the light brown dirt mounds that mark chuck dens. Most of this land will be privately owned. Even if it's posted against hunters, a *polite* query will usually result in permission to hunt. Don't walk up to the farmhouse with gun in hand; this is calculated to make anyone a bit nervous. But let the owner know what equipment you have, and impress him with your good sense about shooting direction and the fact that your bullets disintegrate upon contact with the ground.

To ensure a return welcome, bury carcasses in their burrows instead of leaving them to create a stench and perhaps become fouled in the farmer's hay harvester. Then always check out with the farmer. Thank him and let him know that you have eliminated some of the pests that he abhors.

Because long-range chuck hunters sometimes have trouble, due to recoil, in spotting their hits and misses, two hunters can join forces—one spotting with binocular or scope while the other shoots, then trading off. Both will score better and more often, as the spotter can tell just how much Kentucky windage or holdover will explode the next pill right in the chuck's boiler room.

Slowly scanning promising territory with a big-X binocular will often turn up dens invisible to the naked eye. Often the hunter has his glasses glued to the high-level front doorstep of the chuck's den, while the chuck is observing him just as intently through a screen of grass or brush around at one of the emergency exits, which are dug from the inside and have no telltale mound. When startled into flight, the chuck may seem to just vanish when he reaches one of his hidden holes. With his funny waddle and his abrupt disappearance, he has been likened unto a fat commuter, late for his train, suddenly falling into an open manhole.

Heavy hunting pressure has driven many pasture pigs from their opulent open-air dens into neighboring forested areas and brushy, tree-lined river banks where they den up under tree roots and overgrown hedgerows. These chucks cannot be hunted by the traditional means of gaining some high vantage point from which to scan surrounding clover fields. You can't see much farther than 50 yards at any given point in the rabbit brambles and gnarled oaks inhabited by this new breed of whistle pig.

They must be stalked Indian-fashion by camouflage-clad nimrods, carrying guns chosen for their muted report rather than boardinghouse reach. Armed with a .22 rimfire shooting high-speed hollow-points, you can pick off these close-in ground hogs and double with a few tree squirrels for the evening dinner.

From the wind-swept, rock-strewn Great Plains westward into the Rocky Mountains, the woodchuck's hardier cousin the rock-chuck (*Marmota flaviventris*) holds sway. He makes his abode in the crevices among rocky outcroppings on remote talus slopes. He abandons the safety of his rocky fortress only long enough to visit the alpine meadows on the valley floor, there to dine on long lush grasses, blackberries, serviceberries or, if the opportunity affords, tilled crops.

The rockchuck is no more fond of his own kind than the soli-
tary woodchuck, but he is forced by the nature of his apartment-
house dwelling to live in close proximity with others. However,
each individual jealously guards his own den against intrusion.

Rockchuck colonies will reside in the same rock pile for generation after generation, unless some cataclysm destroys their source
of food. Then they move on to greener pastures. They seldom
range farther than a quarter-mile in search of food and water.
Never completely shoot out a rock pile. As with the woodchucks,
it behooves the hunter to leave breeding stock for the next season.

The rockchuck loves to sun himself on the top of his rock pile,
letting the wind ripple his dark brown, grizzle-tipped fur. But he
is even more alert than his eastern cousin, being on the bill of fare
of every four-footed predator, plus bears and the golden eagle.

This yellow-bellied marmot is "hunted," in a very real sense,
just as you would hunt bears or mountain goats. (In fact, rockchucks require more skill in both stalking and markmanship to
hunt than most big game.) Some scouting can be done by vehicle
over rutted back-country roads, especially if you use a four-wheel-
drive, but eventually you'll be clambering on foot over rugged,
rock-strewn mountains, trying to be inconspicuous.

Any hint of intruders is greeted by the rockchuck with shrill
whistles that are immediately echoed by his companions as one
and all dive for the nearest rock crevice. Rarely will you be able
to approach closer than 200 yards without alarming your quarry.
Chucks are endowed with super-keen eyes, acute hearing and a
suspicious nature. More often than not, the nearest cover you'll
find will be 300 to 500 yards from the chuck's rocky pinnacle.

An often-overlooked factor in this mountain shooting is the
matter of up or down angles affecting trajectory. A hunting companion once solemnly assured me that I should hold higher than
normal on downhill shots and lower on uphill angles. I explained
to him that regardless of whether your shot at a sharp angle is up
or down, the amount of drop is reduced; therefore the holdover
should be less than normal for that range.

As in woodchuck hunting, it is helpful to make a fairly detailed
map of rockchuck-hunting areas, showing colonies, best paths of
approach and preferred shooting angles. Whenever possible, record the range and prevailing winds.

Rockchucks are host to the tick that transmits deadly Rocky Mountain fever; thus, defunct animals are best examined without touching, lest you become an unwilling substitute for the dead chuck.

On the flatlands below the craggy domain of the rockchuck lives the most plentiful pest of all, the prairie dog. This diminutive, gregarious critter booby-traps the rolling plains with a labyrinth of tunnels and holes. His voracious appetite for prairie grass, which stockmen think should be reserved for cattle, has led to widespread government poisoning that has literally eliminated the cunning little burrower from many areas formerly occupied by "dog towns" hundreds of miles square. Enough remain to provide excellent shooting for varmint hunters—who offer a much more humane way of controlling the pest than wholesale slaughter with poisoned oats.

Prairie dogs are named for their habit of barking an alarm in

Prairie dogs, once poisoned nearly into extinction in many places, have made a comeback in some areas. These were taken in Wyoming. Shooting poses no threat to the survival of these animals.

falsetto, like an excited terrier, when anything alien appears on the horizon. They can be approached in an old pickup truck, being accustomed to seeing ranchers rattle across the grassland, but no way can you "Indian" up on them! Shooting is usually from 200 yards to infinity.

A minute-of-angle rifle just won't cut it with this tiny target. Your rifle must group three-quarters of an inch or less at 100 yards to stay on a two-by-four target at 300 yards or better.

Prairie dogs don't hibernate and thus provide year-round targets, but they must be hunted before the prairie grass grows so tall that it conceals their dens.

Predator hunting takes on many varied forms, from the traditional coon hunt behind baying dogs in a Louisiana canebrake to horseback coursing of hounds after a fox over the rolling green hills of Virginia.

The premier predator target is the canny coyote. The coyote gets its name, *Canis latrans*, or "baying dog," from its habit of joining the "boys" nightly for harmonious serenades. This mournful sound is one that I never tire of hearing! To any lover of the out-of-doors, it is a lullaby.

This prairie wolf is one creature that has managed to adapt to man's steady encroachment on his habitat, even threading his way into small undeveloped areas around suburbs. To residents of the Friendly Hills section of Whittier, a suburb of sprawling Los Angeles, the sight and sound of coyotes are a daily occurrence.

Despite man's determined efforts to exterminate him, including an all-out campaign carried out on the Great Plains during the 1850s when early settlers poisoned thousands of buffalo carcasses with strychnine, the coyote has not only survived, but extended his range with every year. The National Geographic Society's 1918 *Wild Animals of North America* reported the eastern limits of the coyote's range as west Texas and Iowa. The 1960 edition reported sightings well into upstate New York. Later reports place the coyote in the New England states and Florida!

One reason for the coyote's tenacity is his natural built-in compensation. When hard pressed, coyotes have been known to breed twice in one year, and litters increase from the usual five to seven whelps. Bitches generally mate at two years of age. Normally, coyotes mate for life and make exemplary spouses. They breed in

This coyote was called in close and dropped with a single shot from a .243.

February and March, later in the cold northern climes, earlier in the warm South. Gestation takes sixty-three days, and the pups are born fully furred, with eyes closed.

Within eight to nine weeks, they are weaned and learning to hunt under the watchful eyes of their doting parents. By early fall, they are off to establish a range of their own. Youngsters travel as far as a hundred miles to find favorable habitat; this accounts for their continual seepage into new areas. A coyote's home range, once established, may cover only a few acres if food is plentiful, or it may sprawl over several hundred if life support is lean.

Coyotes are omnivorous, eating fruits, berries and melons as well as meat, with occasional garbage-can forays into inhabited areas. Coyotes prefer a mild climate, at altitudes of about 4,000 feet. They like open flats located between mountain ranges, where they can course rabbits and rodents, staples accounting for two-thirds of their diet. And coyotes won't turn up their long, thin noses at carrion—a fact that has led many a devious prairie wolf to his undoing when he ran afoul of one of Uncle Sam's dead baits liberally laced with 1080 poison.

Coyotes often hunt in twos and threes and share their successes, so that each is assured of a meal. A favored trick is for one coyote to run game, such as the fleet-footed antelope, forcing the prey to circle back to where another waiting coyote takes up the chase—then a third, and so on until the antelope drops from exhaustion.

I remember one frigid morning when a companion and I heard coyotes howling atop a hill. We called from the base and watched as two gray ghosts worked their way down the near slope, with first one, then the other darting warily from bush to bush like a military infiltration team. It had sounded like a trio serenading us from the hilltop, but only two answered our invitation.

As the dubious duo neared gunshot range, I dismissed all thoughts about a third animal and concentrated on getting my cross hairs centered on one of the shifting targets. A whisper away from a trigger squeeze, I heard a hysterical yapping from down-wind, behind us. The result was immediate, as both coyotes to the front made a wild scramble into reverse, each kicking up sand in his own getaway path. No amount of coaxing on the call would entice them back. A few minutes later, they barked derisively at us, giving us a coyote "horse laugh" from the ridge.

The coyote demonstrates its admirable adaptability by surviving in the desert—an environment for which it is ill fitted with its heavy fur coat and poor heat-dissipating system. A naturally diurnal, or daylight, animal, the coyote simply switches to the night shift, thereby escaping the torrid temperatures and assuring itself a diet of nocturnal desert creatures.

Coyote coloration and size vary with the environment. Desert dogs are sand or slate gray and generally somewhat smaller than their dark-colored mountain cousins. Weight varies from 20 to 50 pounds, averaging about 30. The Indians called the coyote "God's Dog," and predicted that it would be the last living creature on earth. Could be!

The coyote's smaller canine cousin, the fox—red, gray or diminu-

tive kit—covers much of the United States and Canada. Foxes are
considered too-easy prey by western varmint callers, being real
suckers for the call of the dying rabbit. After shooting a few as a
novitiate, the average caller west of the Mississippi will hand foxes
a free pass, preferring to match wits with the cagey coyote. In the
East, where the coyote is still a comparative rarity, the fox is the
principal predator and is taken more seriously. There the fox is
still coursed with horse and hound, as in the days of George Wash-
ington. Those not possessed of such luxuries have to follow the
hounds on "shanks' mare," or stalk the woods hoping for a chance
encounter, or scan snow-clad hillsides, searching for the "rusty tin
can" that shows up as Br'er Fox through a rifle scope. In the rural
Midwest, drives are sometimes organized to rid the area of foxes
that have been raiding hen houses.

When varmint-calling clubs hold a contest to measure ability, a
bobcat trophy rates a higher point score than a coyote. Bobcats
are harder to bag—because there are fewer of them and because
these cautious cats never wax overeager and come storming in to
a rabbit call, as do coyotes on occasion.

Save for a circumscribed area in the central and eastern United
States, the bobcat (*Lynx rufus*) is widely distributed coast to
coast, spilling over into Mexico on the south. In the northern
reaches of the continent, the cold-loving lynx (*Lynx canadensis*)
roams the wild forests. The lynx is distinguished by its longer
legs and ears, thicker pelage and somewhat greater body weight.

An average bobcat weighs in at 20 to 25 pounds, but makes up
for its lack of bulk in pure ferocity. It is a four-footed buzz saw of
claws and fangs! Many people refuse to believe that a bobcat can
kill a deer, but scientific studies have proved that deer constitute
a significant part of the bobcat diet, especially in the Eastern
states and during winter when the deer's running speed is hampered by deep snows. When desperate or cornered, a bobcat will
take on any animal, *including man!*

Eastern bobcats frequent brushy thickets along stream beds,
swampy areas and southern canebrakes. Western bobcats prefer
rugged, rocky, boulder-strewn terrain crisscrossed by dry washes
and arroyos, and bushy draws of piñon, juniper, sagebrush and
manzanita. Western bobcats like to den up in hillside rock piles
that offer a wide view of all surrounding territory. Here they can
find the rodents that constitute a large part of their diet.

Bobcat range varies with the relative abundance of food, covering only four or five square miles if prey is plentiful or spreading to several times that when times are hard. Bobcats make their rounds along the same paths each day, with regular trees for claw sharpening and established spots for defecation.

Watch for these signs in bobcat country. Look for tracks along sandy washes, around muddy potholes and along stream banks. The tracks resemble those of a domestic tomcat, but measure about 2 inches across, spaced 10 to 12 inches apart. No claw marks show, the claws being sheathed except in combat.

Before the sport of varmint calling became popular, few bobcats were seen except by hunters using trained dogs to run and tree the furtive felines. Large numbers of bobcats can live in an area and the natives will swear that none exist. Recently, ranchers near

Here is an overenthusiastic—and now defunct—bobcat that was taken in by the sound of a rabbit in distress, produced by a skillful caller.

Bridgeport, California, felt the inroads of bobcat and coyote depredations on livestock and domestic fowl and hired a professional trapper. After sixty days, the local game warden was convinced that the area had been cleared. However, a weekend hunt by members of the California Varmint Callers Association netted twenty-three critters, many of them bobcats.

The most difficult problem for varmint callers is choosing fruitful terrain. Most losers at the sport defeat themselves before they start by calling areas that lack game. If the animals aren't there, obviously you can't call them!

One way of pinpointing promising territory is to search for tracks along dirt roads or on the soft shoulders of main roads. Other coyote "freeways" include sandy washes and wind-swept ridges. Coyote tracks resemble those of your pet dog, showing four toes and claw marks, approximately 2 inches wide by 2½ inches long, but usually with dirt tossed up behind. Coyotes travel most often at a "dogtrot" that eats up 5 to 10 miles an hour. Coyotes in a hurry have been clocked in excess of 40 miles an hour! This mobility makes tracks an indication that a coyote *was* there, but is not necessarily still around. Dog-like droppings, composed mostly of hair, are a certain sign of coyotes in the area.

Coyotes have an affinity for open flats surrounded by rolling hills or mountains. There they can spook rabbits out of brushy draws and run them down across open ground. In the early morning, they will often be returning to hillside dens from such hunting forays. This is the time to be sitting high on the face of the mountain—preferably on a rocky point with your back to a cliff, so that your quarry can't circle your position and wind you. Also, predators answering a call seldom look up until they near the source, and the caller has good vision over a wide area.

When calling on the flats, avoid a stand near a dry wash that will allow the critter to slip unseen downwind of your position. If possible, call with your back to a cliff, river or highway.

When choosing a stand, allow the critters some brush in which to approach within gunshot range. Coyotes and bobcats dislike crossing open ground that affords no cover. Sometimes they will hang around just inside a brushy patch, afraid to cross an opening, but loath to go away.

Shallow marshes where ducks sleep on the water at night provide excellent coyote hunting. Prairie wolves aren't fond of bathing, but they will swim out to catch ducks slumbering near the water's edge—though how they manage to catch the ducks unaware escapes me. One night a friend and I called up three "dogs" in about ten minutes around a broad marshland, and I went wading above my knees in search of one of our trophies. Every few yards, an alarmed duck burst from the water, almost at my feet, quacking an irate protest. It must have happened a dozen times, but try as I might to steel myself, I was startled out of my skin with each noisy flurry of wet feathers.

You can often find good hunting locations by querying farmers and ranchers in likely-looking areas. You can request permission to hunt on their land at the same time. Farmers and ranchers usually welcome polite, serious-minded varmint hunters; on a national scale, they suffer millions of dollars in property damage and stock losses annually from predation, especially of lambs and calves. Coyotes, bobcats and foxes are also death on ground-nesting birds such as quail, sage grouse, prairie chickens, pheasants and chukars.

When you go varmint calling, you are trying to outwit animals whose perception of sight, scent and sound is far beyond your own feeble capacities. It seems incredible that a coyote so distant you can barely make him out through a 7x35 binocular can actually *see* you hunkered down in the shade of that broad bush. But you better believe he can! The success of your hunt depends on accepting this fact. Total camouflage is the only answer, including jacket, pants, hat, head net and netting gloves. Incidentally, the camo pattern must match your surroundings. Bright green blotches stand out just fine against dry brown foliage. A practical answer is a reversible outfit offered by Kamo (Camouflage Manufacturing Company, Jacksonville, Fla.). The cotton sateen jacket and pants are a mottled green on one side and patchy brown on the other. They can be quickly turned inside out to match your background of the moment. If your local sporting-goods store doesn't handle Kamo, write direct to the company or to Burnham Brothers, Marble Falls, Texas, for their catalogue of varmint-calling equipment.

Holes are handy in the head net, to permit unobstructed vision. An elastic band sewn across the back will hold the net in

place. If head nets bug you, even though they are good protection
from bugs, the National Scent Company, Garden Grove, Calif.,
makes a BO Cream for hands and face that performs the double
duty of masking the skin color and the "man" smell as well.

For years, professional trappers have brewed noxious concoc-
tions from well-aged coyote or bobcat urine and diced intestines,
simmered for days to an eye-watering purée. Modern commercial
scents, such as those made by National Scent, have somehow
managed to retain their effectiveness with animals without being
offensive to people. Scents come in handy plastic spray bottles
labeled COYOTE and BOBCAT and can be sprayed on boots, trouser
cuffs and bushes around the stand. If an animal is suspected of
approaching from downwind, you can launch a fine spray into the
air, both to mask your own odor and to attract the animal.

You might as well sound an air-raid siren as smoke on a stand!
Even smoking in the car beforehand is bad; the stench permeates
your hair and clothing and oozes out for hours afterward. Also,
stay away from perfumed deodorants, after-shave lotions and
hair gook. Odorless mineral oil can be used to hold hair in place,
and a shower followed by a generous spraying with an unscented
deodorant will keep you from spreading "man" musk around your
stand.

If you hope to drag coyotes and bobcats in by their ears, you
must learn how to use a call. Most lung-powered calls consist of a
wooden or plastic tube, about 1 inch in diameter by 4 to 6 inches
long, containing a metal reed that vibrates to create a banshee-
like wail. Calls come in different pitches to imitate the gravelly
squall of a jackrabbit or the higher-pitched squeal of a cottontail.
Close-range coaxers emit the sounds of rats and mice, particularly
attractive to bobcats and foxes but also used to draw coyotes in
closer after the rabbit call has brought them within sight.

With the aid of training records from the Burnhams or Johnny
Stewart, of Waco, Texas, to show you the way, you should get the
hang of it in one season.

Solid-state tape and disk players, backed by extensive libraries
of prerecorded tapes and disks, offer the novice caller a decided
edge right from the start, allowing him to concentrate upon spotting and shooting the critters. The players tirelessly amplify a
wide range of rabbit and bird calls, with never a sour note. For an

With practice, determination and more practice, anyone can master these mouth-blown calls.

added asset, the speaker can be placed some distance from the hunter, drawing the critter's attention away. A mouth call pulls the animal's eyes right to the caller, but you can reduce this problem by giving only an occasional low, hard-to-locate squeal on the coaxer as the animal nears your position.

Most callers start their stand with a series of loud squalls to alert distant game, then drop to normal volume for about three minutes, then reduce it to lure critters close. I use low tones for a few minutes before the loud series, on the theory that close animals won't be frightened off by them. If nothing shows up, no harm done; then try it loud.

Excluding an occasional puma, the coyote is the largest predator on his range, making him bold and fearless—of all save man. If the call fools him, he will come barging in with all stops open to snatch that screaming rabbit from its captor. Smaller predators approach more stealthily, especially the bobcat.

Young coyotes are liable to run from the call, until they learn to hunt and identify the rabbit cry. Then they may be totally naïve and practically run the caller down in their anxiety for a free meal. But shoot and miss, and they'll never forget! I suspect that an educated coyote can communicate his knowledge. In areas where a coyote has escaped my shot, I've found it useless to call again for a season or two. *All* of the coyotes are wise to the call!

Once the calling area is chosen, drive as close as is practical to your planned stand before hoofing it. A moving vehicle is less alarming to animals than a man on foot. Try to park your car or truck where it will be screened from view by brush or trees, preferably in a low spot such as a ravine or dry wash.

Shut down your vehicle with as little racket as possible. Open your doors quietly while you're rolling to a stop and leave them slightly ajar. The slamming of doors, or even the soft click of a gently closed door latch, carries hundreds of yards and instantly alerts any game within hearing. Palaver between hunting partners should be carried out before leaving the vehicle, not en route to the stand.

Walk into the wind, far enough to leave the popping sounds of cooling metal and the smells of oil and gasoline well behind you. *Never* walk across the area that you intend to call over. Take the shortest practical route to your stand, avoiding crunchy gravel and dry brush. Don't allow binoculars, rifle and other gear to clink together. Load your rifle before proceeding to the stand; then raise the bolt handle to make it safe.

Having chosen your stand, back into the shade of a bush or against a tree to break up your silhouette. Scuff the ground with your toe to roust spiders, snakes, *et al.* that were there ahead of you. Rocks and stickers overlooked in your haste to start the stand can later impress you with their presence in a most discomforting way! Avoid cramped positions that you must inevitably squirm out of just as a sharp-eyed coyote is looking you over. Wait a few minutes before calling, so that birds and small game can forget your presence and return to normal activities.

Learn to sit immobile and let your eyes do the searching. A swiveling head is a dead giveaway. Keep your shiny rifle barrel down low, or better, wrap it with camo netting. Before calling, study the area around you and fix it in your mind. Later you may find a "bush" that wasn't there before. If it has a white patch of fur on its chest, fire away!

A blind fashioned of cardboard or chicken wire on a light frame covered with camouflage netting allows you some freedom of movement by hiding all but your head. You can even afford the comfort of a low folding stool. If the wind rises, you may have to tie the blind down.

A howling wind is not calculated to improve calling anyway. The sound of the call can't reach far upwind, and downwind it carries your scent with it.

Sometimes the call will set coyotes to howling in the distance, indicating they're interested. When they stop howling, they are on the way. However, if they bark at you, you might as well pack up and move out—they're on to you! I've never been able to call in a coyote after it barked at me. And I can't recall one barking from upwind. It always happened after they had my scent.

The length of time you remain on a stand depends upon your confidence in it. A good stand should be worth twenty to thirty minutes of your time, perhaps more if your quarry is bobcats. Bobcats, because they are *stalking* animals, usually approach far more slowly than coyotes. If you have ever watched a house cat stalk a bird, you have some idea of how patient bobcats skulk from bush to bush, pausing to study the situation interminably before moving. Use your watch to time your stands. Sometimes ten minutes seems like thirty.

Bobcats usually answer the call much faster under the cover of darkness. However, night hunting is not for the uninitiated. To begin with, it's a pretty eerie business even in familiar territory, and unexplained sounds from the darkness can make your skin crawl! Don't walk without a flashlight. In the Southwest, rattlesnakes are out in force on balmy nights. Also, you can step off into a gully or dry wash—or an abandoned mine shaft. But there's no denying the thrills and beauty of night hunting, with that jeweled canopy overhead and shooting stars lacing the sky.

Beginners would do well to hunt on moonlit nights, although there is a popular prejudice that contends varmints don't answer as well as in the dark of the moon. Wear dark, soft-finished clothing that won't rustle, and use the same precautions regarding concealment that you would in daylight.

Keep your hunting party down to a maximum of three, to avoid too much conversation and to keep from getting in one another's way. One man should operate the call and light, while the other two shoot—each with a well-defined arc of fire. Stay close together to be near the light and to facilitate silent communication.

Always keep the position of your vehicle firmly in mind, to spare yourself the embarrassment of a hole in the radiator or perhaps having to wait for daylight to find your way back.

Range is hard to judge at night. It's better to pass up those long shots, for two reasons: First, you can't identify the animal positively, and you don't want to shoot a deer or some rancher's dog. Second, if you do hit your quarry, he'll be difficult to find. The chap holding the light should remain at the stand, directing its beam toward the downed animal until it's recovered.

A long-held "trade secret" of pioneer predator callers is a red lens over the light, which allows them to put the main beam directly on the animal rather than having to use only the fringes. Thus fewer critters can sneak in under the light and escape detection, and they aren't spooked by the red light as they are by a bright white beam. Avery Corporation, Electra, Texas, offers a red-lens head lamp, held on the forehead by a wide elastic band. It comes complete with belt battery pack, which holds a switch and variable condenser to adjust light intensity. Dialed low, it reveals bobcat eyes at 40 yards. Dialed high, it lights the entire body for certain identification, and the eyes become fiercely glowing coals.

Also from Avery comes the Mini Gun Light, a tiny high-intensity light with a self-contained power source. It attaches directly to the gun barrel and doesn't change the rifle's point of impact. The shooter can press a microswitch attached to the fore-end when ready to fire. The light projects a concentrated beam right down the line of sight.

Any cartridge adequate for predators is ample for varmints such as chucks and ground squirrels, but the opposite is not necessarily true. For instance, the .22 rimfire Long Rifle launching a 37-grain hollow-point at 1,365 fps is fine for rabbits, squirrels and chucks out to 100 yards, but to use it for predators would be overreaching, even on smaller species at relatively close range. Sighted in at 75 yards, it drops but 3 inches at 100. The looping trajectory is formed between 100 and 125 yards, when the tiny slug hits a sudden downdraft and sinks almost a foot.

Until 1930, when the monopoly was broken by the .22 Hornet, the lowly rimfire was the only small-game cartridge around. The Hornet had its limitations too, shutting off at about 150 yards.

There followed a genealogy of successively larger centerfire small-bores, culminating in the .220 Swift, which is still a fine predator/vermin cartridge even though orphaned by its makers. After World War II, a lethargy settled over the manufacture of .22 centerfires, with many old-timers just fading away.

The Hornet, the .219 Zipper and the .218 Bee are little more than fond memories today—but there's little profit in wasting tears, since the .222 Remington with its 50-grain soft-point moving at 3,200 fps does everything they did, only better. The Bee and Zipper were limited to about 175 yards maximum range on chucks, whereas the "Triple Deuce" can nail vermin in its tracks to 200-plus. However, this added muscle still doesn't qualify the .222 as a coyote/bobcat cartridge. Some hunters fail to appreciate the tremendous stamina and incredible will to live exhibited by the coyote. He can survive wounds that would be fatal to most deer.

Marginal for predators but fine for vermin up to 300 yards are the .222 Remington Magnum and the .223 Remington. These small-bore ballistic twins add 5 grains to their bullets and give them a 100-fps-faster send-off. In 1970, the .222 Magnum followed the Hornet, *et al.* into oblivion, when Remington stopped chambering it (into the Model 700) in favor of the .223, known to the military as the 5.56 mm. Actually the two, together, were redundant.

A .22 trio that effectively handles all manner of varmints, large and small, is the .224 Weatherby, .225 Winchester and .22/250 Remington. A year after Winchester dropped the Swift and introduced the .225, Remington countered by factory-loading and -chambering a cartridge that had enjoyed three decades of unprecedented popularity with bench-rest shooters and varmint buffs as a wildcat—the .22/250.

Roy Weatherby started the triumphant triumvirate three years earlier, in 1963, with the introduction of the .224, a belted-head case with double-radiused shoulder which looked for all the world like a .300 Weatherby that had shrunk in the wash. The fine vehicle for the .224 Weatherby is the Varmintmaster rifle, with a short action scaled down from the original Mark V to the exact size required to house the new .22 centerfire. The rifle is light, 6½ pounds, and short, 43¼ inches, and even with the 24-inch barrel, it swings like a baton but hits like a recoilless cannon. The Varmintmaster retains the Mark V's abbreviated 58-degree bolt lift, interrupted-thread locking lugs and fully enclosed case head.

For populated rural areas where the throaty blast of a .22 centerfire is unwelcome, the muted-voiced .22 Winchester Magnum Rim Fire (pushing a 40-grain jacketed hollow-point at 2,000 fps) or the bottle-necked rimfire Remington 5 mm (zipping its 38-grain Power-Lokt hollow-point with serrated jacket along at 2,100 fps) offers 150-yard effectiveness on vermin and small predators.

Sighted in at 100 yards (midrange trajectory about 1½ inches), the .22 Magnum drops almost 6 inches at 150 yards, compared with about 4 inches for the 5 mm, showing a clear edge for the latter. Remaining velocity for the 5 mm at 100 yards is 1,605 fps, compared with 1,390 fps for the .22 Magnum. Despite the obvious ballistic advantage displayed by the 5 mm, there appears to be just about a tossup at the target, with the added bullet diameter and weight of the .22 canceling out the velocity advantage of the 5 mm. Either one of these cartridges is an excellent choice for the occasional varmint shooter, especially the youngster who hasn't evolved into a dedicated varmint buff as yet. And both provide relatively economical hunting for nonreloaders.

For an added plus: both are free of the danger of ricochet always present with .22 Long Rifles—a welcome feature for shooting around grazing stock or near farm buildings.

Way out West, "where you have to walk sideways to keep from flyin'," .22 bullets, however fast, adopt two trajectories when the wind blows: one down; the other *sideways!* That's when we reach for our .24-bores! A recent popularity poll among California varmint callers showed the .243 Winchester outnumbering the runner-up better than 2 to 1. The 6-mm Remington had a substantial following as well. Factory ballistics are about equal for the two rounds, but the slightly longer case with somewhat longer neck of the Remington 6 mm makes it more appealing to reloaders, who can take advantage of the slightly greater powder capacity.

The distinction of having the greatest powder capacity among .24-bores goes to the .240 Weatherby Magnum, my own choice for best combination varmint/deer cartridge. You can subload the

A .240 Weatherby accounted for this plump ground squirrel. The .240, and others of the 6-mm family, are effective out to 500 yards plus.

versatile .240 to a whisper, using 60- and 75-grain bullets, for shooting vermin in rural areas, or soup it up with 80- to 90-grain bullets to lift predators right out of the saddle! It pushes big slugs, such as the Speer 105 grain, at velocities calculated to drill a black bear end to end. Even elk and moose have been taken with the .240 Weatherby, but I don't recommend it.

By loading to overall cartridge length of 3¼ inches, instead of the recommended 3¹⁄₁₆, you can seat the long 105-grain Speer in the .240 without intruding into the powder space below the shoulder, as you must with either the .243 or the 6-mm Remington. There is ample space in the magazine and chamber leade of the Weatherby Mark V for the longer cartridge.

Remington made varmint news in 1971 by introducing the .17 Remington, a mini-bore necked down from the .223. All external dimensions remain unchanged save for the neck diameter and the shoulder, which has been pushed back .087 inch farther from the case mouth to allow a longer neck. The 23-degree shoulder angle

was retained. Remington shrank its Power-Lokt bullet down to
.1725 caliber and 25-grain weight. It requires 280 of these tiny
pellets to make 1 pound!

This leaves the muzzle of the 24-inch stainless-steel barrel of
the Model 700 BDL short bolt-action at 4,020 fps. With the rifle
sighted in at 200 yards, it rises above the line of sight just 1.2
inches and drops only 6.3 at 300 yards. By then the tiny bullet
has lost half of its velocity. Despite that, vermin still come vio-
lently unglued because of the high rotational velocity imparted
by the 1-in-9 twist.

Those chuck/squirrel hunters who reject all shots under 200
yards and delight in picking off tiny targets at 400 to 600 yards
require heavier bullets to maintain velocity and resist wind drift
at extreme ranges. For them, there are the .257 Weatherby, .264
Winchester and .25/06 Remington. Every missile launch from
one of these titans is calculated to rattle the windows in farm-
houses leagues distant, as well as rattling the shooter's teeth some
—leading to complaints from both.

These benighted souls usually arrive in the field toting war-
surplus Army range finders and portable anemometers, the latter
in a vain attempt to outwit the wind. The wind has two effects
upon the varmint hunter. First, it tries to bowl him over and
grabs fitfully at his rifle barrel. Then, when he manages to get off
a shot, the wind gleefully snatches the bullet and drags it off
course. A heavy rifle, tight sling and low shooting position help
offset the first problem, but the second is overcome only by pro-
longed and astute observation of wind and its effects upon bullet
flight.

A 10-mph cross wind, which is barely enough to ruffle your
hair, displaces a 55-grain bullet from one of the three high-
velocity .22 centerfires well over a foot at 400 yards. Displacement is directly proportional to wind velocity. Thus a 20-mph
wind has twice the effect, 5 mph half as much, and so on.

The perplexed shooter may be sitting in a dead calm, but who
knows what evil eddies lurk between him and his target? Relatively mild breezes wafting up converging mountain valleys can
clash and boil upward in an awesome updraft, lofting the bullet
into a reverse trajectory that puts it well over the head of any
chuck. In shooting across wide, deep valleys, the usual wind in-

dicators—such as waving grass and mirage—are lacking. A spotting scope can reveal motion of trees and brush at the target to give the shooter a hint of wind direction and velocity.

Boiling mirage, itself a villain in the field, can become an unwitting ally in doping of the wind. Observed through a spotting scope against a light background such as a brown hillside or the sky, its antics reveal wind direction and velocity. In still air, the waves from mirage rise straight up, but they bend to follow the wind. The more wind, the sharper the angle, up to about 15 mph, when the mirage is blown away.

The best solution, if your object is ultra-long-range shooting, is to load the heaviest bullets practical in a given caliber. That means 60- and even 70-grain bullets in the top .22s, 80- to 100-grain slugs in the 6 mms and 117-grain bullets in quarter-bores.

The best wind guesser in the world won't be any threat to distant vermin unless he has a rifle that delivers better than minute-of-angle accuracy. That means either a bolt-action or a single-shot. The latter suits the relaxed pace of vermin shooting. The Ruger Number One comes in a 9-pound varmint version with heavy barrel, already topped by target-scope mounting bases.

Varmint-weight bolt-actions are offered by most of the major makers. Remington has added the 40XB heavy barrel to its field-style Model 700 BDL in .25/06 caliber, also with scope blocks attached. It's hard to imagine a finer rifle than this for the purpose! From Winchester comes the Model 70 Varmint, weighing in at a formidable 9¾ pounds with heavy barrel.

Weatherby offers his Mark V rifle with No. 2 contour 26-inch barrel on the .224 Varmintmaster, and also his .240 and .257 Weatherby Magnums. Any one of the three will drop vermin as far as the eye, with the aid of 20X optics, can see. Both the .240 and the .257 can double as big-game rifles as well. The Mark V is also available in a mirror version for port-siders.

Those vermin buffs who think nothing of hauling a portable bench rest into the field with them are not troubled by rifles that scale nearly a dozen pounds. But predator hunters, who are wont to scale cliffs and clamber over bluffs in pursuit of wary meat eaters, are likely to temper their desire for accuracy with the need for a lighter rifle. Standard-weight or even featherweight bolt-action rifles better meet their needs.

When the shooting becomes close and fast, the varmint caller reaches for a pump- or lever-action, or even an autoloader. Among the autos that measure up are Harrington & Richardson's Ultra Automatic in .243, Remington's Model 742 in .243 or 6 mm Remington and Browning's BAR in .243.

A "new sport" is calling predators into handgun range. To get them within a radius of 50 yards or so requires every trick of the caller's trade, plus a working knowledge of practical pistoleering with any of the "big three" magnums, the .357, .41 and .44. This is a postgraduate sport, open only to callers who have worked out their apprenticeship with rifles first.

I don't believe in scoped handguns, but scopes are essential to any long-range rifle accuracy. Vermin hunters require the highest possible power level to hold on pop-bottle-sized targets at 300 to 500 yards. For them, a Redfield 3200 Target scope, available in fixed-power 12X, 16X, 20X and 24X, represents about the ultimate. The 3200 is made tough enough to withstand recoil, so that it can be mounted solidly without any provision for slippage during recoil. Windage and elevation adjustments are internal, rather than built into the mount.

Predator callers prefer to use variables in the 3X-to-9X range, such as the Bushnell ScopeChief (with Command Post, which comes in very handy at night or in late evening).

Whichever phase of varmint hunting you prefer, you'll quite often find yourself skunked by a temperamental rifle, a varmint that won't cooperate or just plain bad luck. Perhaps these factors account for the enthusiasm of most of the varminters I know. Tomorrow, they believe, will be different. And sometimes it actually is.

5

CLOSE-RANGE
BIG-GAME HUNTING

BY BOB HAGEL

BY TODAY's standards, hunting situations in which the ranges do not normally exceed 100 yards can be considered close-range. Modern rifles, cartridges and sights have made it easier for a reasonably good shot to hit an animal in a vital spot at over 200 yards than it was for hunters a generation or two ago to connect at 100. But for several reasons, even though the 200-yard shot is not nearly as difficult as it once was, it is not close-range shooting. The difference in the kind of game that is normally hunted at close range, the kind of country it is hunted in, the conditions under which it is shot, all contribute to a different set of problems. This is especially true in the consideration of rifles, cartridges, bullets and sighting equipment.

Obviously, most close-in hunting will be done in heavily timbered or brushy country where the stuff is too thick to permit the hunter to see game at any great distance. There are chunks of this habitat in nearly every section of the country where big game is found, from the whitetail woods of the central, southern and northeastern states to the rain forests along the Pacific Coast. In between, you have the brushy bottomlands of the Midwest and uncounted miles of heavy stands of Douglas fir, cedar and lodgepole pine interlaced with alder, birch, willow and dozens of smaller shrubs that cover much of the high country of the western mountain states. Farther north, there is some pretty thick country in the Canadian game lands from coast to coast, and the tangle that makes up the forests of southeastern Alaska is second to none in bringing the hunter and quarry nose to nose before either is aware of the other.

Consider the vast area where close-range hunting is the rule and the great variety of game found there, and you begin to realize the diversity in the kinds of hunting ordnance required. There is a lot of difference between hunting white-tailed deer and black bears in thick stuff, stalking elk in an Idaho lodgepole patch and trying to snoop out an Alaskan brown bear in the alder and devil's-club jungles along a southeastern-Alaskan salmon creek.

By far the greatest share of close-range hunting is for white-tailed deer. It matters not where the action takes place; most whitetail hunting is done in the brush. There are many forms of pursuit, but invariably the shooting is at close range—often so close that it can be done with a shotgun.

For hunting game in the weight class of whitetails, you do not need especially powerful cartridges, nor do you need heavy rifles to fire them. This is perhaps where the famous .30/30 won the title of having killed more deer than any other cartridge. This is not to say that there is no better cartridge for hunting whitetails than the .30/30—but, everything considered, it is pretty hard to find one.

The main thing is that you do not need high velocity because the range does not require flat trajectory. Neither do you need great penetration or wallop, because the game is small in size and light in weight. Great accuracy is not a necessity except for the occasional head or neck shot, because at ranges from a few feet to 100 yards, 3-inch groups are more than adequate.

What you do need is a cartridge that will reliably expand its bullets, and bullets that will reliably expand at the velocity the cartridge develops yet give enough penetration to reach the vitals on angle shots and completely penetrate on most body hits.

You also need a rifle that is fairly light, fast and handy, one with which you can get off a shot at the buck under the flag before there is nothing but the flag in sight. This is why the Model 94

The eastern whitetail buck is not a large animal as a rule—150 pounds on the hoof is quite respectable—and does not take much killing. However, he is almost always hunted in dense cover such as this, and at short range. The best rifle, therefore, is one that fires a fairly heavy bullet at moderate velocity and offers a fast repeat shot. (Photo courtesy of Winchester News Bureau)

Winchester became so popular, and why the Savage 99, along with the lever-action Marlins, followed closely. The pumps are also fast and quite handy, and so are the autoloaders, but they are heavier and not as compact as the flat-sided, short, light lever guns.

In spite of its popularity, I personally find one great fault with the Winchester 94: it is not well adapted to scope sights. The Savage and the Marlins yes, but not the 94. I know there are still uncounted numbers of hunters who look down their noses at scoped rifles for the whitetail woods, but this does not make iron sights—especially the open, factory-installed variety—the best sights for even close-range hunting. A good compact scope in from 2X to 3X is a far better choice, especially for older eyes. You don't need a lot of power, but you do need a wide field and clarity that will bite deep into the shadows of dark woods.

If you insist on iron sights with an open rear notch, the wider and shallower the V is, the easier and faster it is to pick up the front sight. Actually, the wide, shallow V is more accurate than the tight V or the U notch, especially in poor light, because it blurs less and makes it much easier to tell how much front sight is showing. The best open rear sights I have ever tried are those used by the British on their double rifles for dangerous African game. Their V notch is very shallow, running from side to side of the leaf. There is usually a white line below the center of the V that draws the eye there instantly.

For nearly any hunting at close range in this country, the aperture, or peep, rear sight is far superior to the open variety. Take the disk out, leave a big hole to look through and you'll be able to pick up the front sight quickly. Don't worry about centering the front sight in the aperture; your eye will do that automatically.

With a little practice, the scope is just as fast as iron sights for deer shooting, and a lot more accurate. Not only that, but you will avoid hitting a lot of twigs, brush and small saplings that you would never see with iron sights. You may also avoid shooting a doe or your hunting partner in the belief you're cutting down on a buck. Don't make light of this; it happens every hunting season.

Even though the .30/30 has undoubtedly killed more whitetailed deer than any other cartridge, this doesn't necessarily make it the best load for whitetail hunting. There are a number of cartridges in the same class that are just as good for brush hunting, and perhaps some of them, like the old .35 Remington and .358 Winchester, are even better. If you want to hunt whitetails in the bushes with your .270, .30/06 or whatever, there is nothing wrong with that, either. I'd suggest the heavier bullets fired at lower velocity, and the round-point may not be deflected by twigs as badly as the pointed form. But mostly you don't need high velocity, and lack of it will spoil less meat on angle shots. As for brush bucking, do not try to shoot through brush with *anything*; no bullet will plow through much of the stuff and land anywhere near where you point it—and this goes for *any* brush hunting for *any* game with *any* cartridge and caliber or bullet weight.

The greatest likelihood of hitting a tree or branch occurs in shooting at running game in heavy timber. This is hard to avoid when you're letting go at an animal running across the line of fire. Just when everything looks right, your swing puts something be-

Even though mule deer are often shot at long range, a hunter is frequently required to try for one close up, and with brush or trees in the path of the slug, as in this case. To handle both situations, the gunner needs a bullet that carries well over great distances, but has enough weight to buck brush. (Photo courtesy of Winchester News Bureau)

tween you and the game and the bullet slams into it. The only chance of avoiding this is to pick an opening ahead of the game and try to let off when the animal crosses it. Sometimes it works, sometimes it doesn't.

There is little use in trying to tell anyone how much to lead a running buck zipping off to right or left. First, as in shotgun shooting, no two shooters do it exactly alike; some snap-shoot, some use sustained lead, some swing by. Second, who knows how fast the animal is going, exactly how far away it is or at what angle it is running from the gun? You'll have to dope that out, and quick.

Also, there isn't anything wrong with a bolt-action rifle for a

whitetail or black bear in the thick stuff. The bolt rifle doesn't
handle quite as fast as the lever guns, autoloaders and pumps, but
for the first shot it's hard to find any difference. Forget the idea
that you should be able to squirt out successive shots in a ma-
chine-gun burst of firepower. A well-aimed first shot is worth a
dozen later snap shots at where you think the deer should be.
You'll come up with a lot fewer cripples if you try to make sure
of *every* shot you fire, and a bolt-action will do very well for this
kind of work. When you start hunting large and sometimes dangerous game in heavy cover, you'll likely be forced to use a bolt
gun because it is the only one chambered for the magnum cartridge you wish to use. (The exception being the Browning BAR,
magnum version.)

For hunting black bears in the brush, you don't need much more
power than for hunting deer in the same place, but when you go
to heavier game that likes the deep, dark woods (game like elk,
moose and the big bears—mountain grizzly or Alaskan brown),
the rules change. Here you're opposing so much bulk, weight,
bone diameter and tough muscle that shots fired at adverse angles are not going to plow through into the vitals as they would
in a whitetail with the same cartridge and bullet. And as you gain
experience in hunting big animals in heavy timber and brush,
you soon find that it is the rare shot that is offered with the animal
in classic broadside position. Normally, he is quartering one way
or another, or is moving with either nose or tail pointed at you,
although you may not be able to see either. If he has heard you
or sensed your presence, the chances are he is pointed south for
a quick getaway, with his north end on his backtrail and eyes
peeking over his rump.

I've followed elk around in thick timber and heavy brush when
I was less than 100 yards from them most of the time, usually
much closer, but could not get a decent shot. I would catch a
fleeting glimpse of patches of hair, a twitching ear, the ivory-
tipped points of massive antlers or, if I squatted low enough to
look under the branches, black legs seemingly without a body.
But never did I see anything solid to shoot at.

On one occasion I saw a big patch of tan hide through a hole.
I watched and became aware through another hole that there was
a leg sticking down below it, and by the shape I knew it was a

front leg. I knew that if I held into the tan patch above the leg my bullet would go *somewhere* into the shoulder/lung area. What I didn't know was which way it would go into the elk after it struck. Was the elk facing toward or away from me? Or could it possibly be broadside? Would the bullet go straight into the heart/lung area, where little penetration was needed, or would it have to plow through the heavy shoulder muscle and bone to get there? Or maybe that was the off leg I was seeing and the tan patch was far back in the rib section, requiring the bullet to plow through part of the soggy mass of grass and water that is the paunch to reach the boiler room.

When you sit before the fire the next winter telling someone

Elk, hunted in heavy timber, often have to be shot at from less-than-ideal angles. Powerful loads are recommended, such as the .333 OKH Belted cartridge and 250-grain Barnes heavy-jacket bullet that accounted for this trophy.

about it, or if you tell your stories with a typewriter, the solution
is easy: don't shoot under those conditions. But when you're looking at the elk after many hours of stalking, often with water running out of the tops of your boots from crawling through rain- or
snow-drenched brush, the chances are that you will shoot. And
if you do, you had better have a cartridge of adequate power,
with the right bullet to get inside and tear things up.

Even if you are lucky enough to catch the elk in an opening
where you can see all of him, the law of averages is against his
being broadside. Even if he appears to be, he probably isn't, and
for your bullet to get into the vitals, it may have to penetrate a
lot more elk than you think. Remember that the bullet that
worked so well on the whitetail buck that weighed 150 to 300
pounds on the hoof may fail miserably on the bull elk that goes
near half a ton. Anything we've covered here regarding elk also
applies to moose in thick cover, and a big bull, especially the
Alaska-Yukon variety, may go from 1,500 pounds to near a ton.

Without too much thought it is obvious that the cartridge and
bullet that worked so well on deer and black bear are less than
adequate for the heavy game. It is not a matter of what cartridge
will do the job under *ideal* conditions; it boils down to what it
takes to do the best job under *adverse* conditions.

Actually, many of the cartridges of yesteryear were pretty
damn good close-range numbers. Most of them were of large caliber and fired bullets of good sectional density that gave fairly
deep penetration. By today's standards, they were of low velocity.
Their bullets expanded into classic "mushroom" form, yet held together well enough to give deep penetration. These were cartridges like the .38/55, the .45/70, the .35 Winchester, the .405.
Winchester and the .30/40 with the original 220-grain bullet.

Today we use cartridges delivering much higher velocities,
and we also have many bullet weights for nearly every cartridge.
The magnums drive even the heaviest bullets at velocities that
tear them apart at close range, unless they are extremely tough
and well designed. This is not conducive to the deep penetration
needed against big game at close range; but the high velocity also
produces energy that is vital to quick kills if the bullet gets inside
where it will do some damage.

It is fine to have a special rifle for every kind of game and

Moose like to feed in willow patches so dense it's hard to see more than 50 feet in them. Under these conditions, long, heavy bullets are needed to buck the brush. This Idaho bull was taken with a 275-grain .338 bullet.

hunting condition, and many hunters own an arsenal to cover all situations; but how often do you take several guns on an extended hunt in the back country? You may hunt sheep, antelope and mule deer (where long-range shooting is the rule) on the same trip on which you hunt elk and moose in the brush. If you are in the North, the long-range shooting often associated with sheep and caribou is usually mixed with moose and grizzly hunting that will frequently take place at close range. The same cartridge will do nicely for both if you don't go overboard on the small-bore end and use the right bullet for the conditions and game hunted. In some cases where the caliber is adequate you can get by nicely with one bullet weight for both kinds of shooting if the slug is of the right design.

For serious close-range shooting of heavy game, especially in the brush, the 7-mm magnum is about as small a caliber as should be considered, and then only with 175-grain bullets. Of course, weight alone does not make it a good slug for heavy game; the design has to be right. First, in order to kill quickly, the bullet must expand enough to create a fairly large frontal area—at least double the original caliber—but it must not expand to the point at which it loses its core and disintegrates. To penetrate deeply in heavy muscle and drive through big bones, the shank must stay in one piece and retain weight enough to drive the expanded front end into the vitals. When you consider that it may take from 2 to 3 feet of penetration to do this against elk and moose on quartering shots, you can see why the bullet must be heavy and of good design.

The same situation exists even with the largest calibers, including the .375 and .45s. Even a 300-grain .375 or a 500-grain .458 bullet will not give deep penetration if it blows up. In fact, a well-designed .30-caliber bullet of 200 to 220 grains would be preferable and would give deeper penetration. These .30-caliber bullets fired from big cartridges that churn up a lot of energy are good close-range medicine for any North American game. Actually, the deepest penetration I have ever achieved with any cartridge has been with the .338-bores like the .338 Winchester Magnum, the .340 Weatherby and several wildcats, all with 250-grain bullets. These are ideal cartridges for close-range shooting of the heaviest American game, and are also extremely flat at longer ranges, especially with lighter, better-shaped bullets. There are few .35 cartridges made today, even though they are ideal for close work on heavy game, and fewer good bullets in that caliber.

Actually, there are not too many bullets made in any caliber that are ideal for close-range work. Some of the heavy bullets from various makers will work quite well if velocity isn't too great, but many of them will come apart at close range where velocity is still high. Of the commercial ammunition, my vote goes to the Remington Core-Lokt in heavy weights. For the handloader, the Nosler is available in most calibers and has no peer for reliable expansion and deep penetration. The newer, custom-made Bitterroot Bonded Core gives outstanding performance, but is available in only a few calibers and is hard to obtain.

So far we've dealt with game that is not dangerous; but what about the big bears that on occasion do fight back, provoked or otherwise? The fact is that none of them should ever be shot at what would normally be considered long range for other game. My old friend John Porter, who guided for several years in the grizzly country of interior Alaska, always said that you should never shoot at a grizzly beyond 150 yards, and never at under 50 yards unless it had to be done. Good advice, but hard to follow on the close end in brushy country. In fact, it doesn't have to be especially brushy for you to find yourself entirely too close to a big bear.

On the last hunting trip I made with Porter in the Johnson River country on the west side of the Tanana, I had an experience of that kind that could well have been my last one.

Another hunter and I were prowling along the river bar one morning looking for a trophy Dall ram when we spotted a she-grizzly eating blueberries and working down the slope toward the mouth of a small side canyon. My companion wanted the bear, so we headed up the glacial gut to try to head her off when she came out on the bench above. We made it just in time to catch the bear as she came out of the alders into an opening at a range of 50 feet. Everything would have been fine if my partner had been using the right bullet for this close-range work on grizzlies. He whacked the rather small bear in the neck just ahead of the shoulder as she quartered toward us. She went down but didn't stay, and came end over end down the slope right on top of us. A couple more shots didn't hit anything vital, and when she was 15 feet away I started backing out of the way. Seeing the movement, the old girl decided I was what had bit her and charged. That was one time I would have been happy without a scope; all I could see was hair! But the bullet took her in the point of the shoulder and damn near tore it off, and she reared up and came down 5 feet from my boot toes.

We were both using .30-caliber rifles—his a .30/06, mine the then-new .300 Winchester Magnum. But my companion used Winchester 180-grain Silvertip bullets, while I had 180-grain Noslers. His first shot failed to penetrate the neck and get into the off shoulder. All it did was knock the bear silly for a minute or so. If his bullet had held up under the velocity of even the '06 cartridge instead of coming apart, there would have been no trouble.

This Alaskan brown bear was killed at 130 yards by a 250-grain Bitter-root bullet fired from a .340 Weatherby Magnum.

Most mountain grizzlies are, of course, shot at longer ranges in the open, but your bullet still has to get inside to stop one, and it takes a bullet designed for close-range deep penetration to do it.

In the case of big brown bears in southeast Alaska, much of the shooting can take place at ranges of only a few feet. This is especially true when you're hunting in the fall along the salmon creeks with their tangled jungle of brush that comes right down to water's edge. Here you need a cartridge delivering plenty of energy—but even more, you need a bullet that will break up a lot of bone from any angle and get inside and tear hell out of the internal machinery. The more bone you can break up, the more likely you are to immobilize the bear—something that's highly desirable at close quarters.

Even when you're hunting the beaches there is a good deal of close-range work. You may spot a bear a mile away, but when you get there he may suddenly appear around a rock or clump of brush within spitting distance. In these cases you never feel overgunned!

The sport of close-range big-game shooting actually comprises several different situations—the game varies in size, and it is dangerous or nondangerous. For the smaller, deer-size animals, about any cartridge will do, with emphasis toward a heavier bullet at lower velocity—something that will expand quite rapidly, yet give fairly deep penetration. If the bullet goes on through the animal, so much the better; it will leave a good blood trail to follow if the animal moves out of sight, and it usually does.

If the game is large, you need plenty of wallop, and to get it you have to have either a very large bore with heavy bullets shot at low to medium velocity or a smaller bore with long, heavy bullets and fairly high velocity.

If the game is big and dangerous, you never go amiss by having a bore of .30 caliber or up, preferably larger; plenty of bullet weight in the right design and a large helping of velocity to give it authority. As I said, there are times when you don't feel overgunned no matter what you're carrying.

6

LONG-RANGE
BIG-GAME HUNTING

BY WARREN PAGE

PERHAPS the easiest piece to write is the one damning the hunter who shoots at long range. It is comfortable, like upholding motherhood, to ridicule him as being unsportsmanlike; to cuss him out as an optimistic chance-taker who defies the law of gravity and so, presumably, all the known facts about both man performance and rifle performance. At least one gun-writing notable annually takes a swipe at the gent who shoots, or claims to shoot, at game at ranges beyond, say, 250 yards, and in the swiping obviously gratifies himself with that holier-than-thou feeling.

But such are the conditions of modern hunting, and such are the qualities of modern equipment, that our concept of what constitutes proper sporting range merits a fair amount of study. When rifles used simple iron sights and blew lead balls out of their tubes, the wise hunter got as near to tomahawk-throwing range as possible. A try at 150 to 200 yards was then hardly sporting, save for the likes of Daniel Boone or Lew Wetzel or Simon Girty. The buffalo killers who a century later operated on our western plains could hit and kill with acceptable surety at considerably greater range with their black-powder semi-cannon, however. Precisely how far, of course, depended on whose story you read. They outstripped everyone save, perhaps, the snipers of the Civil War period who, with special rifles and Malcolm scopes, got amazing hits with the Minié ball. The big changes came later. With the development of the unit cartridge of small bore, velocities in the Mach III area, effective smokeless powders and efficient optical sights, the idea of taking game at long range but by reasonably sporting methods has altered significantly.

Modern military thinking is, of course, committed to an idea alien to riflemen—that of spewing masses of bullets at the enemy rather than of directing single unerring shots. I suspect a partial reason for this is that it's too slow and costly to train men to remain cool under hammering and to use a rifle as a rifle rather than as a garden hose. Yet even the modern military has found time and money for a sniper program in which men are trained in long-range riflery, equipped with range-estimating scopes of Redfield persuasion and 7.62 NATO rifles of a high degree of accuracy, whether modified Remington 40X single-shots or worked-over Garands. They kill enemy personnel with great regularity at 600 to 1,000 yards.

But we are not here concerned with military problems, and I mention this only as an indication of the capabilities of modern equipment. There are plenty of civilian signs. For example, in the past few years records have been badly smashed by a 7-mm magnum rifle that poked, as I recall, 43 consecutive Xs into the 20-inch center ring of the 1,000-yard target. It used the Sierra 168-grain boattail bullet, right out of the box. At the same time, a group of accuracy bugs centering in Pennsylvania have been pleasuring themselves by firing from a rest at a known 1,000 yards, tightest 10-round group to win. It ordinarily takes between 10 inches and 1 foot to win, but the world record, held by a gal named Mary DeVito, is only 7.687 inches. That's close to two-thirds of a minute. It becomes evident that we now have cartridges and sights that could make hitting an elk's chest at a known 1,000 yards almost a sure thing.

But I am not here holding forth about shooting such game at 1,000 or so yards, unknown range; rather, about what is indeed long range for contemporary hunting equipment and mere mortals—more like 400 yards. Sometimes 500. Beyond that, we may well have to wait for even further betterments in either man or his shooting gear.

As of now, however, it is quite possible, with the right man, rifle and cartridge, to *expect* to make killing hits at ranges between 350 and often 500 yards, assuming conditions are in the hunter's favor. Note that the statement is heavily qualified. You can't do it offhand or with a .35 Remington deer rifle unless you are as blessed by fortune as the man who makes eleven straight passes at Las Vegas. Everything *must* be going your way, and the name of the game in long-range shooting is to *make* everything go your way.

I call to mind a far-out kill—admittedly too far out, perhaps, to be properly sporting. In Les Bowman's Wyoming elk country, we were packing in to Pass Creek, up the Ishawooa. At that point, roughly halfway in and some three miles below a steamside flat where Les had a camp he called Cut Coulee, the Ishawooa roars deep in a vertical-sided canyon, the trail edging along the topmost northern bench. Opposite, at much the same elevation, are three steep grassy parks or benches. At first, when Les suggested I bust the six-point bull managing his harem of six or eight cow elk on the middle bench, I thought he was joking; but eventually the challenge of the situation as a shooting problem took hold, and we began the adventure that has since, between Les and me, been known as the "six-mile shot."

With only thin canyon air between us, judging range to the elk was pure guesswork. Les and I could only hope we were right in agreeing on 600 yards. What little wind there was drifted up-canyon, left to right, and wouldn't shift a bullet much. But at the canyon lip reared the tangle of a wind-twisted juniper which, after a certain amount of jiggling around and branch-breaking, became a rough approximation of a bench rest. I had a steady rifle, and that rifle was an old friend, the accurate 7-mm Mashburn Magnum whose trajectory I knew like my own back stairs out to 500 yards. So several of the elements of a long shot were on our side.

Waiting until the bull stood perfectly broadside, moving very slowly if at all, I swung the cross hairs into steadiness about 6 inches forward of his withers to allow for the wind and any forward step that he might take during the almost three-fourths of a second it would take the bullet to cross the canyon. I put the horizontal hair fully at the top of his rack to handle the added 4-plus

Success on big game at long range calls for good glassware: a powerful spotting scope (15X to 60X), a 7X to 10X binocular and a 4X to 6X rifle scope. (If a variable scope is preferred, the 2X–7X is best.) The rifle in the foreground is Page's 7-mm Mashburn Magnum—"Old Betsy No. 1"— with a 4X Redfield scope.

feet of drop I expected beyond the 300-yard zero, and touched off. At that point Lady Luck took over. The bull pitched, falling into the brush. It was not until we had ridden three miles upstream to the first possible crossing, then three miles back down along the high southern bench—hence the "six-mile shot" business—that we discovered the bullet had taken off the major arteries topping his heart as perfectly as if I had fired at rock-throwing range.

Risky? Yes. With the possibility of hitting and later losing a splendid trophy animal, since we couldn't possibly get over there to check out the shot in less than two hours? Yes. Unjustifiable? Probably. But I did have everything going for me save yardage.

And whenever you attempt a long shot on game, the odds must be the prime consideration.

That the cartridge must be up to the job is self-evident. And here we are talking not only about trajectory factors but also about that combination of bullet-expansion reliability and energy delivery which is the basis of killing effectiveness.

It is as easy to hit a big-game animal at 400 yards with a .22/250, say, as with the .300 Weatherby or some like cartridge—easier, in fact, because the lighter recoil of the varminting number makes it easier for most humans to shoot. And while the .30 caliber's heavy bullet has some obvious advantage in terms of wind, in trajectory flatness the difference between a 55-grain .224 bullet starting at around 3,700 fps and a well-shaped 180-grain slug leaving at 3,200 fps is zilch: something like a theoretical inch at the 500-yard post. Yet, obviously, the 1,800-plus foot-pounds of striking force exerted out there by the bigger bullet must outstrip the 400 foot-pounds or so of the zippy varmint combination as far as shocking the animal, tearing up vital tissue or penetrating to reach those vitals is concerned. If the target is a prairie dog or even a coyote, the hot small caliber is fine; if it's a deer or a heavier creature, we need a more authoritative caliber, perhaps in the regions over .277 diameter.

At this point, incidentally, a lot of people fail to understand the rationale of a writer who has long been involved in controversy —my respected friend Elmer Keith, the big-bullet man. Elmer is a devotee of the thumb-sized slug for close-in work, but the greatest strength of his argument comes with the middle-sized calibers (like the .333-.338 clan, for example) when the target is on the next hill. When some 220-plus grains of bullet arrives at the 500-yard post with the authority of roughly a ton of bullet energy, it is working out there with all the force of, say, the conventional 130-grain .270 loading at about the 200-yard mark, and nobody has ever questioned the effectiveness of that combination on normal game.

Of course, not everyone can shoot 200 to 300 grains of bullet at magnum velocities! Some of us who are mere flesh and blood have to mess with calibers no greater than .30, and preferably under!

Though I don't want to labor the point, it is the compromise situation of recoil vs. bullet weight that has led me into deeming the various 7-mm magnums as top dogs for work at long range. By and large they hurt me less than they do the game, yet are high enough in ballistic coefficient or aerodynamic factors to be really effective both close in and far out.

Another too-far kill was almost assuredly made possible by one of those rounds—the same rifle and loading, in fact, I had used on the Ishawooa. This took place near Kondoa in what is now Tanzania. We spent four or five days working on one bull kudu who lived in a cup-shaped valley surrounded by hills. Most of the time he was also surrounded by 18 to 20 cows whose devotion to him was exceeded only by their alertness. By no means could we stalk him in the semiburned brush and elephant grass of his valley. I finally fixed his wagon and nailed a Rowland Ward head by much the same combination of luck and preparedness that had some years earlier made the Ishawooa elk possible.

It happened one morning when he incautiously left his harem for a stroll. From a high point we discovered him walking a faint

This Barren Ground caribou, a top-ranker in the Boone & Crockett lists, was dropped at 400 yards with a single shot from a 7-mm Mashburn Magnum.

trace that would cross below us at what the professional hunter (and most professional hunters in Africa are pretty lousy judges of range at any yardage where distance becomes critical) likewise figured was in the 600-yard class. A stump, two rocks and some ingenuity gave me a dead-steady rifle, on a sort of bench rest. Wind, nil. Angle, down; not worth considering, since it was way under 30 degrees—probably something like 5 or 10. Hold, at the top of his 50-inch-plus horns and enough forward of the withers to account for a slow step, say 15 to 20 inches.

He did not go down with the bullet thump, but when we discovered him later and found that the slug had smashed through the liver, sure but slow to kill, we realized that the range was probably a trifle shorter than I had figured, and he had probably been moving a mite faster, to shift the impact a foot or so behind expectation. But the very large amount of tissue damage that was caused and his very short travel were made possible only by a rather heavy spitzer bullet (175 grains) of very high ballistic coefficient (about .425) for a projectile able to deliver a lot of smash without terrorizing the shooter into a flinch. That it was a surely expanding Nosler design helped a good bit, I am sure.

Sheer velocity, then, is not the sole characteristic of a sporting rifle for use on game at long range. It must be complemented by bullet heft and form for energy delivery and by good design for far-out expansion. Hosea Sarber once showed me a box of used 220-grain outer-belted round-nosed bullets such as Peters used to make in .30 caliber. They had been effective on Alaskan brown bears because the bulk of the shooting was done at tight ranges, with impact speeds high enough to push back the collar that makes those bullets tough. Over long range, with their inefficient point shape and tough construction, they'd not be worth a hoot, because none of them would ever expand. That job calls for spitzer and spire-point contours, plus the expansion surety at least of the Remington PSP or present Hornady and Nosler types.

If all animals were the same size and of the same anatomy in respect to nerve and muscle structure, it would be easy to state flatly that one cartridge, or certainly one class of cartridge, would be the ultimate for far-out shooting. Or we might, in this utopian situation, say that a minimum of x foot-pounds of residual energy or y foot-seconds of velocity was needed. But not all animals are

One of Warren Page's favorite cartridges for long-range work on light game is the .240 PSP (Page Sooper Pouper) loaded with a 105-grain 6-mm bullet at 3,100 fps. The combination accounted for this New Zealand sika deer at 350 yards.

moose, tough enough and lethargic enough to require very large damage indeed as evidence of a good hit; nor are all animals Coues deer, that version of the whitetail which usually dresses out well under 100 pounds. Obviously, the .243, 6-mm Remington, .240 Weatherby or .25/06, which might seem just dandy on a 90-pound pronghorn way out across the sage, is all too puny for a bull elk at barrel-stretching range.

I am not, then, of a mind to list sixteen or eighteen calibers, with or without two "secret" loads for each, that constitute first-flight long-range combinations. It all depends, and you, dear reader, are expected to do a little thinking on your own account.

Obviously, for example, far-out shooting with a caliber using velocities very far under 3,000 fps gets pretty chancy. I do, however, strongly feel that in the far-out department the hunter must always err on the overgun side, if indeed there be such a thing as overgunning here. The chaps who shoot deer in central Pennsylvania at 400 to 800 yards across the gully complexes below Galeton seem to prefer items like the various .300 magnums in Improved form, the 7-mm magnums, some 6.5 magnums at the lightest, because they want minute-of-angle accuracy, drop characteristics of, say, 35 to 40 inches at 500 yards on a 200-yard zero and residual energies of over 1,200 foot-pounds at 500 yards—all this for use on an animal that seldom weighs over 150 pounds on the hoof. At normal or 200-yard ranges, any such cartridges would be almost absurdly potent on small whitetails. At double or triple or even quadruple that range, the situation changes markedly.

Perhaps the Pennsylvanians are straining things a bit. Yet they do not lose wounded game, their shooting being done almost entirely with snow on the ground and with the distant deer seldom showing any tendency to run out of the country when only wounded—apparently because the animals do not connect the hurt with the remote noise as evidence of man-presence. And these hunters' reasoning as to cartridges makes very good sense.

Any man who expects or plans to take a shot at pretty fair range can take a second leaf from their book. The Pennsy distance shooters operate from old railroad grades, originally cut along the hillsides to get out hardwoods once used in charcoal and alcohol making. They tote considerable duffel—spotting scopes, special range finders (of which more later) and sandbag or similar rests for rather cumbersome heavy-barreled rifles. All this is impractical for, say, an elk hunter. He certainly will lug no 40 pounds of error-eliminating gear.

However, he does have available and should use the terrain to help him hold precisely. He must learn one basic truth: the last yards of a stalk are not to get a few feet or yards closer to a game animal but rather to get into a surer shooting position—to an anthill in Africa, a log or rock or lump of tundra or even a ridge edge on our own continent. Any hunter should be willing to trade, say, 50 yards of distance for a rock pile or tangle of tree roots that will permit dead-steady holding. I certainly will, even when the shooting situation is hardly one that could be termed long-range. The ultimate end, after all, of both hunting and target riflery is to place the bullet precisely.

Exemplary situations come to mind that occurred one Wyoming hunting day. Early on, we spotted my bull bugling up a storm on the next one over of five fingerlike ridges that ran down off a mountain. Had we sneaked over onto his ridge we'd have been blinded by brush. The shot had to be taken from our finger to his, a yardage that, after some discussion, appeared to be between 400 and 435—call it 425. Sitting, I could not even hold the cross hairs surely on his forequarters. Prone with the sling, I could hold much better; but I was not 100 per cent sure how the rifle would shoot out of a tight sling (a fault which I later, by careful experiment,

The Wyoming elk shown here was shot at slightly over 450 yards. The rifle is a Champlin in 7-mm Remington Magnum. Page's 175-grain Nosler bullet broke the near shoulder and killed the bull where he stood.

remedied as far as that musket was concerned). Prone, with the
rifle fore-end resting on two or three folds of jacket sleeve over a
handy rock and my left hand curled back under the buttstock so
that opening and closing my fist gave very precise elevation control, I could keep the cross hairs very steady indeed, the horizontal
wire floating with just a hair of daylight between it and the bull's
withers. With the rifle zeroed at 300 yards (plus 3 inches at 100
yards for that load), I knew the bullet should strike 9 to 11 inches
low at 400, perhaps 12 to 14 down at 425. The bull died within
seconds of the impact.

Later that same day, my companion had a whack at a bugling
bull only a little way downslope from him. Within 2 feet of
where he crouched was an overturned tree; he could have used its
roots for a rest and surely bagged his six-pointer. A great salesman
but a poor rifleman, he elected to stand on his own two feet and
shoot like a man. So he missed the bull clean. The moral common
to the two anecdotes is obvious: take advantage, every possible
advantage, of the terrain until you can be assured of a hold that
is bench-rest steady.

The long-range deer shooters of Pennsylvania use target-style
scopes, with windage and elevation factors set according to the
estimated range and wind conditions on the basis of settings pre-
established for known ranges. This is hardly practical for the
hunter and his hunting-scope equipment—not because his internally adjusted scopes are not capable of correct movement (although only the best of them are), but rather because a hunter
does not often have the range data at his finger tips, or even pasted
onto the buttstock of his rifle, and seldom does he have time or
opportunity for such extended calculation. He has to proceed,
usually, in a more instinctive fashion, guided by the dictates of
Chinese windage, as it were.

Sensibly, he should set up or zero his rifle and sight in a fashion
that will get the best out of the rifle for full-range operation—at
least out to that yardage where bullets begin to run out of effective
steam or become unreliable in expansion. For about 90 per cent of
today's hunting rounds, what I have long termed the Rule of
Three is probably the handiest way to operate.

This scheme is based on the experience that for modern open-
country hunting, cartridges operating in the muzzle-velocity

range of from 2,700 to about 3,200 fps with reasonably well-contoured game bullets—and the scope set so that the impact center at 100 yards is 3 inches above line of aim—will keep the bullet inside a theoretical 6-to-7-inch pipe (a trajectory of plus 3 to minus 3) clear out to a point well beyond 200 yards. In some instances the "pipe" will extend to a full 300, and provide for a back-line hold on an animal the size of an elk or mule deer out to as far as bullets can normally be expected to give sure expansion, which is to say 350 to 400 yards, depending on the combination. Since the man doesn't live who under ordinary hunting conditions can hold steadily inside a 6-inch circle to, for example, 300 yards (although over a rest and with a good rifle many can do it), this "shoot through the pipe" system is a neat way of minimizing problems of range estimation. It furthermore puts minimum strain on your memory. As you note from the table on the next page, all you need remember is the effective point-blank range (the distance out to which the bullet stays within roughly 3 inches either way of your line of aim) and the 1-foot-holdover yardage—at which you are shooting about as far as that man/rifle/bullet combination has a reasonably proper degree of surety.

To use the table, zero your rifle and hunting load to hit 3 inches up at 100 yards; then memorize only the "Hold Dead On" and "Hold Over 12" yardages for that load. Dismiss other trajectory factors as merely confusing matters. If your pet cartridge is not listed, pick the one nearest to it in velocity and bullet weight, adjusting the yardages slightly as the relative speeds indicate. In other words, for the 180-grain .308 Winchester load, use the 180-grain .30/06 data and reduce the ranges by 10 to 20 yards—not enough to upset matters when you are shooting under hunting conditions. If you shoot handloads, the small speed difference will mean little change. I have used this plan successfully for years. It is simple and practical.

At this point somebody raises his hand to ask, what about the situation of the shot, with a rifle so sighted, on a buck that pops up at 84 yards? Well, what about it? At that range the bullet will be a theoretical 2-plus inches high. But you'll be shooting offhand, probably. So can you hold within 2 inches offhand, brother? And what about a low-velocity number like the .35 Remington? The answer is equally clear. That's a short-range item anyway, pretty

SIGHTING BY THE RULE OF THREE FOR
SCOPE-SIGHTED SPORTER RIFLES

Cartridge and Bullet Weight*	50 Yds.	100 Yds.	Trajectory Peak	Targeted for	Hold Dead On to	Hold Over 12 Inches at
.243—100	+ 1.5	+ 3	3.3 at 180	275	325	400
.257—100	+ 1.6	+ 3	3.3 at 150	230	270	350
.257—117	+ 1.7	+ 3	3.0 at 125	200	240	310
.264—140	+ 1.3	+ 3	3.5 at 170	300	340	425
.270—130 (and .280—125)	+ 1.4	+ 3	3.4 at 170	265	310	400
.270—150	+ 1.4	+ 3	3.1 at 140	215	255	330
.280—150	+ 1.4	+ 3	3.2 at 140	240	290	375
.30/06—150	+ 1.3	+ 3	3.2 at 150	245	285	370
.30/06—180	+ 1.6	+ 3	3.0 at 125	215	260	340
.30/06—220	+ 1.6	+ 3	3.2 at 115	190	230	300
.300 H&H—180	+ 1.4	+ 3	3.2 at 140	250	290	370
.308—150	+ 1.5	+ 3	3.0 at 150	230	275	350
.300 WM—180	+ 1.4	+ 3	3.4 at 170	290	325	400
7-mm Mag.—160†	+ 1.3	+ 3	3.4 at 170	290	325	400
.30/30—170 RN‡	+ 1.0	+ 1.5	1.5 at 90	150	180	250
.35 Rem.—200 RN	+ 1.0	+ 1.5	1.6 at 90	150	180	240
.358 Win.—200	+ 1.4	+ 3	3.0 at 100	195	230	300
.375 H&H—270	+ 1.4	+ 3	3.0 at 150	220	260	340

* Data based on calculations; exact yardages rounded for practical use.

† Based on assumed muzzle speed of 3,100 fps, feasible with most of the short magnums when fully loaded.

‡ Bullets save those marked RN assumed to be at least as well shaped as Winchester Western Silvertips or Remington Pointed Core-Lokt.

sorry beyond 150 yards, and the sights for it should be set accordingly.

Now, what of shots beyond the 400-pace range? First off, in most cases they shouldn't be taken anyway; and second, in any event those really long ones, as I've already spent several thousand words in trying to make clear, should be attempted only by the right rifleman in the right situation with correct equipment of known range performance.

Actually, of course, the toughest part of any long-range problem is that of estimating distance. You need be no mathematical genius to realize that while a high-speed bullet follows a marvelously flat curve to a couple of hundred yards and a useful one to beyond 300, out around the quarter-mile mark that old devil gravity really gets in his licks, and a misguess on range of only a few yards can mean a total miss. Let's take one of the commonest and best long-range cartridges, a .300 super magnum, say the .300 Winchester version, with a 180-grain bullet of first-rate shape and a ballistic coefficient well above .400—one as good as Hornady's spire-point, for which the flight index is .434. Muzzle speed, a bit under 3,100 fps. With the rifle zeroed at 200 yards, just for instance, the added drop at 300 yards is about 6½ inches, at 400 a mite over 18, at 500 about 38 inches. You think 400 is the range to the buck and hold accordingly. But it's a misty day and the beast is really at 500, so you miss.

Or if we put into the computer the figures for a less efficient round, as for example the standard .308 Winchester, even using a bullet with the same aerodynamics but with a muzzle speed down around the 2,500 to 2,600 mark (remember that most .308 rifles are rather short-barreled), we get a situation in which if you again zero at the conventional 200 yards, the added drop at 300 is almost 11 inches, at 400 nearly 30, at 500 over 60. Now, even if you hold for 450, say, and the animal is really at that 500 mark, you're going to shoot under his chest rather badly. A less efficient bullet would only make you miss farther.

So your yardage estimate must be, if humanly possible, correct to within not 50 yards but 25 yards, and if you can get it within 10 you are really cooking on all burners. Bullets do bend badly when you get out to bragging distances.

In our day of fancy technology, the easy answer should be optical range finding in the scope itself. One system involves paired spanning wires in the reticle (as earliest used in the Weavers), with which you have to do a small calculation as to the range; another has paired spanning wires in the scope which are hooked up to the power-varying element so that spanning gives a yardage read-off from an indicator within the scope field (as in the Redfield designs); and a third uses spanning wires that are hooked up to the mount through a bullet-trajectory cam so as to give the effect of scope resetting for the distance to the game (as in the Realist scheme) in order to eliminate any need to know exact range.

Any or all of these can work *if* and *when*: the game stands around to be scanned; the animal does indeed happen to be the

required 18 inches deep (or whatever depth that species supposedly is); you have three hands so as to hold the rifle steady
on some kind of rest and titivate the scanner at the same time; the
cam is right for the specific load—etc., etc. Frankly, they all work
better in the store than they do on the mountain, although the
Redfield scheme, or an adaptation of it, has been used effectively
by the military in far-out sniping in Vietnam.

Or the range finding can be away from the rifle scope—done,
for example, by one of the two-eyed split-image focusing devices
widely offered for the purpose. These are highly accurate on still,
sharp-edged objects within about 250 yards. At a fuzzy roundish
target moving around at 500 yards they are darned near useless.
A good guesser can do better.

What nobody yet (as this is written) has done is to put the ranging device where it ought to be, in the binocular. It is with the
binocular that the hunter finds his far-out game in the first place,
and while he may or may not have opportunity to check it out
with a spotting scope, it is primarily with a binocular that he
counts the points and, with or without his guide, makes a shoot-
or-no-shoot decision. If that binocular contained spanning wires,
or a similar reticle device, perhaps located off-center of one lens
barrel so as not to interfere with normal uses, the range estimation would then be made with relatively steady glasses and during
a time when the game is being viewed with higher power than
that found in most hunting scopes. Thereafter, the hunter could
turn to his rifle and devote his energies to the shooting problem
alone. At least he would need only the normal complement of two
hands, and would be compartmentalizing the viewing, ranging
and shooting actions where they belong. If some first-rate binocular outfit puts this simple idea into production (after all, artillery-
men's binoculars are usually equipped with a mil scale, which is
nothing but a ranging reticle), I plan to push a peanut down Chicago's Lake Shore Drive. However, it's too reasonable, not gim-
micky enough.

In the long run, of course, the top-notch hunter must become a
top-notch estimator of distance. He should practice constantly:
on a golf course, where the yardages are readily known from the
club score card; on the street, where distance can be checked out
by pacing (with a known fudge factor, or correction percentage,

worked out for his normal stride); during midsummer woodchuck or crow expeditions or by constant and repeated guessing
of distances during the hunt itself. There's a buck—not good
enough, but how far is he? Guessing yardage is an *acquired* skill.
It is not something you are born with.

Many guides, in fact, are lousy range guessers, either because
they simply have never checked out the distances involved or because they are trying to bamboozle their customers into happy
hotshots. The tales returning hunters tell about 500- and 600-
yard shots—range courtesy of the guide—for which they held dead
on the heart, thereby defying the law of gravity if nothing else,
are equaled only by the bunk I see about wildlife on the TV tube.
The first-rank guide, who may well himself be your outfitter, often
tells a different tale. So too does the *Jaeger* of central Europe. In
Austria a few years ago, my *Jaeger* in the Donnersbachwald
Hirsch (red deer) and chamois country, a third-generation professional, never conducted me into position for a possible trophy
without making it absolutely clear that the range was *"drei hundert Meter"* or *"ein hundert fünfzig."* And he was, as far as I could
see, right on the button every time.

That *Jaeger* would never, I am sure, have let me take a truly
long shot, it being against the tradition of his guild to risk wounding any game animal. He did let me stretch one at 350 meters,
some 385 yards, on a stag *Hirsch*, one size smaller than a bull elk,
when it was obvious we could never get closer. I had a perfect
dead-rest situation, and he had already seen me shoot the 7x64
Steyr-Mannlicher for three consecutive perfect kills—yet that
much range would, I suspect, rate in the exception column. Their
tradition calls for getting in as close as is reasonable for a shot that
is, above all, sure.

Yours should, too. The long shot is only to fall back on in case of
necessity. The name of the game is to be ready for that necessity,
however. Know your own capability, the limits of the rifle and the
relationship of range and trajectory, and the long kill becomes far
less a matter of luck than of preparation. And it is better to be prepared than to take stupid chances, since in my book only the prepared hunter has his prayers answered.

Handgun Shooting

7

HANDGUN
TARGET SHOOTING

BY STEVE FERBER

OBSERVE any handgun buff plinking away with his favorite pistol and you will immediately know whether he has had some formal training or he hasn't. The fellow who fits the latter description might be seen shooting from the hip, consuming the contents of his cylinder or magazine with a rapidity seldom seen even on *Gunsmoke*, ventilating empty beer or peanut cans.

His jaws hurt from the intense grinding he has applied to that part of his anatomy while shooting many shots rapid-fire. And each time a bullet finds its mark, he's pleased beyond all reason. This (admittedly exaggerated) stereotype never took the time to learn something about the sport that obviously gives him so much enjoyment.

You needn't be a competitive pistol shooter to be a good handgun hunter or informal plinker; but once you're indoctrinated into the ways of formal competition, your overall shooting performance is bound to improve. This is because the target shooter concerns himself with one vital concept: shooting the smallest possible groups under controlled conditions. There is probably no other practical way to realize how accurate handguns are than by shooting groups at paper targets at established distances.

It is a predictable, uncompromising experience. You *always* have a reliable target, and you never have to estimate distances. When you miss, it isn't because you were forced to shoot from behind a swaying sapling at a hunk of game running fast for the horizon. You miss because your concentration wasn't perfect. Discipline has a tendency to increase in competition shooting, as does determination. And to achieve a reasonable amount of both, hard work is the key.

Although certain police-type combat matches and events are included in the general category of "competitive handgunning," the ultimate purpose of such training is effective, practical gun fighting. I will limit myself here to conventional-type competition shooting and international-style competition. The majority of pistol shooters in this country compete in conventional events, so I'll detail this aspect first.

All conventional targets are scored in exactly the same way. The highest numerical value for any given shot is 10. Within the 10 ring is a smaller X ring, and this is used to break numerical ties. The rings are perfect concentric circles, the outermost one having a value of 5.

There are various types of targets, and for outdoor shooting the standard distances are 25 and 50 yards. The 25-yard timed- and rapid-fire target has black 9, 10 and X rings. The 50-yard slow-fire target has the black area extended to the 8 ring. The black area on any target is called the "bull," or "bull's-eye," but the objective is to shoot 10s and Xs, not just to "keep them in the black."

For each 10-shot "string," the highest possible numerical score is 100. When you hear "six-X possible," it means the shooter fired a perfect score, with 6 of the shots inside (or touching) the X ring. And scoring is simple. If a bullet hole just "cuts" or touches the ring, the shooter is given the total value of that ring—even though most of the hole might be outside it. When a shot is so close to the ring that there is question as to whether the hole is actually cutting it, the shooter is given the benefit of the doubt.

If a shot hits the target but isn't within—or doesn't touch—the outermost 5 ring, it is termed an on-the-paper miss. You might just as well have put the round through the bench, because the value of the shot is zero and you have lost 10 points.

Here, firing as a member of the Naval Reserve Pistol Team, Steve Ferber is using a .45 automatic fitted with an extension rib. This lengthens the sight radius and decreases the severity of errors in sight alignment.

There are only three courses of fire to learn. All conventional matches are composed of these three, in whole or in part. They are slow-fire, timed-fire and rapid-fire. Slow-fire means just that. You shoot slowly. From a distance of 50 yards, each competitor is given ten minutes to fire 10 rounds. At a command from the range officer, each shooter on the firing line loads 5 rounds. The officer then asks if the firing line is ready. If no one raises an arm indicating otherwise, he calls out the command "Ready on the right, ready on the left, ready on the firing line." About three seconds later he gives the final command, "Commence firing." And everybody does. The second 5 shots are loaded and fired at will. At the end of the ten-minute period, the command "Cease fire" is given, all guns are locked open with magazines removed or cylinders opened, and the guns are placed on the bench. When the range officer knows the firing line is "safe," the command to go forward and score is given. The commands and sequences are the same for all events.

"Timed-fire" is really a misnomer, since all events are timed. It means shooting 5 rounds in twenty seconds. Timed-fire (and rapid-fire) events are fired from the 25-yard line in outdoor competition. Most outdoor ranges have turning targets, giving each shooter the same opportunity. That is, after the last command from the range officer, the targets turn toward the shooters (up until that time they were at right angles to them, with only the target edges visible) for twenty seconds. At the end of that time the targets automatically turn away again. Each man must aim, squeeze, follow through, recover five separate times, all in twenty seconds or less. When you hear a shooter moan that he "ate a round," he means that after the targets turned away, he still had one round in his gun.

Timing is obviously important. Most good shooters develop a rhythm to their shooting pattern: each shot almost precisely equidistant in time from the last, and in timed-fire, the 5 are usually downrange in from twelve to sixteen seconds.

Rapid-fire is more difficult. The shooter is given only ten seconds to fire 5 shots. It's considerably harder to recover, aim and squeeze—five times—in ten seconds. Most good shooters in this event get their 5 shots off in barely under ten seconds.

There are four distinct matches in conventional competition. The slow-fire match is a 20-shot event. After each 10 shots (in some instances after only 5) the scores are recorded and the targets changed. The highest possible score in a slow-fire match is 200.

The timed-fire match is also a 20-shot event, as is the rapid-fire match. Again, the highest possible score in either is 200. Targets are usually recorded and changed after the first 10 shots. The final event is called the "National Match Course," or simply "The Course," and is a 30-shot match incorporating 10 shots each of slow-, timed- and rapid-fire. Since it is a 30-shot event, the highest possible score is 300. These four matches comprise what is known as an "aggregate." Each aggregate has a total numerical value of 900 points.

All-day matches are usually 2,700-point aggregates, or "2700s." They are conducted this way: The first 900-point aggregate (90 shots) is completed with the .22 rimfire, as detailed in the four events described. The next 90 shots are fired exactly the same way, but the competitor *must* use a centerfire gun. The .38-caliber is the usual choice. For the final 90 shots (possible 900 points), a .45-caliber gun must be used. The .45 ACP is the choice here, and the aggregate is fired exactly like the previous two. In

These are the basics for a .22-handgun competitor: "ear muffs," stop watch, shooting glasses, scorebook and spare ear plugs (in the cylinder). The pistol is a .22 Long Rifle Smith & Wesson Model 41, one of the top rimfire target autos.

the middle, or centerfire, aggregate, a .45 may be used, and many shooters prefer it for a couple of reasons. First, the .45 makes a bigger hole than the .38, and a shot that would, say, be an "almost" 10 with the .38 would definitely be a 10 with the wider .45 bullet. By using the .45 in both the centerfire *and* the .45 event, the shooter gets twice as much practice and has only two guns to worry about. The total number of shots for the day is 270, having a total possible score of 2,700. No one's fired 2,700 yet, but more than fifty men have fired scores over 2,650.

A .22 pistol, ammo, targets, ear protection and a score pad are a must for beginning target shooters. A spotting scope and a "pistol box" which will hold your gear are recommended and for the serious competitor are also a must. A staple gun will be needed to replace targets, and some sort of carbide lamp (or spray can of a blackener) will be necessary to blacken the sights. A pencil to record each shot (after the 10-shot string has been completed) and a screwdriver for sight adjustments will be needed. A base-ball-type hat will serve to keep the sun out of your face and eyes, and *good* shooting glasses, tinted to your preference, should be used. Eventually you will need a centerfire gun and/or a .45 ACP.

Tremendous importance must be placed on the selection of your target guns. Although an infinite variety of handguns is available, you need consider only two brands when it comes time to purchase the rimfire pistol. With the possible exception of certain customized .22s (like the Clark-made Ruger, for example), the best choice is the Smith & Wesson Model 41. This comes in two barrel lengths, and my preference is the longer, standard-length barrel over the short "bull"-barrel model. The Smith Model 46 is essentially the same gun, but has plastic grips rather than wood.

The "41 Smith" is a big favorite. Its accuracy is without peer, and it handles and functions extremely well. But the other superb target gun to be considered is the High Standard—any one of that company's top-quality target grades would be good. The Smith probably has a very slight accuracy edge over the High Standard, but the latter gun has a totally different "feel," and since it can be had with military (.45-type) straight-style grips, it approximates very closely the feel of the .45 ACP. Standardization of "feel" in all your target guns can be important—but not for all people. Some shooters like the feel of the High Standard over that of the

Most competition handguns are customized by their owners. In recent years, though, the manufacturers have begun offering extensive lists of options, available from the factory. This gun is a High Standard Super-matic Citation equipped with custom grips, a muzzle brake and an extra-long barrel. It is chambered for the .22 Long Rifle cartridge.

The U.S. Army's service pistol for over 50 years, the Model 1911 Colt .45 has been refined into a highly accurate arm. This is the Gold Cup MK IV, a commercial version designed solely for competitive shooting. It's equipped with an adjustable trigger and sights, a hand-honed action and a special barrel bushing to aid consistent accuracy.

Smith & Wesson Model 41, and select it mainly for this reason. But if you can't make up your mind—get the Smith.

Of course, both brands are semiautomatics. Don't entertain the thought of using a revolver for conventional target shooting. Think back for a moment to the timed- and rapid-fire events. It's hard enough to get those five shots off without having to take additional time to manually recock the hammer each time, and shooting double-action is unthinkable.

The only ammunition to use on the target range in .22 events is standard-velocity Long Rifles. Hi-velocity rounds aren't nearly as accurate for serious shooting, and they also weaken semi-automatics' recoil slides. Match-type bullets do shoot a little better than regular ammo, but it will take a long time until you notice the difference. Nonmatch, standard-velocity .22 Long Rifle ammunition will shoot groups around 1 inch or under all day at 50 yards when fired from the Smith 41 or one of the better High Standards.

There are several good and reliable pistolsmiths who will build you a custom .45 ACP for about $300, depending on what you have done. This route isn't necessary for most people, because we're only talking about shaving off an additional inch or so at 50 yards. So get the more accurate custom gun only when it will really make a difference.

The best factory gun available today in .45 ACP is the Colt

Gold Cup Mark IV. It's about half the price of a good custom gun. The trigger is usually fine (and can always be adjusted), and the gun will shoot groups 2½ inches wide or under from the 50-yard line. Many individual specimens will punch 2-inch groups or better. This is the *only* commercial gun to buy.

The Smith & Wesson Model 52 is probably the best bet for a commercial .38 Special. It costs about $200 and shoots as well as —or better than—the Colt Gold Cup Mark IV .45 ACP. All the guns mentioned come equipped with very fine adjustable sights— which is a must, too.

Unlike the serious competitive rifle shooter, you won't go wrong using factory centerfire ammo. Excellent handloads *can* be made for pistol competition, and just for economy reasons should be used in practice, but factory .38 Special wadcutters and factory .45 semi-wadcutters are extremely accurate and are widely used.

Begin with the .22 rimfire semiautomatic. Learn technique with this gun and don't even pick up a centerfire pistol until you have considerable confidence, and some expertise, with the rimfire. Start out at the 25-yard line and use *only* official 25-yard NRA targets. Shoot slow-fire and wait until you can keep all your shots in the black before trying timed-fire.

Target shooting is an exercise in precision. Take advantage of what absolutes there are. The target is one. In competition, the size of the target, the black area, the ring diameters never change. So don't penalize yourself from the beginning by trying to adjust to several types of targets.

Load five rounds in your magazine, insert it into the gun and release the slide. One round will be chambered and you are ready to fire. The desired "grip," and the one you want to maintain, should be firm but not overly tight. Place the stock well into the palm of your hand, "rolling" the flesh between your thumb and index finger slightly under as you do it. Always use your non-shooting hand to place the gun; never try to get the correct grip by just picking up the gun with your shooting hand. The thumb should ride naturally, parallel with the slide or slightly above or below the parallel. The thumb performs *no* function in gripping. The gun is being held by the inside of your hand and lower three fingers. The trigger finger is never used to grip or support the gun. It must become the only moving part of your hand, to oper-

The stance of a competition shooter should be as easy and natural as possible, since muscular strain lowers scores. Note here that the pistol is raised to eye level, rather than the head being lowered, and the left hand is tucked into the gunner's pocket.

ate the trigger exclusively. When you squeeze the trigger finger, the other fingers *must not move*; and never squeeze your palm when you are operating the trigger.

Situate the first pad of your forefinger—or the first joint of the finger—on the trigger. No other portion of the finger should be touching the trigger. When you squeeze the shot off, come straight back with the finger.

Stand at a slight angle to the target—perhaps 30 or 40 degrees—*close your eyes*, take a deep breath, release part of it, hold the rest of the breath and bring the gun up to where you think the target should be. Open your eyes, and if you are to one side of the target, *move your body*, not your arm, until you are pointing at the target. Try this a few times until you find your most comfortable position. Put your free hand in your pocket—and forget about it.

Shoot with both eyes open. It might seem strange at first, but this is the best way. While you are experimenting with your position—bringing your arm up and pointing at the target—don't tire yourself unnecessarily. You can rest by lowering your gun to the bench, while maintaining your hold, and allowing it to carry the total weight of the gun.

Aligning your sights properly is crucial. An error here of just $\frac{1}{100}$ of an inch will move the point of impact about 3 inches at 50 yards. Good sight alignment calls for tremendous concentration, which will come, in time, with determination. Sight alignment means the attitude of the front blade in relation to the rear notch. When you have your gun raised in the firing position, look through the rear notch to the front blade, and attempt to keep the front blade exactly in the middle of the rear notch and in a straight line across the horizontal plane. In other words, don't allow the front blade to rise over the rear notch, or drop below it either. The top of the left side of the rear sight, the top of the front blade and the top of the right side of the rear sight should form a straight line. This is sight alignment.

Sight *picture* means something else. Whereas alignment incorporates two reference points, the front and rear sights, sight picture includes an additional reference: the target. But sight alignment is vastly more important to learn.

In conventional shooting, the "6-o'clock" hold is best. That means that your aiming point—for all matches, for each event, for every shot you deliver—is at the bottom of the bull, where white meets black. There's a good reason for using this aiming point. Everybody knows that the human eye can't focus on more than one point at a time. Since a shooter has three things to think about—the rear sight, the front sight and the target—you actually focus on the front sight, keeping that in perfect alignment with the rear sight. You do not focus on the target. The rear sight will appear slightly hazy, which is fine. When you put the aligned front blade at the bottom of the bull, the target will register as an indistinct gray ball which appears to "sit" on the front blade. This is the sight picture you want. If you get into the habit of holding "center bull," it will be harder for you to achieve a good sight picture because you will have lost the round reference point, the bull. Remember that when you're focusing on the front sight, the bull will appear gray and hazy. It will be far less distinct if more than half of it is hidden, which would be the case if the front sight were in line with its middle. And you would never be quite sure that you were holding exactly in the middle.

The match pistols I have described come with adjustable sights, for both windage and elevation. If you are shooting to the left, move the sight (only the rear one is adjustable) to the right. If you are shooting high, move the sight down. Adjust your rear sight so that when you are holding at the bottom of the black at 6 o'clock, the bullet will hit dead-center X. When you are certain your sights are adjusted correctly for 25 yards, you might semi-permanently fix your "zero" by painting a narrow line of nail polish across the adjustment screw to the sight itself. When you start shooting at 50 yards and have to move your sight up a few clicks, it will be an easy matter to return them once again to your 25-yard zero by just aligning the dab of nail polish.

But even when this is done, by no means retire your screw-driver permanently to the back drawer of your shooting box. Lighting conditions fluctuate during the course of the day, and they can often play havoc with your sight setting. A different brand of ammo might shoot differently from the type you used when you set your sights. Any number of causes can move the impact point of the bullet—including an inconsistent grip on the gun. If the shots aren't hitting where you think they should hit, move your sights. That's why they are adjustable.

Suppose you are shooting from the 50-yard line. Your sights are aligned well and you have perfect sight picture as the shot breaks. You didn't jerk the gun and you followed through well. You call a dead-center X. But you look through the spotting scope and see a 9-o'clock 8. The hit was a full 4 inches to the left of center. If you had real confidence in the shot, you'll immediately move the sight to the right. But if you weren't *that* sure of the shot, you'll fire again at the same setting. If the second shot was delivered well too but if the hit is near the first shot, get the screwdriver out. With some experience you'll be able to "call your shots" well, and you'll know just when to make sight adjustments.

The correct amount of pressure to apply to the trigger is that force necessary to disengage the trigger/sear mechanism—care-fully, so as to prevent movement of the gun itself. Each shot must be thought out. By that I mean you must properly align the sights, then get the sight picture, and when the trigger breaks, you must follow through with the shot. By far the best way to squeeze the trigger is in one continuous pull. Naturally, this works best only if your sight alignment is consistently good for the fraction of a second it takes to squeeze off the shot. The second way, which works fine too, is to squeeze the trigger (remember not to move or apply pressure with any other part of your hand) when you have good alignment as in the method first described, but to abort the squeeze if you lose proper alignment. If your arm begins to "wobble," put the gun down on the bench to rest, while still maintaining your hold; then bring it up and try again when you think you're ready. Eventually the shot will break, and it will be a good one if alignment was correct at the critical time. Never bring the gun down in timed- and rapid-fire events, but you can and should follow this procedure in slow-fire.

In the faster 25-yard events, strive for alignment and timing. Even though you may not have the perfect sight picture (the front blade, for example, might be a little high into the black, or a little low into the white), get the shot off anyway as soon as possible. Only practice will reduce your wobble area to acceptable limits. But understand this: If your sights are not aligned and your sight picture is not perfect, you will have severe error—even at 25 yards. But if your alignment is good and your sight picture is just slightly off, your error won't be much at all. Practically speaking, in the latter instance, if when the shot breaks your aligned front sight is, say, an inch into the black (high, but still at 6 o'clock), you will probably hit a high (12 o'clock) 10. But if your sights were *not* properly aligned when the shot broke, the hit could be well into the white.

Follow through with each shot by "riding" with the recoil to a certain degree. In rapid-fire events you have to recover much faster than in slow-fire or even timed-fire; nevertheless, don't ever fight the recoil. In rapid-fire, when you have only ten seconds to shoot 5 rounds, ride with the recoil if only for a fraction of a second. The amount of recoil is consistent with each shot, the amount of ride and follow-through should be consistent and the amount of time required to find your sights again should be consistent. Eventually, you'll find the right combination to deliver the five shots accurately.

The correct amount of trigger pressure will come automatically, and you won't have to concentrate hard on that. Your concentration will be fixed almost entirely on aligning the sights properly, and everything else—trigger control, sight picture, timing—will take care of itself . . . after a great deal of practice.

There has always been an enthusiasm for the international-type handgun-shooting events, and many ranges around the country host these competitions. The main international competitions in which handgun shooting is included are the Olympic Games, the Pan-American Games and the World Shooting Championships. These competitions have come to include air-pistol tournaments in recent years, but the three most important events are still the 50-meter "free"-pistol match, the centerfire competition and the rapid-fire event. The guns, targets and rules are far removed from the conventional disciplines in both free-pistol and rapid-fire pistol, while the centerfire event is not really much different from its conventional counterpart. The concepts and skills learned in conventional shooting can be readily applied to the international variety. To wit: concentration and sight-alignment principles are much the same. The main transition to be made is in timing.

The free-pistol target is fired at from 50 meters only and is divided into ten circular zones, scoring 10, 9, 8, 7, etc., points. Zones 10 to 7 are black, and this forms the circular aiming point. The 10 ring is much smaller than the conventional 50-yard 10 ring; it measures 50 mm. There is no X ring.

The course of fire allows 15 sighting shots and 60 shots for record. These record shots are fired in six 10-shot strings, and the time allowed is a full three hours. Shooters are permitted to fire sighting shots before any 10-shot string or at any time between strings.

The most common free pistol used by Americans in competition is the Hammerli. Sako also makes a free pistol now, and it is available on special order from the Garcia Corporation. A few custom-made free pistols are in existence too. All are .22 rimfire single-shots having the lightest of triggers, long barrels with an extra-long sight radius and wrap-around grips. However, it is forbidden to have the grip of the pistol extended in such a way that it might gain support from any part of the arm other than the hand. Even the wearing of wrist watches is banned for the same reason.

International rapid-fire is conducted at 25 meters. The course for rapid pistol shooting incorporates a line of revolving silhouette targets. These are placed in groups of five, and all turn simultaneously for one shooter. This too is a 5.6-mm (.22 rimfire) event, and special automatic pistols are used. These are designed to fire .22 Shorts.

The event is carried out this way: After the shooter loads, he says "Ready" to the target operator. A few seconds later, the five silhouette targets are rotated from a side-on position to a facing position. Only then may the competitor bring his gun up to fire. He fires one shot at each target in a specified time—eight, six and four seconds are time limits in this event. At the end of the time period, the targets turn away again to the side-on position.

Sight alignment is vital, obviously, as is timing. It's very easy to get off only 3 or 4 rounds in the four-second event (remember you have to shoot 5 shots, one on each target, which requires moving your arm five times) and unhappily watch the target bank turn away.

The firing is carried out in two courses, each of 30 shots. Each course is fired in six series of 5 rounds. Two series last eight seconds each, two six seconds and two four seconds. The object is to place 1 shot in the center of each of the 5 targets during each series. Before each course of 30 shots, the competitor may fire 5 sighting shots in eight, six or four seconds or, if he wishes, without a time limit.

International centerfire is a two-phase contest which includes precision (slow-fire) shooting on 10-ringed bull's-eye targets and rapid-fire shooting on 10-ringed silhouette targets. Separate ranges are usually used for the two phases, but the shooting distance is always 25 meters. Ranges for the precision phase may be equipped with stationary targets, targets that can be raised or lowered, or targets that can be turned away.

For this event, the international precision target looks much like any other handgun target with a bull's-eye. The black aiming area is 20 centimeters and includes the 10, 9, 8 and 7 rings. Any type of semiautomatic pistol or revolver may be used, but the .38 Special is the right choice. Since the bullet size must not exceed

Competition air guns, such as this Winchester Model 363, are rapidly gaining in popularity. Limited in range, power and noise, they are extremely accurate at short distances.

9.65 mm, the .45 ACP cannot be used. The trigger pull must not be less than 3 pounds, and certain other restrictions pertaining to sight radius, type of sights and barrel lengths are enforced, but virtually all conventional U.S. match guns fall within these boundaries.

International centerfire is the only nonconventional event in which the use of a revolver would not be a handicap—provided it was accurate enough. I've had good success with the Colt Python in this event, and I've also used a semiauto—the Model 52 Smith—but my preference is the revolver. Many military shooters also use the .38 AMU, the .38 Super or various custom-accurized .38 Special Colt autos.

The precision, or slow-fire, phase consists of a 30-shot course fired in six series of 5 shots each. The competitor is allowed six minutes to fire each series of 5 shots.

The second phase, rapid-fire, is likewise a course of 30 shots fired in six series of 5 shots each. The silhouette (same target as in the .22-caliber rapid-fire event) is shown five times, and each time it faces the shooter for three seconds. Then it turns away. The interval between appearances of the target is seven seconds—ample time to manually recock a revolver. One shot is fired during each three-second appearance. A sighting series of 5 shots is fired before the shots for record.

The air-pistol course is fired at a distance of 10 meters (33 feet). Only .177-caliber projectiles are allowed, and the match consists of 40 shots. These are fired on a "reduced" target, the 10 ring measuring not much wider than the pellet itself. There is absolutely no room for error. At the same time, the special guns developed for this match are extremely accurate, capable of shooting 10s consistently from that distance.

One of the most popular handguns used is the German Fein-werkbau, imported by Daisy and called the Daisy/FWB. Walther manufactures an excellent match pistol too, the Model LP-2, as do Hammerli and a few others.

Besides the international event for air pistol, there exists a fine conventional course called the "NRA-333." The distance is the same, 10 meters, but it's a 30-shot course rather than 40.

The real beauty of match air-pistol shooting centers around the fact that practice can be carried out virtually anywhere: the back yard, the basement, or even the living room. That, plus the facts that it is noiseless and that ammo is so inexpensive, makes the match air pistol an extremely desirable training gun. If you own one of these, the basics of good match shooting can be learned, really, in your own living room.

8

HANDGUN HUNTING

BY JEFF COOPER

DESPITE the enthusiasm of a small but devoted following, hunting game with a pistol remains a pretty esoteric business. Its satisfactions are great, but its practitioners are few. This, of course, makes for a good deal of resistance to the whole notion, based upon the dismally egalitarian attitude that anything the "average guy" cannot do should not be encouraged. It is asserted that this average guy (whom neither you, nor I, nor anyone else has ever met) cannot shoot a pistol well enough to take game humanely. Excellence, in marksmanship or anything else, is rare. An excellent pistol shot is a humane hunter—certainly more so than a bad rifle shot. Derogating handgun hunting because it is exacting strikes me as unsportsmanlike, and we might reasonably ask that those who cannot measure up to it just quietly drop the subject.

But it is certainly not my intention here to complain about the opposition. It is rather to point up the positive side of the matter by way of a certain amount of explanation combined with a somewhat larger portion of illustrative anecdote. Hunting with a pistol is perfectly feasible, highly rewarding and great fun—always provided you are a fine pistol shot. It should be understood that, however "average" he may be in other ways, our pistol hunter must be far better than an "average" pistol shot.

There are several reasons why a man might wish to hunt with

147

This is an excellent holster for a scoped handgun, since it affords ample protection to both the sight and the arm itself. In selecting a scabbard for any sporting handgun, remember that the fast draw is almost never a factor in shooting at game—but shielding the gun from the elements is important.

his side arm, and the first is perhaps the challenge of the thing. A pistol is roughly three times as hard to shoot well as a rifle, and is effective at only one-third to one-quarter of the latter's range. A good modern rifle is so good that, in the proper hands, its accuracy is as certain as taxes. Its efficiency is so great that taking game with it is just not much of a problem. The pistol is efficient too, but it calls for quite a bit more study and application before its potential can be realized. And it takes real woodcraft to get close. The successful pistol hunter has thus brought off more of a feat than the rifleman, and that is a point of satisfaction.

Secondly, a pistol is convenient. It is much easier than a rifle to pack on a galloping horse or when you're climbing a cliff or wading a river or pushing through a thicket. In icy wind or a snowstorm it rides warm and handy under your parka, and your fingers do not stiffen from exposure. On a fisherman's belt it permits fishing and hunting to be combined on the same outing (seasons permitting), and this is a rare pleasure. Anyone who has ever packed a deer out of rough country can tell you how much he needed both hands free; and the backpacker, who designs his load to save ounces, can certainly appreciate cutting the weight of his main battery by two-thirds.

Thirdly, anyone who has an interest in self-defense (admittedly a ridiculous notion in these peaceful times) can certainly sharpen his practical skill by taking his side arm out hunting. Clearly there are a lot of so-called "protection" pistols lying around that would be of no value in the field, but the best combat handguns are great game-getters, and probably the sooner a shooter finds out that his "house gun" will not perform for him, the better off he will be.

In the last connection, I must point out that proper ammunition, of flat-point-lead or other energy-transmitting design, must always be used on game. The military-type bullet, with its hard jacket and rounded nose, slips through game—especially small game—without much impact effect. You can lose a rabbit to a GI "hardball."

Any *good* pistol is a good hunting pistol, assuming its cartridge is appropriate in power and design to the game sought. By "good" I mean accurate and reliable, with sharp, square, adjustable sights and a fast, crisp trigger release of from 3 to 4 pounds. (You can go lighter in special cases.) The defensive advantages of the auto over the revolver are not critical in a hunting pistol, and the problems of double-action control may not matter much either. Any really good revolver man shoots without cocking, but we common people usually cock a revolver for a precise shot, and game shooting calls for all the precision you can manage.

In this respect, one of the greatest aids you can enlist toward steady, accurate shooting is a set of grips that fit *your* hand. Men with short fingers often cannot get a secure grasp on the oversize "magnum" grips furnished with many heavy-caliber revolvers, and the same is true for gents with meat hooks, who find that slim stocks get lost in their grasp.

The solution is to invest in a set of handgun grips that fit you perfectly. Sometimes, you can buy them over the counter. Firms such as Herrett's sell several models that are widely available through gun stores, and it is no great trick for a good pistolsmith to carve you a pair to order. Beware, however, of target-style woodwork that offers great support but makes fast gun handling nearly impossible. Remember that punching holes in paper and hunting are two different things, and equipment for one generally will not serve for the other.

For the smallest ground game, as well as for most birds, the .22 rimfires are fine. The bottle-necked .22 centerfires will do nicely for animals of up to 30 or 40 pounds, though they do tend to tear up a lot of good meat. Better for quarry of this size are the .30s (.30 Mauser, .30 Luger, .32/20), though they are currently out of favor and difficult to find in proper condition. A modern exception is the S.I.G. 210 Swiss target pistol in caliber .30 Luger (7.65 mm). This is a sweet field gun, ready as sold without customizing, and with good handloads it is just about perfect for small game.

For beasts in the 50-to-100-pound range, the .36s (.38, .357, 9-mm Parabellum) can do a good job, though there are a couple of problems here. The .38 "shorts" (.380, .38 S&W) must be discounted, as must the .38 Special unless it is loaded very hot or limited to smaller game. (The .38 Special target wadcutter load is just great for rabbits and birds—killing cleanly without much meat destruction.) The Parabellum and .38 Super must be used with special ammunition not readily available across the counter, so the .357 remains the best bet in this power range. It will do as a general-purpose deer gun. At moderate range, with perfect placement, it will down even a big deer cleanly.

For anything much over 100 pounds in weight, it is best to go to the .40/200/1,000 formula: *"Not less than .40 caliber, not less than 200 grains of bullet, not less than 1,000 fps in initial velocity."* (Note that we do *not* favor an "energy floor," as kinetic energy is a deceptive index of killing power.)

For really big animals, we have the .44 Magnum revolvers of Smith & Wesson and Ruger, and the recently introduced .44 Automag. Arms of this power have cleanly killed beasts in the 1,000-pound category, and while they may be a bit much for our mythical "average guy," they are in no way uncontrollable. The auto kicks distinctly less than either revolver, but the blast is the same.

In recent years, a good many telescopic sights have been fitted to pistols, mainly as hunting aids, and I have tested most of them. As of this writing I consider them to be a .22-only proposition. This is not a matter of strength or durability, but simply one of tactics. In general, *sighting* is not a problem with a pistol. Big

Long barrels offer distinct advantages for the handgun hunter. They reduce muzzle blast, increase velocity and cut down on sighting error. The upper gun here is a Ruger Super Blackhawk in .44 Magnum with a 7½-inch barrel; below it is a Smith & Wesson Model 29 in the same caliber with an 8⅜-inch barrel.

animals at pistol ranges are easy to *see*. It is only when you're tracking a mouse in a brush pile that vision is much of an issue. For that, a glass is fine, but we generally shoot such *animalitos* with .22s. A glass sight unbalances and "uglifies" a pistol, it causes complex holster problems and it is really no help in planting your shot in the shoulder of a buck deer at 43 paces. So I use a telescope on my .22 auto, but not on my .44s or .45s.

It matters not whether you prefer iron or scope sights—the cardinal rule for accurate handgun shooting in the field is: *Use two hands!* Firing with one hand may look fine on television, but it's strictly for actors. The way to use the two-hand hold is as follows: Assuming you're right-handed, grasp the gun in your right hand in the usual manner. Now grasp the gun with your left hand, the fingers of the left overlapping the fingers of the right, left thumb lying above the right thumb. You are, in effect, grasping your right hand with your left.

"The more support the better" is a cardinal rule of handgun hunting. At left, note that both hands are supporting the gun, and that the right arm is braced against the tree trunk. At right is another illustration of the "maximum support" principle. Both hands are supporting the gun, and the right arm is braced on the right knee.

Using this hold, you'll find that you must face your target square on—forget about the old duelist's stance. Keep both eyes open (if possible), spread your feet wide apart and concentrate on your squeeze. You'll find that the two-hand hold works well standing or sitting and that, as a rule, the closer to the ground you get, the steadier you are.

To shoot sitting, ease down on your backside, feet planted on the ground in front of you with your knees at shoulder height about shoulders' width apart. Rest your arms on your knees and proceed as usual.

Hunting bullets should transmit energy in such a way as to deliver all of it to the vital zone of the target. A bullet that slips through and blasts a hole in the ground on the far side is not transmitting well; but, on the other hand, a bullet that breaks up and stops on the near shoulder blade, there expending all its kinetic energy, is not delivering it where it counts. So we ought to use a little thought in matching our bullets to our targets. Terminal ballistics, the study of bullet performance on impact, is a complicated and uncertain subject at best, and one that changes from year to year as new products are designed and promoted. About all we can say is that any plain, round-nosed bullet is poor, and that a round-nosed jacketed bullet is particularly poor. Even this is not *always* true, as a heavy, big-caliber RNJ bullet may be indicated for especially tough, thick targets—like crocodiles.

In general, however, the standard semi-wadcutter (SWC) bullet, with its flat point of soft lead and its bore-diameter cutting shoulder, has given long and dependable service. Hollow-points are okay, when they work. I have known many that did not— mashing shut on impact with no expansion.

Much is written on trajectory, borrowed mainly, I believe, from the rifleman's lore. At pistol ranges, however, it matters very little. Whether you shoot at a small animal such as a squirrel or at a large one like a moose, the range at which you can hold reliably on the sure-kill zone is going to be less than the range at which the projectile is going to depart significantly from the line of sight. Very few people can print a group, on demand, smaller in diameter than double the distance from the trajectory to the line of sight. The maximum ordinate of the .357 is only 2.5 inches over 100 yards, and that of the .22 Long Rifle, 3.3 inches. You can't hold that close, and you certainly should not try any shot on game that is farther than you can hold. Even the slowpoke .45 hardball departs only 1.6 inches from line of sight at 25 yards when zeroed for 50. Ranges at which bullets from correctly sighted pistols have dropped far enough below the line of sight to cause a miss are too great for the holding ability of the marksman, so trajectory is something we can safely leave to the lab men.

Range is the heart of the matter. If the pistol hunter stays within sensible ranges, he will have no trouble. What range is sensible will depend upon the size of the vital zone and the grouping ability of the marksman. He can check this easily by firing a series of ten-second 5-shot groups with the hunting pistol, using hunting loads and an unsupported firing position. The range at which 90 per cent of all shots fired fall within the sure-kill zone of the beast pursued is the range within which he must work. It will vary from 150 yards for a master shot hunting moose down to less than 20 yards for a novice hunting rabbits, but it should always be determined in advance and never exceeded.

For a pretty good pistol shot, we can set up a simple ground rule for sportsmanlike hunting ranges. Using a ⅛-inch front sight and a medium-length barrel, point at the target. If you can distinctly see portions of the sure-kill circle above and on both sides of your front sight, you are within range. If you can't, pass up the shot and get closer.

From this it is clear that the pistol hunter hunts at short ranges, only very exceptionally over 75 yards. While this does rule out certain types of game—most notably the antelope—it is not nearly so restrictive as one might think. The brilliance of our long-range rifles and sights, plus a certain amount of exaggeration on the part of their owners, has led many hunters to feel that 300 yards is about standard for a shot at any worthwhile target. A little investigation will show that this just isn't so. A lot of game lives in brush or forest where long shots do not present themselves. In such terrain a good pistol shot, with a good pistol, is quite capable of handling the shooting chores.

Last fall, for example, the elk, when we finally located them, had quite sensibly retired into as thick a stretch of woods as the country afforded. The only place you could see 50 yards was along a trail. The only bull encountered by anyone in the three parties that found those woods was shot at from 35 paces—and he was missed clean with a rifle!

Among our small-game animals, the best sport for the handgunner is afforded by rabbits. If you know of a farm that is pestered by a tribe of these voracious, prolific and tasty little dodgers, you are in luck. The big thing about the cottontail is *speed*, and if you can anchor one bunny in three, drawing the gun from its holster as he bursts out of cover and flashes through the weeds, you are an accomplished *pistolero*. Because rabbit shots are very difficult, careful placement is almost out of the question, so I favor a centerfire pistol properly loaded with square-point solid ammunition. High velocities and hollow-points can spoil much meat if the projectile expands, so medium- or big-caliber *target* ammunition is indicated.

The jackrabbit of the West is also a good pistol target, but unless he is overly plentiful, you won't get many shots at him at practical ranges. Alfalfa farmers will love you for thinning out their jackrabbits, but of course you must always ask permission first, and keep your ricochets away from the buildings and stock.

Tree squirrels, where legally taken, make good .22 targets, as the shot is usually stationary and can be directed at the head. This is one game that does call for a glass sight, since while the treetop may not be very far away, a squirrel's head is a small and well-camouflaged target.

Where I live, the ground squirrel must be controlled, because he is both a crop destroyer and a plague vector. The government people do this with poison—which is hard on my chipmunks and tree squirrels, among other things, so I prefer to forestall them, if possible, with my pistol. If I can keep the population of ground squirrels down by shooting, I can avoid the poison program. They make good targets, both while running and while peeking over a rock at greater distance, and while they're not much to eat, a good afternoon's bag is at least ecologically satisfying.

The marmot tribe, which includes the ground hog, the rock-chuck, the whistle pig and such, is rewarding to the handgunner. In the East these beasties are coming back, which fact may cheer the hunter even as it dismays the gardener. It is important to note that all marmots are very good eating, provided that (1) they have not been feeding on rank vegetation, and (2) the musk glands in the hind legs are removed immediately. And they are rugged. A .22 will very often fail to anchor a marmot, and if you don't anchor him he's usually gone, since his hole is never more than a couple of jumps away.

I have very fine memories of rockchucking in Wyoming. My father was a fly fisherman and could spend a whole day whipping a stream in complete contentment. I, on the other hand, can get all the trout fishing I want in a fairly short time, and I was delighted to find out about the rockchuck situation. I packed a Super .38 in those days, tuned up with a set of fancy sights, custom stocks, a trigger shoe and the like, and I turned to the pot-shooting chore with enthusiasm. I had, of course, the wrong ammunition, for until recently it has been impossible to find anything else. (You still—at this writing, at least—cannot buy anything over the counter for the Super but RNJ "hardball.")

Still, the effort was a success. After a good many hours spent sneaking around like an amateur Indian, I finally figured out a way to close the range by the right combination of wind, light and cover. Shooting one-handed, as we all used to do before the enlightenment, I was able to put a slug right into the center of the shoulder of the downwind sentry at about 30 yards. To my considerable discomfiture, he leaped off his perch, hit the grass running and popped down a hole 10 feet distant. Maybe that hadn't been such a good squeeze after all! Actually, it had been okay. He was stone dead about 2 feet down that hole, and I was able to haul him out with no difficulty. Having read the book, I got the scent glands out at once as I cleaned him, and packed him deep in a drift of old snow to cool.

Two days later we roasted him in a Dutch oven with onions, carrots, potatoes and red wine. Ignoring threats of excommunication from all the trout fishermen, I claimed it was the best meal of the trip.

Limiting myself thereafter to head shots because of the ammunition problem, I got only one more animal on that trip. On other occasions, when I used a .357 with lead semi-wadcutters, the chucks I hit properly stayed put.

In Central America, one of the best pistol targets is the iguana, called *garrobo* in some places. Where the local people know how good they are to eat, these big lizards are scarce, but happily, many *campesinos* scorn them as food. A friend of mine in El Salvador told me that *garrobos* used to be plentiful on his land until the Peace Corps came down and ate them all. In the backwoods of Puebla State in Mexico, I was solemnly assured that the flesh of the iguana was poisonous, because of his fondness for eating scorpions. When I mentioned that pigs also eat scorpions, I was confronted with a blank stare. Had I been a bit more sophisticated, I would have agreed that the lizards were indeed poisonous to eat, and quickly popped a couple of aspirin tablets as an ostentatious antidote. This might have helped the iguana population— but perhaps not. It is well known in the *monte* that all gringos are insane. That they eat iguanas could well be taken as excellent corroborative detail.

The iguana is not very resistant to shock, and no great power is needed to down him. He is most common along the banks of arroyos, with or without water in them, and usually does not stray far from cover. Quick shooting is usually necessary, and I have never known an iguana to stop and look back after being alarmed, as rabbits often do. Mexican brush rabbits tend to be as tough on the platter as parrots. If you kill both a rabbit and an iguana on the same evening walk, give the rabbit away and eat the iguana.

Hunting birds with a pistol can be a fine sport, though here particularly one is hazed to and fro by the vagaries of nitwit regulation. Most states of the Union flatly prohibit bird hunting with a pistol, and if you ask why, all you get for an answer is, "There's no reason. It's just our policy." Fortunately, there are exceptions, so those are the places we go.

· Turkeys stand out as pistol targets, and you may recall that the lead story in Colt's wonderful little book *Colt on the Trail* concerned a turkey adventure.

At one time I served on a huge military reservation in the Southeast that sported a large and inviting turkey population. On field exercises I always carried a Colt "Ace" .22 in my holster in place of my duty .45, as I was a G-2 type and spent a good deal of time on reconnaissance away from my unit. I didn't reduce the turkey count much, but I had great fun trying.

Crow shooting is not generally subject to regulation and offers fine handgun sport. Sitting shots within pistol range are nearly unheard of, so you have to zap these blackbirds on the wing. This is obviously not easy, but it can be done. A flock of crows will circle in a mobbing-type operation involving an owl or a house cat. You wait until you catch one turning end-on and, with a good squeeze, you've got him.

In general, wing shooting with a handgun is impractical, but there are various exceptions, such as the following illustration. In 1962, we camped by the estuary of the Río Balsas in central Mexico, a region which at that time had a reputation for peril. Perhaps it still does. At any rate, we walked a bit wall-eyed then. As we set up camp, a party of three shaggy-looking countrymen rode in among us, two with shotguns and one with a carbine across his saddle. We greeted them in friendly fashion and asked about the fishing. Good, they said, but one needed meat for bait. And here arose a chance to establish something.

Sweeping up the estuary in line abreast came a flock of fish ducks, flying evenly and steadily 3 feet above the water. It was obvious that they would pass us some 40 yards out, in a lateral enfilade presenting a solid target the size of a Volkswagen, moving at perhaps 30 miles per hour. No big deal. I managed the kind of smooth draw that looks much quicker than it is when you're not expecting it, swung from a good stance through the flock just as they came breast, led about 2 feet and squeezed gently while continuing the swing. At the pop of the big auto, one unlucky duck plopped into the shallow river. "There's meat, *amigos!* Let's wade out and go fishing." This sort of thing is a fine way to make points in a gun-toting environment.

But stunts aside, there is one bit of wing pistoling that I really want to arrange sometime. I was once confronted by a very grand and exalted British shotgunner with the proposition that shooting pheasants over dogs is not sporting, in that it is too easy. He asserted that a spooked pheasant will, more often than not, tower up to about 10 feet, check and then fly straight away. At the check it is, in effect, stationary for a half-second and thus no fit target for a scattergun. He further stated that he had proved his point by taking a limit on the wing with a .22 rifle—somewhat illegally, but all in the interest of scientific demonstration.

Now then, gentlemen, if this fellow could do that with a .22 rifle, why can't it be done, from the leather, with an honest combat pistol? That's my project. I want to follow a good dog, have him point up a cock ringneck, leave the pistol in the holster until the bird is flushed and then take him clean with one round of .45 ACP right at the top of his rise. Maybe I can't do it, but I think I can, and I sure aim to try.

Teddy Roosevelt opined that the only proper way to hunt pigs is with a spear. Sir Samuel Baker liked to hunt pigs with a knife. Great doings! But in a chapter on pistol shooting I must respectfully submit that pig hunting with a pistol is fun, too. Pigs, both large and small, are particularly good pistol game in that they are active, gregarious, mainly diurnal, nervous, shortsighted and *fast*.

These things tend to provide an abundance of quick short-range shooting—just right for a handgun.

The big *Sus scrofa,* which is a true pig and has interbred freely with domestic hogs, is an import into this country and must generally be hunted on preserves. My pistol-shooting friends have not been very successful in locating him, so I don't have many pertinent anecdotes—apart from the experience of Walt, whose camp was invaded at first light and who zapped a big boar from his sleeping bag.

On the other hand I have had much fun with the native peccary, called javelina in the places where you find him. One renowned pistol master tagged out a whole party in one virtuoso demonstration a few years back. Hunting a canyon bottom between two rifle-toting companions, he spooked a big herd. He dropped the leader with one round from his 8⅜-inch Smith & Wesson .44; then, as the riflemen could not see to shoot quickly enough, he splashed another as it ran. Still waiting for a rifle shot, he heard only shouts of interrogation. It was the last day, and hunter success on javelinas is only about 20 per cent. As another boar appeared beyond the mesquite, he shot again. Three pigs, all running, with three shots! That's about as good as you can get.

The .44—Magnum or Special—is really too much gun for these beasties, which rarely scale over 40 pounds, but we use it because the guns themselves are so nice. Mine, also a long Smith, has a trigger like a wish and shoots like a theodolite. It gave me a bad moment, though, on my last pig.

I was working up a ridge when a nice boar topped out from the opposite side about 40 yards uphill. Javelinas have poor eyesight, but I was moving and he saw me. He said, "Chuff!" in a loud voice and came straight downhill, flat out. He wasn't charging, of course, but the effect was nevertheless dramatic. I snapped the pistol forward out of the Berns-Martin holster just as fast as I could, cocking as I drew, and lined up on the center of his chest. As it turned out, I cocked the piece so hard that the cylinder rotated right on past the bolt, so that when the hammer fell it missed the primer. A click when you expect a bang is one of the more distressing experiences. The pig went by on my left almost close enough to touch. I lucked out as he departed with a shot that took him under the ear.

My favorite pig adventure doesn't even involve any pigs.

The javelina makes a challenging target for the handgun hunter. This animal is relatively small and extremely fast on its feet, so it requires rapid and precise gun handling.

Around Tombstone, Arizona, there are many holes in the ground —both old mining galleries and natural caves. We were assured that the pigs liked to shelter in these holes on cold nights, and the dawn was cold. We had engaged an Apache who was said to know all about pig hunting, but who did not communicate much. We were a party of six, all using .357s or .44s, and we all piled into the truck and drove up to the head of a canyon where our Apache knew of an absolutely first-rate hole. Before we had even un- loaded, the Apache disappeared into the ground. Not knowing that his plan was to flush the animals out, I ducked in after him, followed by the others in our party. The hole did indeed smell musky—pigs had been using it, though not necessarily that night. We went on in, using our flashlights.

About 100 yards underground, I got a funny feeling that we weren't doing things right. I stopped. Five hunters immediately bumped into me from behind, much like the cars of a braking freight train. Six magnum pistol barrels clattered in the gloom. If just one pig had come sprinting down the gallery at that point, he would surely have won the "battle of Tombstone," single-hoofed. The concussion alone would have caved in the tunnel. Very gently we got all pistols holstered, reversed ourselves and crawled back out of the hole, feeling decidedly foolish—not without cause. I have since wondered if that Apache wasn't trying to tell us something.

Both white-tailed and mule deer are, normally, cover-loving animals. You encounter them more often under 75 yards than over. This is pistol range, and deer are great pistol game. While the .357, loaded all the way up, will do for deer in many cases, I strongly urge observation of the .40/200/1,000 rule in selecting your deer-hunting handgun. This limits you to the .44 and .41 magnums using factory loads, and to the .44 Special, .44/40, .45 Colt, .45 ACP and .45 AR (Auto Rim) using handloads. In several of the better-organized states, the calibers of the pistols you may use are specified by law. My friend Ray has now taken four deer with four rounds of .44 Magnum, using a variety of loads but all in the 240-grain, 1,600-fps range. Such ammunition is probably ex- cessively powerful for the purpose; but however you achieve it, a clean one-shot kill is the aim of the game.

The problem in deer hunting, with either rifle or pistol, is readi- ness. Only some of the time will you be able to spot your buck be- fore he spots you. More often, sighting will be simultaneous; he will see you at the moment you see him, and then you face the very difficult problem of getting on him before he spooks. A bounding deer is too hard a target, and when a man brags about

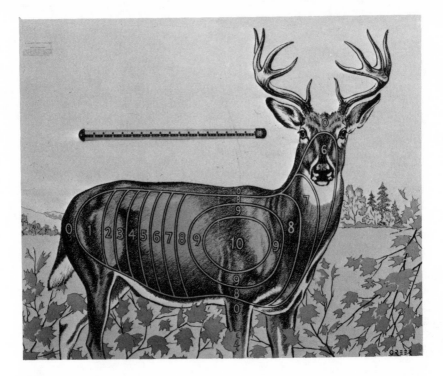

This deer target, sold by Stoeger, is highly useful for an aspiring pistolero.

bringing off this sort of shot he casts doubts upon his sportsmanship. Missing clean is okay, but the chance of wounding is too great.

Drawing on an alert deer is one of the real spine-tinglers. Any sudden movement and you've lost. You must *ease* the piece out and up, moving gently and very smoothly, fighting the tendency to go for broke every inch of the way. Even when you do it perfectly, your chance of a stationary target is none too good. And this exercise is quite common, as only rarely are you prepared for the contact with your pistol out and "aimed in." Under this pressure, the necessarily perfect squeeze is a real achievement. You can be proud of yourself when you manage it.

It *is* possible to see a buck first—especially if he is preoccupied. One beautiful morning a few years ago, on the San Carlos Reservation in Arizona, I was offered the perfect deer shot. Of course, I was hunting pigs at the time, and the seasons do not coincide, so

for all I know he is still there. I was glassing an open canyon from
a bed of wild flowers, while the quail called all around, when a
group of does and fawns appeared down to the right, followed at
about 200 yards by one of the handsomest buck mule deer I have
ever seen. His was a grand rack, and still on even in February. He
was screening his harem from a coyote family, which appeared in
due course, following the deer unhurriedly in hopes of a straggler.
The scene unfolded as if it had been written for a Disney production: a perfect naturalist's scenario.

From my post it was 60 yards, no more, to the saddle over which
all three echelons of the column would pass. After the does had
trotted by, I gently eased a cartridge out of the cylinder of the
long-barreled .44, and waited with an empty chamber under the
cocked hammer. The buck appeared, splendid in the morning sun
as he stopped and posed exactly in the saddle and looked back
toward the coyotes. The square, red-filled front sight steadied exactly in the center of his massive shoulder. Gentle pressure on the
trigger—and a whisper click. No venison that time, but every other
satisfaction I could ask.

In the Central American isthmus south of Mexico there lives a
small but handsome race of whitetails, fond of thick forest and
reasonably plentiful in the wilder regions away from paved roads.
It is customary in those parts to hunt them with dogs—a procedure
I regard as noisy, sweaty and prejudicial to the flavor of the venison. I was told that you just don't see the *venado* without dogs,
but it turned out that this is a matter of how well you use your
eyes. I have now taken Central American whitetails with both
rifle and pistol, but the rifle shot was not over 50 yards and could
as easily have been made with a side arm.

Having been skunked on both tapirs and wild cattle, I had
about given up hunting, and the rifle was packed up for transport,
when the pistol opportunity arose. You don't wander around naked
in that country, and my old friend the .45 auto, loaded with 215-
grain hard-cast SWC bullets and 7.8 grains of Unique, was never
out of reach.

I was actually bird watching rather than hunting. The birds in
that mountain forest are pretty unbelievable. A running river
covered the sound of my movements, and I walked right up on
two bucks drinking on the opposite shore. As they scrambled up

the bank, the old pistol slid out. A running shot was declined, but the larger of the two stopped at the top to look back. Range, 35 yards. At the crack, I saw all four hoofs in the air, just as if the .45 had turned him upside down. I've never seen a more instant kill. And the meat? *¡Pero que sabrosa!*

As a boy I acquired the old-fashioned frontier notion that anything with sharp teeth was a varmint, to be shot on sight as a protection for the grass-eaters. With maturity I have discovered that I, a predatory carnivore myself, am a comrade of the wolf, the mountain lion and the fox, rather than an enemy. One can make friends with a coyote or a raccoon, but nobody ever made a buddy out of a bighorn or a bison. So now I regard the grass-eaters as prey·and the carnivores as brothers-in-the-hunt. This personal view is admittedly a bit eccentric. I mention it merely to explain why I do not have a lot to say about hunting predators.

Certainly both of the great cats of America, the cougar and the jaguar, are better pistol than rifle game—if you must hunt them. The cougar is customarily treed with hounds, while the jaguar is bayed or called in. In either case the range is bound to be very short, and the power of a big pistol is quite sufficient for animals of this weight. If one is fortunate enough to make it to the Mato Grosso, where it is said that the jags grow to enormous size, the full-house .44 Magnum or Automag is indicated; otherwise, the .40/200/1,000 rule will do very well.

Likewise with bears, which I don't consider to be game animals but which at times can become a nuisance. Ordinarily the American black bear (*Euarctos americanus*) can be classed with the mule deer in regard to what power is necessary to take him. The Alaskan race of *E.a.* may, however, be another matter. There were a number of "accidents" with these in the 1960s, which lead one to believe that campers and fishermen are well advised to be wary of them. (These incidents were not accidental from the bears' viewpoint.)

I recall that once in my youth I had cause to speculate upon the disposition and wound resistance of a black bear. Chasing lions, we had inadvertently run a bear up a tree. As we proceeded to

haul the hysterical hounds off to a safe distance, ol' bear decided
to come down. I was packing a .357, very new at the time, and
almost had to check it out then and there. Everybody knows that
black bears do not attack people, but there was some question as
to whether the bear knew that. There was really no problem, as
all but two dogs were tied up by the time he hit the ground and
we had a good grip on those two. Bear took off, target angle
180 degrees, at a high rate of knots, and nothing further was
decided.

To round out this dissertation on handgun hunting, I think I
cannot improve upon a recounting of the Adventure of the Petersen Bear. Bob Petersen is a great hunter and an excellent pistol
shot, and has as good a claim as anyone to the title of foremost
pistol hunter of big game. He has taken moose, elk, polar bear and
Alaskan brown bear with his 6½-inch .44, in addition to much
lesser game. The brown bear episode was particularly stimulating.

It happened near Becharof Lake on the Alaska Peninsula. The
streams in that region are bordered by thick willow tangles, so
that wading is simpler than travel along the banks, for either bear
or man. So Bob wore regular trout waders as he hunted the stream
lines. The encounter took place as Bob was going upstream and a
trophy brown was coming down, making such a splash racket that
he could be heard round the bend. An Alaskan brown bear is not
something you want to bump into suddenly at rock-throwing distance, up to your knees in water and with no place to run even if
you could. Particularly not with a pistol—even if it is a .44
Magnum.

Bob waded to the bank as quickly as possible and rammed himself backward into the willows. He made 7 yards from mid-
stream before the enormous bulk of the bear loomed abreast of
his improvised tunnel in the willows, almost blotting out the day.
At 7 yards he had no marksmanship problem, though problems of
other sorts may occur to you. Bob put a 240-grain, steel-clad, flat-
nosed Norma right behind the shoulder, and then another as
quickly as the pistol could be realigned. The animal's roar seemed
louder than that of the gun as he crashed forward onto a gravel
bar. There was no back door to the tunnel if he had come up it,
but he charged straight ahead and fell. Petersen fired one more

shot after the bear was down, for safety, but it wasn't necessary. Two .44s through the heart are enough for anything.

The pistol is not the best arm for dangerous game, but in this case it did everything a rifle could. I do not advise hunting the great bears with a handgun, but it is interesting to know that, under proper circumstances, it can be done.

Shotgun
Shooting

9

TRAPSHOOTING

BY DICK BALDWIN

THE FIRST mention of trapshooting appears in a 1793 English publication called the *Sporting Magazine*, and it is there referred to as a "well established recreation." In those days, wild game was plentiful, so there is no doubt that shooting at the traps was indulged in largely for the purpose of gaining proficiency in the use of the gun.

In the early stages of its history, it would seem that trapshooting was purely an English sport, as no Continental records of it have been found. Residents of the southern and midland counties of England met near London to engage in a sport called "Old Hats"; they were among the first organized groups of pigeon shooters. "Old Hats" was so named simply because pigeons were placed in holes in the ground and covered with large old hats until they were released to fly as targets for the gunners.

Later, the rendezvous was changed to the "Red House" at Battersea, which was more easily accessible to the Londoners who were the chief followers of the sport. The "box," which was a shallow hole about a foot long and 8 or 10 inches wide, replaced the "Old Hats." The box was provided with a sliding cover to which a string was attached. At the command of the shooter, the string was pulled, liberating the bird. Trapshooting became one of the most popular of British sports.

The first record of this type of shooting in America is found in the history of the Sportsman's Club of Cincinnati, beginning in 1831. This is the earliest known mention of trapshooting in the United States, and good evidence that the Queen City is the birthplace of trapshooting in this country. At the time, wild pigeons were abundant, and these birds were used in the sport, though the records of the club indicate that it was not unusual to replace them with English sparrows. The sport quickly spread to other areas. The Long Island Gun Club was formed in 1840, and soon after, the New York Sportsman's Club was organized in that city. No doubt travelers returning from England helped to promote the sport.

In old-time championship matches in the late nineteenth century, it was not unusual for a good shooter to score 100 straight at wild birds. These matches were shot in such places as Detroit, Buffalo, Rochester, Syracuse, Cleveland and Windsor, Ontario. Great shots of this period included Cook Cozens, John Long, Ira Paine, Seth Greene and C. W. Bradford, all active in the sport and founders, so to speak, of today's game.

Bradford and Greene, according to old records, each scored 100 straight more than once, waiting with their guns held below their hips until the trap was sprung. Bradford held the then world championship for several years, finally losing to Edward Gilman of Detroit. Many of the old-time trapshooters did not take kindly to shooting at artificial or inanimate targets when they were first introduced, and although they occasionally took part in such contests, their enthusiasm for live birds remained intact. But as public sentiment against the sport developed, inanimate targets replaced live birds.

For several years, until after the turn of the century, the old Interstate Association held a "Grand American Handicap" using live birds, but discontinued the event after the 1902 championships in Kansas City, Missouri.

What might be termed the "glass-ball era" in trapshooting was inaugurated as early as 1866, when Charles Portlock of Boston invented the glass-ball target as the first popular substitute for live pigeons. From that day on, the new sport gained rapidly in interest and popularity.

The first glass balls were approximately 2¼ inches in diameter and made of smooth, colorless glass. Soon they were replaced by balls made of blue or amber glass. As the sport became more widely followed, numerous varieties of targets were placed on the market. For shooters who liked to see "feathers fly," a ball was manufactured that, when broken, released a handful of feathers. Another ball was made of a chemical advertised as an excellent fertilizer. This was devised, no doubt, as an answer to the problem of the glass-ball fragments that covered the ground after a shoot.

Belcher's Patent Paper Bird was introduced in 1884 by G. F. Kolb of Philadelphia. It consisted of stiff paper, rather oddly shaped, attached to a wire ball. A standard glass-ball trap would send a "Belcher Bird" into the air. After shot perforations were marked, the bird could be reused. There were no pieces of glass or clay left on the ground when Belcher paper birds were used; and there were no shooters, either, for they found them quite inferior to other targets of the era and refused to patronize clubs using them. The projectiles were advertised as "everlasting," and for half a dollar the company would send 50 birds and 1 ball, post-paid.

Chicago's Henry Sears & Company decided to enter the business in 1886 with a superior target called "Powell's Patent Puff Ball." From the description, it differed in several ways from other balls available. There were no broken glass, fragments of clay, explosive compounds or balloon shreds. And no question when a ball was hit, as the instant it was struck by a shot, a cloud of smoke was visible. "Powell's Patent Puff Balls" were relatively expensive, $5 per 100, and 1 ball was good, without adjustment, for 10 hits.

Notwithstanding all the various and sundry target innovations, the invention of the clay target, or "clay pigeon" as it was first called, marked the beginning of a new era in the sport of trapshooting.

In 1880, George Ligowsky of Cincinnati perfected a clay bird that would scale through the air with speed and flight comparable to those of a game bird. He developed the idea after watching boys skip shells over water at a lake near his home.

The first appearance of Ligowsky's clay bird was a demonstration at the conclusion of the New York State Trap Shoot at Coney Island in 1880, and the special showing received much attention and praise. The target, made of finely ground clay mixed with water and baked, was an extremely hard bird, ringing almost like a bell when hit.

For a while, Ligowsky had the field to himself, but as the success of his new venture became assured, others entered the business with targets of similar shape but of different materials. There was the "Best" tin pigeon, which made its appearance in Chicago in 1885 and soon was called the "worst substitute for live birds ever offered." The inventor claimed that a pellet of shot striking the target would release a flange which would, when hanging from the underside of the rim, gradually bring it to the ground like a wing-tipped bird. The theory was fine, but sometimes it didn't work. Some of the tin birds were picked up perforated by shot with the flange still withdrawn, while at other times the jar of the trap would release the flange before the shooter fired.

The first national trapshooting tournament using inanimate targets was held in New Orleans from February 11 to 16, 1885, sponsored by a new organization called the National Gun Association. Although wide publicity had been given the shoot, only forty or so shooters faced the traps.

The Atlantic Ammunition Company of New York offered the "Blue Rock" target in 1887. The target was "the best ever invented," or so the people who made it said. Its flight closely imitated that of a quail or grouse. In shape, it resembled other targets with the exception of a groove in the rim that fitted over the carrier of the trap. It was adopted as the official target of the New York, Illinois and Central Ohio shooting associations in 1887, an indication that perhaps the company's claims had some foundation.

The name "clay" was literally true for early targets, but in later years, pitch, plaster of Paris and fine river sand were used by manufacturers to make the birds strong enough for shipment but brittle enough to be broken when hit.

As inanimate targets improved, so did the numbers and skill of the shooters. There were some great shots already active in the late 1800s and early 1900s. Captain A. H. Bogardus was one of the first of the really great shots in those early years of trapshooting in America. His first recorded public shooting feat was a series of sweepstakes in St. Louis. He shot against Gough Stanton of Detroit for a $200 side bet; the targets were 50 birds propelled from a special trap Stanton brought. Bogardus won the match 46 to 40 and, in the months that followed, met many challengers for side bets ranging as high as $1,000.

Soon after the invention of clay targets in 1880, Bogardus joined Dr. W. F. Carver, another famous shooter of the day, in a tour of the country for the purpose of introducing the new inanimate target to trapshooters. Bogardus and Carver probably did more than all the other shooters of their era to establish the sport we know today.

On June 12, 1900, 74 contestants competed in the first Grand American Handicap at clay targets, held at Interstate Park, Queens, Long Island, and won by Rolla "Pop" Heikes of Dayton, Ohio, a professional who scored 91 out of 100 from the 22-yard line.

"Pop" Heikes was a prominent professional, but professionals were allowed to compete with amateurs in championship events in those days, and it was not until 1915 that they began competing among themselves. Few shooters were better known than Rolla Heikes in the early years of the century. He was a member of the American team that visited Great Britain in 1901 and, at that time, held more records and titles than any other living shooter. Some of them included winning the world championship at live birds (five consecutive times); the target championship (five different times); a world record for breaking 500 targets from five traps; and a world record for breaking 100 flying targets in 2 minutes, 58 seconds.

The Interstate Trapshooting Association, formed in 1890, organized and regulated trapshooting in the United States until 1922. The present-day Amateur Trapshooting Association evolved from these beginnings in 1923, and permanent home grounds were built in Vandalia, Ohio, where the Grand American Trapshooting Championship has been held since 1924.

Recognizing a widespread and growing interest in trapshooting among women, the Interstate Association, in 1915, voted to permit them to compete in the Grand American, the banner event of the trapshooting year. Up until 1915 they were eligible to compete only in some of the less important tournaments—from which many emerged as excellent shots. In any list of famous women trapshooters, Annie Oakley (Mrs. Frank E. Butler) should certainly be one of the first. She was easily the most famous. Annie did much of her preliminary practice at trapshooting on the grounds of the Cosmopolitan Gun Club of Cincinnati and gained international fame for her skill with shotgun, rifle and revolver.

Mrs. Ad "Plinky" Topperwein of San Antonio, Texas, was another of the leading women trapshooters of the early 1900s. On a trip through Utah, Montana, Oregon and California in 1915, she shot at 8,010 targets and hit an average of over 95 per cent. During this trip she made a straight run of 168. In 1916, she shot at 2,690 targets and broke 94.38 per cent of them.

In the 1920s, new names were beginning to appear in the winners' circles at gun clubs throughout the country. They're famous names today—like Fred Gilbert, Mark Arie, Forest McNeir, Woolfolk Henderson, Sparrow Young and J. R. Graham, to name a few. And the '20s and '30s were boom years for trapshooting in America. Records were established, and then broken overnight. People like Joe Hiestand, Frank Troeh, Walter Beaver, Lela Halland and Phil Miller replaced the Bogarduses, Carvers, Oakleys and Heikeses of bygone days. Much has been written about these famous shooters and the tournaments they won, and some of them are still winning.

The grand sport that began almost two hundred years ago with a field of "Old Hats" continues to develop. It is estimated that by 1985, close to a million trapshooters will be toeing the line at gun clubs across the nation.

Trapshooting today is a fast, extremely competitive 12-gauge-shotgun game that gets into your blood and stays there. It's a game you can't consistently master—no one ever has. The man has yet to be born who won't miss his share of targets one day or the next.

Small, disk-shaped objects made of pitch and clay, 4½ inches in diameter, supply the fun. They're called clay targets by some and a variety of other names by contestants who missed enough to allow a silver cup to go home with someone else.

The targets are scaled through the air away from the shooter at speeds approaching 60 mph by a mechanical device called a trap. The machine is housed in a small shed called, appropriately enough, a trap house.

A target can travel at one of seventy different angles. Its com-

The author, a southpaw, has won five national championships and been on seven All-America Professional teams. He was captain of the 1966 team.

plete flight can be from 48 to 52 yards; however, the average distance at which the birds are shot is 30 to 35 yards.

The shooter asks for his target by calling "Pull!" The trap boy, keyed for this call, pushes a release button which electronically releases the trap and scales the target into the air.

A string of regulation trap is 25 targets, with five shots taken from each of five shooting stations arranged in an arc, 16 yards from the trap house. Generally, championship events consist of 100 or 200 targets.

Competitive trapshooting is divided into three events: 16 yards, often called the Singles Event; Handicap, or Yardage; and Doubles (two targets released at the same time). This chapter will deal with 16-yard target shooting, the most popular of the three categories.

There are, strictly speaking, two types of beginners at trapshooting, and these two differ tremendously. The first class, and no doubt the largest, is made up of field shooters, veteran hunters who have no experience on the line trying to break clay targets. Trapshooting participants are generally made up of these people, and many a national champion started his competitive shooting career at the local gun club in a Hunters' Special Event.

The shooter of the second class is the true novice—man, woman or child—who has never shot a gun of any type. If this person has any natural ability, an instructor who knows his business can make him as good as, and often better than, the hunter who has shot in the field all his life. That last sentence will probably raise some eyebrows, but I've seen it happen time and again. When the instructor has started from scratch with a new shooter and taught him the basic fundamentals of lead, follow-through, stance, etc., results on the score pad are usually better than those of the old duck hunter who has spent half his life in the marshes. The reason is simple: Too many hunters try to shoot clay targets the way they shoot in the field, and in so doing they pick up habits that are hard to break. The tyro with a shotgun has never acquired bad habits and will follow the advice of an instructor.

The first and most important item a new shooter must acquire is a trap gun. Just any kind of "Long Tom" won't do, for many a

Here is a typical trap layout, with the shooters competing at handicap yardages.

potential champion has left the sport discouraged simply because the gun he was shooting wasn't right for him.

Clay targets are small and fly at approximately 60 miles per hour. They have no wings to break and put them out of commission. A visible piece must be seen before the shooter is credited with a hit. In the field, a bird that is nicked and downed can often be retrieved and put into the hunting-coat pocket, but even when a clay target is "dusted" lightly, a miss is recorded on the score sheet. One missed target can be costly, and many a national championship has been won or lost on a single bird. Therefore, a dependable gun shooting an even, dense pattern is a necessity.

Experience has taught that a 12-gauge gun weighing in the neighborhood of 7½ to 7¾ pounds is the right weight for trap. Guns of lighter weight tend to recoil too heavily, even with "light load" ammunition.

The stock dimensions of your gun are most important. This is the biggest single factor, aside from ability, that will determine whether you will be a champion or just another shooter. Trap stocks manufactured by leading firearms companies are designed for people with an average build and are generally 14⅜ inches long, with a 1⅜-inch drop at comb and a 1¾-inch drop at heel. (Drop, as applied to the stock of a gun, denotes the distance between an imaginary line extending back from the rib and two specific points on the stock known as the comb and the heel.)

Shooters over 6 feet tall or under 5 feet 8 inches will find average trap stocks too short or too long, respectively, and alterations should be made. There is an old method of measuring a stock by standing erect and putting the butt in the bend of your arm with the trigger finger on the trigger. If the trigger is at your first finger joint, the length is correct; if it's below your first joint by ¼ inch, then the stock should be lengthened that much. When the trigger is above the joint, the stock is too long. It should be pointed out that this test does not take into consideration the shooter's overall physical make-up—the length of his neck and curvature of his face, for instance—which in many cases is important.

The thickness of the stock is another matter to be considered. Generally, a thin-faced man does not require as thin a stock at the comb as does a shooter with a full cheek. The thin man is also less likely to be punished by recoil. When a person puts a gun to his shoulder, brings the stock to his cheek and looks along the barrel, he should be looking straight down the rib to the sights. If he is not, the gun does not fit him and changes must be made.

It is also a good idea at this time to determine which is your dominant, or "master," eye. Shooting with your nondominant eye can cause you to miss most of your targets. For instance, if you have a left master eye and shoot right-handed, you will unconsciously be getting your sight picture at an angle, since the left eye, which is not aligned with the shotgun rib, will be doing the "looking."

To determine which is your master eye, pick out an object across the room and, while looking at it, blink one eye several times in rapid succession. If you're blinking your master eye, the object will appear to move. While you blink your nondominant eye, it will remain stationary. If you determine that you have a left master eye, you must either learn to shoot left-handed or else keep your left eye closed at all times if you shoot right-handed.

A good plan for a beginner to follow in selecting a trap gun is to borrow one for a trial. Sooner or later he will find one with which he can do better than others, and he'll thus have a basis to go on. Many times a new shooter picks one off the rack that happens to be just right. In this case, a big battle has already been won.

Years ago, during the days of black powder, full-choke barrels ranging in length from 30 to 36 inches were used. With faster-burning smokeless powders now available, it's a rarity to see a 32-inch barrel on the line—the majority being 30 inches, with a sprinkling of shorter 28-inch barrels. There is no advantage in shooting a full-choke barrel longer than 30 inches; rather, it is sometimes a handicap, as the long tube tends to slow the swing.

Here are the fundamentals of choosing a trap gun.

There are four basic styles of shotgun used for trapshooting. They are the single-barrel, over/under, pump and automatic. The side-by-side double-barrel, although a popular hunting gun, is seldom seen on the trap line. Let's take a close look at the four basic models.

The single-barrel is by far the oldest type of action found on today's firing line. Modern gun technology has improved its reliability greatly since it first appeared in the early 1900s. Some fine

American gunmakers reaped large profits on the sale of their particular models. Parker, Fox, Baker and L. C. Smith each offered a "single-barrel trap," and their professional shooters were on hand at all major tournaments to talk up the merits of their respective companies' products.

With the advent of the pump-action and eventually the over/ under, the single-barrel's popularity began to decrease in the 1920s and early '30s, and it remained in the distinct minority until the early 1960s.

It was then that smart European and American manufacturers foresaw the need for reliable and popularly priced single-barrel trap guns. Their designers corrected the faults found on older models, and soon advertisements of a half-dozen different companies began appearing in national magazines.

Today, the majority of the large gunmakers offer this type of trap gun, and some have gone a step further. Interchangeable single barrels can now be supplied on an over/under frame, giving the shooter the option of using the same gun in singles and in doubles or in other events requiring two shots.

A single-barrel offers a trapshooter a relatively light, easy-pointing and fast-swinging shotgun. It has one of the safest types of action, as a shell in the chamber is always plainly visible. Some of the new models have extremely short lock time (the time that elapses, measured in milliseconds, between the pull of the trigger and the actual firing of the gun). This is an important feature in any gun and will help the shooter break a target faster. Because of its relatively light weight, a single-barrel has the tendency to "kick" more than other types of trap gun.

The over/under began making inroads in the trap-gun business in the mid-1920s. The choice of two barrels with different chokes greatly appealed to the doubles shooter who needed an open choke for a quick first shot and a tight one for the longer second bird. What was more important to the trapshooter was that he could now use one gun for both singles and doubles events. This eliminated the need for custom fitting of two guns.

Today, there are over twenty manufacturers of over/unders. They range in price from about $300 to well up in the thousands. But to the shooter who enjoys shooting one shotgun in all events, the over/under's price tag is of little concern.

The pump-action (sometimes called the slide-action or "cornhusker") is the real bread-and-butter gun among the trapshooting fraternity. There are few who will dispute the fact that the pump has won more championships than any other type of action. The reasons are basic. It's a fairly low-priced shotgun, and hundreds of thousands of pumps have been sold to trapshooters since the introduction of the first successful model in 1905.

Modern pump-action trap guns offer a great deal at a popular price. Interchangeable parts that can be replaced, sometimes in seconds, make it possible for the shooter to carry spare parts in his shell bag. It's not uncommon to see a man with a broken pump walk off the line, replace the defective part and be back ready to shoot all in a matter of two or three minutes.

Barrels are instantly interchangeable and do not require factory fitting, as was the case twenty-five years ago. Many fast pump shooters prefer a modified choke for 16-yard shooting but switch to a tight full for the handicap event. This barrel switch can be made in less than a minute on modern pump guns.

Their balance, reliability and ease of pointing, combined with low price, also contribute to making pump-action shotguns the favorite of most trapshooters.

The automatic (some call it the autoloader) has increased greatly in popularity over the past sixteen years. It has one big feature that other actions lack—a very noticeable loss of recoil sensation. Today's automatic trap guns operate on a gas-metering system that stretches the "kick" over a longer period of time than do other types of action. Thus the shoulder feels a push rather than a kick. Automatics, too, offer interchangeable barrels and parts that can be fitted in a matter of minutes.

The modern autoloading shotgun can be credited for the entrance of many women and youngsters into the trapshooting game. Its low recoil makes shooting easy and virtually eliminates' bruised shoulders and cheeks. Seasoned shooters say the automatic pays off for them in 200-bird 16-yard events when other actions cause extreme body fatigue.

This is an ideal gun for doubles events, as the muzzle will not have a tendency to jump after the first shot and interrupt a smooth swing toward the second target. Most automatics are priced lower than single-barrel and over/under models, but slightly higher than pump-actions.

So much for the guns themselves. Now, here's how to use them.

The correct position of the body in relation to the trap house is important. The left foot (if the shooter is right-handed) should be positioned approximately 6 to 8 inches in advance of the right. Body weight should be on the left foot, leaning slightly toward the trap. The left hand, on the forearm of the gun, only cradles and points it. It should not be held tightly; this hand and arm should be loose and used only for support and pointing. The right hand does all the work. It holds the stock in place at the shoulder and swings the gun in the path of the target. The right elbow should be held at shoulder height.

Here are some do's and don'ts for when you're on the line:

Pay no attention to what the rest of the squad is doing. Remember, at this point, concentration's the secret; without it, you'll never be a champion.

Call "Pull!" in a sharp, clear voice. The puller is watching you and is keyed to press the button as soon as he gets the word. A slightly fast or slow pull can cause a break in your concentration.

While waiting your turn to shoot, stand relaxed with the gun at waist level. In actual competition, the action of the gun would be open until the shooter's turn to fire.

In the ready position, the shooter leans forward slightly with the weight on his right leg and his right knee bent. Both of his eyes are open.

Raise the gun to your face and back it up with your shoulder. This will give you a comfortable position in which to absorb the recoil.

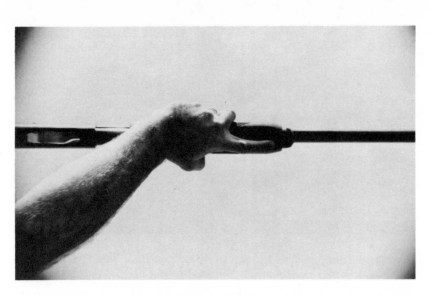

The index finger of the hand supporting the forearm points toward the target.

The hand cradling the forearm should be relaxed. A tight hold will cause a jerky swing.

Here is an example of bad shooting form. The stock should be brought to the face rather than the face lowered to the gun. Keeping the stock this low will cause tension in the neck muscles.

If the man ahead of you misses, wait until his target hits the ground. When the shooting is into a strong head wind, a target previously released can be caught in an updraft that may bring it into line with the one you've just called for.

When a target comes out broken, take the gun down from your shoulder and wait until the bird is out of the way; don't mount the gun again until you're ready to call for a new target. A little extra strain can slow down your swing. Remember, it's the small things that make the difference between 24 out of 25 and 25 straight.

Acquire the habit of following through on each shot. That is, keep swinging the gun as you pull the trigger and after the shot is fired. This will prevent any hesitation in your swing. Remember, if you stop that swing for the smallest fraction of a second, you'll miss.

Remember that you *pull* a shotgun trigger; you don't squeeze it. The instant you have the bird where you want it, slap the trigger.

Shoot with both eyes open, if possible; you need both and sometimes you'll wish you had a third. Years ago, a good many trapshooters closed one eye and squinted along the barrel rib. Many fair shooters still stick to this method, but the real top-notchers keep both open and their scores speak for themselves.

Experience has taught that you hit fast-moving targets best by pointing the gun as you would your finger. Point, don't aim. Time is an important factor in trapshooting, and the gunner who stops to aim with one eye is sacrificing an essential element of success.

For illustration, pick out some object across the room. Quickly throw up your arm and point your finger at it; close one eye and squint along the finger to the object. Now, take your hand down and, raising it again, keep both eyes open and line up the same object. Notice the difference between the time it took to whip your finger directly on the object with both eyes open and the time required to sight with one eye and achieve proper alignment.

A clay target is sometimes hard to see with two eyes open, let alone one. A pool player doesn't shut one eye, nor does a baseball player at bat or a golfer. In all instances, both eyes are on the ball.

Don't aim your shotgun, point it. This one sentence could well be the key to success in trapshooting. The hand holding the forearm follows the eye and instinctively points the gun where you are looking. Disregard the sight on the end of the barrel; it is used for proper alignment before calling for the target. Remember, *"the hand follows the eye,"* and the most important thing to do is look in the right spot—look where you want the pattern to go; the rest is instinctive.

The "lead" of a target is one of the most-discussed questions in trapshooting. It means different things to different shooters. One gunner may tell you he led a target 2 feet and broke it, while another will swear he hit the same-angle target with no lead at all. The reason for these seeming contradictions lies in the fact that some shooters swing their guns faster than others. The one who shot right at his angle target and broke it swung so rapidly he actually led the target unconsciously. A man with good reflexes often does this, while the slower gunner is conscious of his lead.

The point of aim on the trap house before calling "Pull!" is most important. It varies from Position 1 to Position 5. With the right-handed shooter in mind and targets flying in a normal manner (no wind), the following gun positions will break targets at 16 yards.

No. 1 Position

Here the gun is pointed at an imaginary spot between the middle of the trap house and the left front corner, approximately 1½ feet high.

No. 2 Position

At this station the gun is again pointed over the middle of the house about 1½ feet high.

No. 3 Position

The gun should be pointed approximately halfway between the middle of the trap house and the right front corner, about 2½ feet high.

No. 4 Position

At No. 4, point the gun directly over the right-hand corner of the house and approximately 2½ feet above the roof.

No. 5 Position

Here the gun is pointed approximately 2 feet off the right-hand corner of the house and approximately 2½ feet above the roof.

Note that the gun is held farther to the right of the house on Stations 4 and 5 than it is to the left on Posts 1 and 2. The reason? It is harder for a right-handed shooter to swing right than left, and with the gun already pointed to the right, less gun movement is necessary.

On the average, more right-quarter and right-angle targets are missed by right-handed shooters than other angling targets and straightaway birds. The direct opposite applies to southpaw shooters, who must concentrate on targets going to the left.

The more you shoot, the more proficient you'll become. Once you've learned the basics, only practice will put you on top. Learn to study local conditions, especially the wind. If it's blowing in your face, the targets will rise and the possibility of undershooting is greater. The wind at your back will push targets down and chances are you'll overshoot. Keep your eye on the grass in front of the trap house; it can act as your weather vane. In a gusty wind, it sometimes helps to watch the flight of the target ahead of yours. If it goes up, yours probably will too.

Hold your gun higher than normal above the trap house when the birds are rising in a head wind. Lower it when the targets begin to duck.

Above all, do not become discouraged if your scores don't rap-

16-YARD SINGLES

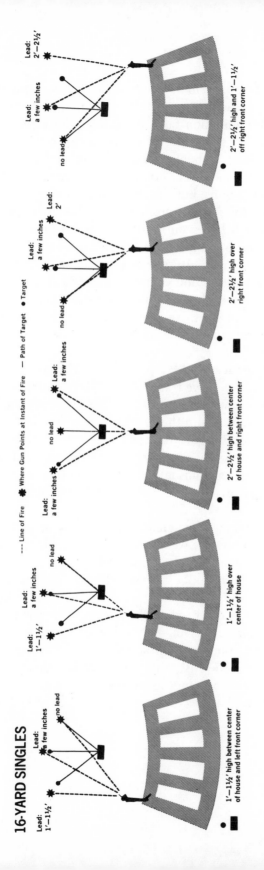

Lead: 1'–1½'
Lead: a few inches
no lead
1'–1½' high between center of house and left front corner

Lead: 1'–1½'
Lead: a few inches
no lead
1'–1½' high over center of house

Lead: a few inches
no lead
Lead: a few inches
2'–2½' high between center of house and right front corner

Lead: a few inches
no lead
Lead: 2'
2'–2½' high over right front corner

Lead: a few inches
Lead: 2'–2½'
no lead
2'–2½' high and 1'–1½' off right front corner

--- Line of Fire   ✹ Where Gun Points at Instant of Fire   — Path of Target   ● Target

While not all shooters use exactly the same aiming points and leads, this diagram gives a good example of what works for most competitors. The figures at the bottom show where the muzzle of the gun should be pointed in relation to the trap before the bird is released. (Diagram courtesy of Remington Arms)

idly improve. Most beginners progress well, but seem to hit a
snag when they reach the 17-, 18- and 19-out-of-25 bracket.
Here's where determination takes over. Don't let a piece of clay
4½ inches across get the better of a member of the human race.
There has never been a shooter who hasn't missed a target.

As in any sport, the correct equipment is necessary. We have
already covered the guns, but the ammunition one uses is equally
important. Every top-notch trapshooter has his own opinion, for
the load with which he's won most often is his personal choice.
Rules limit the shot to no larger than No. 7½. Most shooters prefer No. 8s, with either 2¾- or 3-dram-equivalent charges of powder. Every major ammunition company makes a trap load, and it
is not to be confused with the high- or low-base field loads available in the same shot sizes. Any reputable gun club will have an
adequate supply of ammunition on hand, and plenty of advice is
available with it.

A good shooting jacket with a proper shoulder pad is standard
equipment for a competitive trapshooter. The pad serves two purposes: to absorb some of the recoil, and to help lock the gun in
place at the shoulder. A gun that can't be shouldered in the same
place shot after shot is a gun that can't be pointed consistently.

Until approximately ten years ago, few shooters used any sort
of ear protection. It was unusual to see a man on the line with ear
plugs—and unusual to talk to a good trapshooter who wasn't at
least partially deaf.

Gradually this picture has changed, and now almost 100 per
cent of active trapshooters wear ear protectors, which are available from any of half a dozen manufacturers.

There are few sports today as competitive and demanding of
absolute perfection as trapshooting. It is not enough to do everything right once: you must repeat the performance 100 times and
often far more in order to win. To do this takes endless practice,
attention to detail, concentration and more concentration. There
are times when the game will drive you crazy; but there is no feeling in the world like stepping away from that last station after
every target you fired at has disappeared in a puff of smoke.

10

SKEET SHOOTING

BY HOWARD BRANT

THE CLAY-TARGET-BUSTING game known as skeet is a relative new-comer to the shooting sports; yet during its half-century of existence, it has become an avid pursuit of shotgun enthusiasts throughout the world.

The word *skeet* is from the old Norse word for "shoot." The game had its inception back in the early 1920s when a few New England upland-bird hunters devised a clay-bird game that simulated the darting flight of their favorite game bird, the ruffed grouse.

And so it came to pass that Charles E. Davies, his son Henry and William Harnden Foster of Andover, Massachusetts, soon had their new grouse-shooting game in operation. Originally, it was designed with a single trap and varied shooting positions marked off on a 50-yard-diameter circle.

The trap was positioned at 12 o'clock on the circle and located so as to toss targets in a straight line toward the 6-o'clock position. There were twelve shooting stations around the circle, and each gunner was required to shoot twice from each station, with the 25th shot of each "round" taken from the exact center of the "clock." This newly conceived game soon became known as shooting "around the clock."

Now, the original "around the clock" sport was a good one, but it had one dangerous disadvantage: since shooting was permitted around the entire circle, there was no safety in any direction. After numerous complaints from the local neighbors, Foster came upon a new idea to alleviate this problem. He simply cut the circle in half and added a second trap at the 6-o'clock position. With this innovation, gunners were still presented with the identical shots that were offered in the original game, but it reduced the danger factor by a significant 50 per cent—and we had the beginning of skeet as we know it today.

Soon Foster's game began to receive wide acceptance, and realizing skeet's nationwide potential, he immediately set about to improve it further. The new game had seven shooting stations about the semicircle, with an eighth—center—station midway between the two target-throwing houses. It was also Foster's idea that doubles should be added to Stations 1, 2, 6 and 7—and these, combined with the singles shot from each trap at all eight stations and the shot taken after the first missed target, constituted the 25-shot round of skeet.

In the current state of the game, a round of skeet consists of 25 shots fired at clay targets hurled from a high house (a trap house with the trap installed about 10 feet above the ground) and a low house (where the birds are thrown from about waist level). Single shots are taken at high-house and low-house birds from all eight stations, and doubles are fired from Stations 1, 2, 6 and 7. It used to be that the 25th bird was shot after your first miss, or if you broke every target as you went around the semicircle, you were allowed to take your last shot from whatever station you chose, at either a high- or low-house target. Now, however, the 25th shot must be taken at the Station 8 low-house bird.

In 1926 the "around the clock" game, as it was still called, was introduced to the shooting public via national sporting magazines, and a prize was offered to the person who came up with the best new name for it. The contest was won by a Mrs. Gertrude Hurlbutt of Montana, who suggested the name "skeet," and soon skeet fields were under construction across the country.

It became apparent, however, as skeet continued to grow in popularity, that some sort of national organization should be formed, and in 1935, in Cleveland, the National Skeet Shooting

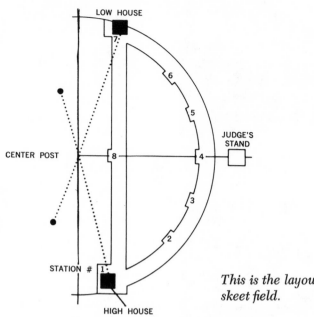

LOW HOUSE

6

5

JUDGE'S
STAND

CENTER POST

8

4

STATION # 1

3

2

HIGH HOUSE

This is the layout of a regulation skeet field.

Association was born—and the country's first national skeet championships as well. Some 113 gunners participated in the first tournament, and in ensuing years the annual event was rotated to various clubs across the country.

But soon the nation was thrown into World War II, and civilian shooting quickly became out of the question as sporting-arms manufacturers turned their attention to the production of the grim implements of war. Skeet shooting as a civilian pastime disappeared.

But skeet shooting didn't die entirely, for the military soon realized the merits of skeet for training aerial gunners. When World War II ended, a dedicated group of shooters, accompanied by a whole new following of military-trained men, returned to civilian life and reorganized the National Skeet Shooting Association.

The NSSA established a permanent home (as well as the permanent site for the annual national championships) at the Dallas Gun Club. But it soon became apparent that competitors were not enthusiastic about the permanence of the Lone Star State tournament setup, and consequently, since 1952 the national championships have been held at different clubs across the country.

International-style shooting requires a low gun position and calls for a delayed release of the bird, making this version of the clay-target game far more difficult than American-style skeet.

The year 1952 also saw skeet adopted by the International Shooting Union, and it has been on the ISU program ever since. During the infancy of skeet, a "low gun" position was required of competing gunners. A "visible" (upward) movement of the gun was required when the shooter called for targets. But this low-gun ruling was changed to permit the scattergun to be mounted to the shoulder before the target was called for. This new regulation immediately made a difference in scores. By eliminating the low-gun handicap, the neophyte gunner found he could break a few targets on his first go-around. The low-gun regulation is strictly enforced, however, in international competition.

In 1963, the NSSA added the International Division (which directs international-style competitions in the United States) to its scope of activities. Today, instead of national championships, it holds world championships, since the event is open to gunners from around the world who use any regulation skeet gun—the all-around 12-gauge, the 20, the 28 or the little .410—with individual and team championships for each category.

Now, let's learn how to hit the speeding clays that leave the trap houses at 50 to 60 miles per hour.

When I was actively touring the competitive skeet-shooting circuit (and particularly during the year I made a clean sweep of every event in the New Jersey State Skeet Shooting Championships), I was repeatedly asked for the "secrets" of clay-bird-busting success. I concluded that there are no "secrets" to the game, but that high-score skeet shooting hinges on the following: concentration, or the "will to win"; personal conditioning; practice and proper gun fit.

Foremost is concentration, or the "will to win," as I call it. You cannot worry about the next target or the score you're building or your competitors' scores—you must obliterate everything from your mind except the one target you are calling for as you step to the line. Once you break the target, only then do you concentrate on the next. Each and every target represents an individual challenge, and your complete attention and full concentration are required to consistently bust it.

You must train yourself not to be unnerved by the sight of a rapidly disappearing target, but to take the necessary time to concentrate on the finer points of gunning form, style and follow-through in order to break it. Even though the clay disk is rapidly fleeting across the field, in reality you have more time than you imagine. Just follow a squad of gunners around a skeet field and watch each target as it appears. You'll be amazed how much time you have to swing your gun, obtain the necessary lead, shoot and follow through (keep swinging the gun after you shoot).

Remember to mount the scattergun to exactly the same spot on your shoulder and in the same manner each time you shoot. Keep your head down on the stock and both eyes open. Many birds are missed by gunners who can't resist peering *over* the barrel at the disappearing target. Keep your face pressed to the stock, both eyes open; swing smoothly and follow through like a golfer. If your shotgun is not moving, you will almost invariably shoot behind every moving target. Remember to grip the scattergun firmly, but not tightly. Once a gunner tenses in anticipation of the ensuing recoil, either he will flinch (and destroy his follow-through) or he will be unable to swing the firearm smoothly. And without this smooth, uninhibited swing, his target will be lost.

Your head should be planted on the same spot on the stock for each shot, and both eyes should be kept open.

Swinging a skeet gun freely is a talent—but a talent that's easily mastered once you acquire the fundamentals. The skeet gun is not swung past a target with your body stationary and only your arms moving. Quite the contrary: your arms merely support the scattergun and move only in conjunction with your torso—you move your hips and turn your body and arms in unison as you *push* with one leg and *pivot* with the other.

Most "top guns" utilize a slight crouch with the feet placed 8 to 12 inches apart, the left foot (for right-handed shooters) slightly in advance of the right.

Try mounting your gun naturally and swinging it to the right as you would on a right-crossing target (left to right). You will feel your body shift naturally or pivot its weight to the right leg, while your left leg acts as a balance or "pusher." Now swing at an imaginary left-crossing target (right to left) and you'll instantly feel your left leg take up the body weight and become the pivot leg, while your right leg then becomes the follow-through or counterbalance leg.

Once you understand this natural method of swinging a scattergun, you will immediately perfect your swing and follow-through, since your entire body will flow smoothly. In the mean-

This is the crouch favored by most skeet shooters.

while, the gunner who merely swings his arms, keeping his body rigid, will find that his swing becomes cramped and erratic and that it is impossible for him to score consistently.

You must also remember prior to each shot to position yourself so that you are comfortable and will be able to swing freely when you have centered the scattergun over the mid-field aiming stake. Most skeet hotshots break their targets in precisely the same spot most of the time, and this spot is somewhere over Station 8. It is in this area that the gunner takes full advantage of his pattern and that his swing is most unhampered.

A perfect example of a hampered gun swing frequently occurs at Station 2 on the high-house bird. Outgoer (the bird is going away from you) 2 is an easy target, but many gunners attempt to break it mere yards from the trap house. Of course this can be accomplished, but not consistently. I've watched many a shooter point his body and gun a few yards from the high house, then call for the target. But before he can catch up to it, it is almost at mid-field and, if he has positioned himself to shoot at it just after it leaves the trap chute, he will find it impossible to swing smoothly at the target when it is sailing over Station 8. In fact, he'll be downright cramped and unable to follow through on it.

Instead, position yourself by facing toward Station 8. Then point your gun at the spot where you can first clearly see the target as it leaves the trap chute. Call for your target and you'll be able to swing smoothly and break it easily just before it reaches Station 8.

From every shooting station, study both trap houses and determine where you can first clearly see the target after it emerges. (Different people will pick up the targets at different points.) Fix this spot in your mind, for this is where you should point your gun when calling for the disk. If you point your gun closer to the trap house than where you can clearly see the target, it will already be yards ahead of you before you can get your muzzle up to it. But if you have the gun positioned at the right point, you can instantly distinguish the target, your muzzle will be right there and you'll be able to assume the proper lead, swing through and break the bird.

Let me digress a moment and discuss your eyes.

First of all, it's a good practice to use some sort of protective glasses when shooting, be they normal spectacles or shooting glasses. Secondly, poor vision is no hindrance to the skeet buff so long as he wears corrective lenses. I've been nearsighted for years, but have no difficulty picking up skeet targets when I am wearing prescription glasses. Lastly, the most important thing to remember is to use both your eyes. Never shoot with one closed. Normally, if you are right-handed, your right eye will be your master eye.

If you are not intimately familiar with the skeet-field layout, the normal flight path of each target, the semicircle's positions and how the game is played (including the NSSA rules), you cannot be expected to shoot championship-caliber scores. If you have to think about what target you are going to shoot next, or where the doubles are shot, you take your mind off the only thing it should be concentrating on—breaking the target you are about to shoot at.

Proper gun fit is another highly important factor in skeet gunning, with prime importance centered on stock length. Most scat-

The shooter at left is wearing custom-made latex ear plugs, which fit the ears precisely and offer excellent protection. The gunner at right is using plugs with an over-the-head band to keep them in place. This type of plug is also good, though not quite as comfortable to wear as the molded variety.

terguns sold over the counter have stock dimensions designed for the so-called "average" man, but these do not correctly fit a great number of shooters.

Proper stock length was of utmost importance in the early days of skeet when a visible movement of the gun to the shoulder was required, and it is especially vital today in international-style skeet shooting, which also calls for a low gun position.

I was never impressed with the significance of correct gun fit and stock length until I encountered the problem during my early skeet-shooting days. I was using a conventional gun of standard dimensions, and I got to the point at which I could consistently break 22 or 23 targets per round. But try as I might, I could not achieve the ultimate goal of 25 straight.

Light dawned when my father, a top-notch wing shot, observed my shooting one afternoon and remarked that I appeared to be mounting my gun rather awkwardly simply because the stock appeared to be too long for me.

"Why don't you remove the butt plate for the next round? Perhaps you need a shorter stock."

Well, I removed the butt plate (which is some ¼ inch thick) and proceeded to go around the semicircle busting my first 25 straight. The stock length had undoubtedly been my problem. Since that time I have had all my gunstocks cut off by the thickness of the butt plate, and these guns now fit me perfectly. By the way, it's far better to utilize a gun with a stock that is too short than to shoot with one that's too long, particularly in field and skeet shooting.

If you plan to take up skeet with any degree of dedication, I recommend that you obtain the services of a qualified gunsmith and have him watch you mount and swing your gun. Let him observe whether it properly fits you, and he will suggest any modifications he should make.

Remember, too, that while any smoothbore in the hands of a qualified wing shot can produce a respectable score on the skeet layout, for championship-caliber skeet shooting you should obtain a scattergun manufactured solely for this sport.

While the trapshooter requires a relatively straight-stocked gun, since he is shooting at a rising target, the skeet gunner needs a smoothbore with more drop in the stock, since he is shooting at a falling target. Gun manufacturers have incorporated into their various models features to meet the demands of field, trap and skeet gunners. Hence, today we have standard or field models, trap models and skeet models.

Perhaps the action best suited for the beginner is the autoloader. It will not confuse the starting skeet shooter with the intricacies of operating a pump-action. However, skeet models are manufactured in over/under, side-by-side double, pump and autoloading action types, and the choice is up to you—each model has its merits. All quality skeet guns have ventilated ribs, come in barrel lengths of 26 or 28 inches and are bored skeet or improved-cylinder. While I recommend starting your skeet-shooting career with an autoloader, as you progress (and only then) you may consider yourself qualified to choose another type.

The lead, or forward allowance, required to consistently break skeet targets is the skeet gunner's most difficult problem. Every shooter swings his gun past targets at a different rate of speed, and consequently lead on flying clays varies according to each person. The fast swinger leads less, while the slow swinger must increase his lead. But remember to pick up each skeet target as it moves across the layout, keep the gun muzzle swinging, move past the bird, pull the trigger as the correct lead is obtained and continue to swing through.

As I've stated, every gunner leads slightly more or less than another. But as a rule of thumb, here are the leads that I have used successfully in skeet gunning; they were given to me during my early years in the sport by the veteran New Jersey skeet ace and sporting-goods dealer Ray Lueddeke. For whatever they are worth to anyone else, here are the leads for each target that I have used for many years.

Station 1, High House—6 inches below target
Station 1, Low House—6 inches ahead of target
Station 2, High House—1 foot ahead of target
Station 2, Low House—2½ feet ahead of target
Station 3, High House—1½ feet ahead of target
Station 3, Low House—3 feet ahead of target
Station 4, both targets—3½ feet ahead of target
Station 5, High House—3 feet ahead of target
Station 5, Low House—1½ feet ahead of target
Station 6, High House—2½ feet ahead of target
Station 6, Low House—1 foot ahead of target
Station 7, High House—6 inches ahead of target
Station 7, Low House—right on
Station 8, both targets—swing and shoot as muzzle covers target

Now that we have learned a bit about the game of skeet, methods employed, stance, lead, etc., let me take you through a round. First, a round of skeet consists of 25 shots taken at 25 targets flying at varying angles to the shooter. There are eight stations around the skeet field, from which the gunner shoots 16 individual, or singly thrown, targets, plus four pairs of doubles and 1 (which used to be known as the optional target) from Station 8.

Single targets, one from the high house and one from the low house, are shot at from each of the eight stations; in singles the high-house target is called for first, then the low-house target. At Stations 1, 2, 6 and 7, doubles are shot, and in these situations remember that the outgoing target is shot at first, followed by the incoming target. Hence, at Stations 1 and 2, the high-house target is shot at first, then the incoming, or low-house, bird second. At Stations 6 and 7, the low-house, or outgoing, target is shot first, followed by the high-house, or incoming, target.

Prior to the introduction of "speed-up" skeet, the squad traversed the semicircle shooting the 16 single targets first, then returned to Stations 1, 2, 6 and 7 to shoot the doubles. But then came speed-up skeet. Here, gunners shoot their doubles at Stations 1, 2, 6 and 7 immediately after they fire at their single targets and before proceeding to the next station.

Let's step up to the line at Station 1. (Remember, we're now speaking of right-handed gunners only. If you are a southpaw, simply reverse the weight-shifting procedures.) As you approach Station 1, make certain your gun's action is open and the firearm empty. (It's a good practice before you shoot for record to call for a single target each from the high and low houses just to see how they are flying. Call for a single high-house target, watch how it travels over the center-station aiming point, then call for the low-house and carefully watch its flight.) Once positioned at the initial station, only then proceed to load the firearm, making sure that its muzzle is pointing in a safe direction. It is best that the beginner load only one shell at a time. Some skeet layouts permit the loading of two shells during the singles shooting, but whatever the circumstances, observe the rules set by the grounds committee.

Once your shotgun is loaded, remember to position yourself comfortably, facing the aiming stake located at mid-field ahead of Station 8. The first target you're going to call for will be the high-house, outgoing target.

You have positioned yourself so that you can readily swing downward and toward the center aiming stake. Start with the gun muzzle pointing to where you can first expect to clearly see the target as it emerges from the high house and call "Pull!" Remember, your weight is on your left leg.

Swing smoothly, and since this target is sailing directly away from you and dropping as well, an underlead of some 6 inches is required to break it. Don't attempt to calculate 6 inches; so long as the gun muzzle is swinging smoothly downward and so long as

This is the correct position for the high-house bird on Station 1. Note that the shooter does not attempt to bring his gun muzzle too close to the house.

you shoot just below the far, or outer, edge of the target, your downward swinging movement will invariably produce a shattered target. Keep your face snugly on the gunstock—don't try to peek up at this target or you will miss it.

Now for the Station 1 low-house, or incoming, target. Again, assume a position that is comfortable when your gun muzzle is pointed over the mid-field aiming stake. Move the muzzle of your gun from the mid-field stake toward the low house at the point where you have previously determined you can easily see the target as it appears from the trap house. Now call for the bird.

You have more time on the incomer, but don't be fooled and wait for it to sail the length of the field before you attempt to break it. The time to pick it off is when it is just past mid-field—swing past the incomer, maintain a 6-inch lead, keep swinging and pull the trigger. Don't overly "ride" the incomer in, as it is easy to do on this bird—break it just this side of mid-field, for the closer this target comes the more difficult it is to break.

Remember, too, that all skeet targets are falling targets and you must be not only ahead of but slightly *under* the clays.

Here, the gunner is awaiting a target from the high house at Station 2. Both knees are flexed to aid in the pivot.

Moving on to Station 2, remember to keep the action of your gun open and do not reload again until you are in position and ready to call for your target.

The Station 2 outgoer has been a bugaboo target for many gunners. But it is an easy bird and should not be missed. Most shooters hold their gun muzzles too close to the high-house chute and cannot pick up the target and still maintain a free-flowing swing in shooting at the bird as it sails over mid-field.

Again, take up an easy, comfortable position pointing over the mid-field aiming stake—this is where you will break your target, not several feet from the trap house. Only after you are comfortably facing mid-field, move the muzzle back to a point where you can clearly see the target as it leaves the high house. Call for the bird, swing past it, maintain the 1-foot lead, pull the trigger and follow through.

Again face mid-field in preparation for the low-house Station 2 target. Point your gun over the center stake, then move the muzzle toward the low house. Call for the bird and don't swing too far ahead of it, but maintain the 2½-foot lead, keep swinging and fire.

Always attempt to break the same target over the same spot on the skeet field; don't wait too long on any of them. Notice the champions at any large skeet event—they consistently bust the same target at the same point near mid-field. They don't ride in on any bird.

Station 3 is nothing more than a duplication of Station 2, but with an increased lead for each clay. The outgoing high-house target requires a lead in the neighborhood of 1½ feet, while the incomer, a deceptively slow-appearing bird, requires a sustained lead of some 3 feet.

At Station 4 you are exactly in center field and at nearly a right angle to your targets. The Station 4 targets account for so many missed birds simply because shooters have a tendency to swing too far past these birds. Here, I usually position myself so that I'm comfortable and able to swing smoothly while aiming at the center aiming stake past Station 8. In other words, I plan to break the bird over Station 8, but on its far side, toward the low-house trap.

For the low-house Station 4 target, I position myself so that I can swing freely past a point on the opposite side of Station 8, toward the high house. Both Station 4 targets require the longest lead on the skeet field—some 3½ feet.

Station 5 is the opposite station to 3, but Station 5's low-house target particularly has accounted for more misses than any other on the field. There is no demonstrable reason for this, for it is not a difficult bird.

The high-house Station 5 incomer here appears as a "floater," but it is traveling faster than it appears to be, so keep a 3-foot lead on this target. The low-house, outgoing target requires a lead of some 1½ feet.

Station 6 is nothing more than Station 2 in reverse. Again, remember to swing properly, pivoting on your right leg for the incoming bird, and maintain a 2½-foot lead. For the outgoing low-house target, lead it a foot.

Station 7 is perhaps the easiest station on the skeet layout, but beware—do not let up on your concentration. I've seen many a championship lost by the gunner's "walking away" from the birds here. The high-house incomer at Station 7 is a floater, but don't be fooled. Break it at mid-field, leading it not more than 6 inches,

At Station 8, drop the gun muzzle below the chute, call for the target, catch up to it, swing past and fire.

and remember to swing smoothly, for an erratic, lackadaisical swing at this station can cause missed targets. The Station 7 outgoing low-house bird is a straightaway—simply place your muzzle right on the bird and pull the trigger.

Many neophyte gunners have an unreasonable fear of the center-field Station 8 target, but in regulation shooting I find it one of the easiest on the skeet field, provided I am set for the target to appear. You must take your time and prepare yourself for this bird. (Under international rules, however, it's the most difficult on the entire field.)

At Station 8, when you are shooting at the high-house target, the bird will appear almost directly overhead and slightly to the right. False-point the muzzle skyward over the Station 8 spot where you anticipate busting the target, so that you are comfortably positioned. Then drop the muzzle directly below the high-house chute and call for the target. Swing quickly, and fire as soon as the muzzle covers the bird. If your gun is moving, the speed of your swing will be sufficient to cause you to connect with this target.

For the low-house target, which will appear over your right shoulder, again assume a position that will enable you to swing freely skyward and to the left; drop the muzzle just under the chute, call for the target, catch up to it with your gun muzzle, swing past and pull the trigger. Remember, both Station 8 targets must be broken before they reach the center of the field and *not* after they pass it.

The Station 8 low-house bird is also the 25th target in a round, so proficiency at breaking it has added significance for the skeet shooter.

Doubles shooting on Stations 1, 2, 6 and 7 should not present any problems once you have mastered singles shooting. In fact, very few doubles are missed in skeet events. Simply remember in doubles shooting to take your time and concentrate on each bird, one at a time. Break the outgoer first; then, and only then, concentrate on the incomer. You have more time than you imagine.

Not only is skeet shooting a game in itself, but once mastered it will vastly improve your scattergunning performance and increase your game bag afield. It teaches you safety, proper gun handling, performance under pressure, correct lead and all the other aspects of successful wing shooting.

11

UPLAND-BIRD
HUNTING

BY PETE KUHLHOFF

IN THE United States, the upland bird in one locality may be the pheasant; in another, the quail; in others it may be grouse of one kind or other, the chukar partridge, the Hungarian partridge, the woodcock, pigeons and doves, ptarmigan or even the wild turkey. It is my good fortune to have had the opportunity to hunt all the kinds of American upland birds, and several others in quite a number of places throughout the world.

The first element to consider is, naturally, the shotgun.

Certainly, one of the most important factors in successful upland gunning is shotgun fit. The reason for this is simple: Invariably, you have to flip the gun to your shoulder, swing and fire all within fractions of a second; there is no time to position the gun, or "wrap yourself around it," as there is with a rifle. Therefore, a good upland gun must literally "shoot where you look."

The way to determine proper shotgun fit is simple: Close your eyes and shoulder the gun as you would in the field. Now open your eyes. Your line of vision should be right down the rib or the center of the barrel. If the muzzle is high or low, left or right, the gun doesn't fit and you'll miss your shot as a result.

A made-to-order stock is one solution, but there are simpler and less expensive approaches to correct shotgun fit. Shortening the stock by cutting it down or lengthening it by the addition of a recoil pad will often give the correct length of pull (the distance from the rear of the butt plate to the trigger); and you can effectively heighten the comb by adding a moleskin patch or lower the comb by sanding it down.

The upland gun should be lightweight. A hunter after grouse, or even chukars or pheasant in some vicinities, will walk distances that may seem like 20 miles between shots, and even more if he is doing kick-up shooting without a good dog. When he is carrying a heavy gun, his arm feels as if it is being pulled longer and longer, finally giving him the proportions of a lopsided ape. For the sportsman who insists on the 12-gauge, there are plenty of guns weighing 7 pounds and under, and even some as light as 6 pounds.

When an individual plans to spend a full day wandering the uplands, he probably will take along a snack for lunch and per-

This is excellent shooting position—the gunner is well balanced, weight on forward leg, able to pivot and follow the bird in any direction. (Photo courtesy of Winchester News Bureau)

haps a small thermos bottle of thirst quencher, plus a supply of
shotshells. With the comparatively small limit on most upland
birds, the number of shells necessary may be only a handful. Yet
in hunting ruffed grouse, I have seen fellows shoot more than a
full box of shells, with nothing ending up in the bag for table use.
So ammo weight may be considered in some instances. A box of
12-gauge field loads with 1 ounce of No. 6 or 7½ shot weighs 2
pounds 6 ounces, while a box of 28-gauge shells with ¾-ounce
loads weighs 1 pound 10 ounces. That's only 11 ounces, or less
than a pound, of difference, but every little bit may help.

For many years, I figured that anyone who used a smaller
gauge than 12 was out of his head and was handicapping himself. Then, more than a decade ago, while hunting ducks on Long
Island Sound, I met two fellows from Winchester-Western. Both
were using 20-gauge guns, and they started kidding me about my
big cannon and the little bitty ducks. (The ducks, mostly mallard
and common blacks, were not so small, averaging at more than 3
pounds.) Anyway, the next day I sneaked out with a 20-gauge
and did about the same on the quackers as with the 12. After lug-
ging the 20-gauge in various upland fields, I was completely sold
on smaller bores than 12 gauge and sort of nailed-in on the 20.

About that time, I was looking over several of W. W. Greener's
books, including the fifth edition of *The Gun and Its Development*. In one of the volumes, some almost unbelievable accounts
of activities with the 28-gauge caught my attention. I figured that
if the little gauge was so deadly in the 1870–90 period, now, with
modern improvements, it would be even better. So I obtained
several for tryout.

My first use of the 28-gauge was on quail, then chukars, over
dogs. The average shot was probably not over 25 yards, and I
don't recall missing a shot or losing a bird. The payoff came one
day, in excellent pheasant cover, when several of us decided,
somewhat hesitantly, to give these larger and tougher birds a
try with the 28-gauge. Using a variety of loads, we had no problems. From the standpoint of knocking down the birds, no difference in effectiveness was noticed. We lost no wounded birds, and
my longest shot that day was at a measured 43 yards to the point
where the shot charge overtook the pheasant and knocked him
cold. The guns were mostly choked for skeet, with a couple of

Here is the wrong way to shoot. The hunter is leaning too far forward and, an even more serious fault, her head is not down on the stock of the gun. (Photo courtesy of Winchester News Bureau)

doubles bored improved-cylinder and modified choke. Many times I have heard that about 25 yards is the limit of sure killing range of a skeet-choked gun. So perhaps we were lucky—consistently! Since that time, I have used the 28-gauge at field trials and again had no problem. To give myself an out, I will say that our tests cannot be considered as conclusive, but *I* am completely sold.

One fellow did miss a fast-flying and fast-rising chukar on take-off by shooting under him with both barrels. Which brings up another point in upland hunting. Most birds are rising when shot at, so a slightly straighter stock than one with average field dimensions will help some shooters. Maybe not as straight as the trap-gun stock, but about halfway between. You can experiment by using a lace-on Monte Carlo cheek pad.

To get an idea of what has happened in the shotgun-shell field, let's compare shotshell loads of fifty to sixty years ago with those we have today. For brevity we'll consider primarily 12 and 20 gauges. Back in 1913, shotshells were regularly loaded in four weights of shot charges in 12 gauge: ¾, 1, 1⅛ and 1¼ ounces. Now, in 2¾-inch 12-gauge shells, 1, 1⅛, 1¼ and 1½ ounces of shot are loaded, while in 3-inch shells we have 1⅜-, 1⅝- and 1⅞-ounce loads available. In 20 gauge (1913), ½-, ¾- and ⅞-ounce shot loads were factory-available. Now, in 2¾-inch 20-gauge shells, we have ⅞, 1 and 1⅛ ounces, and in 3-inch shells we have 1 3⁄16- and 1¼-ounce loads.

This means that today we have some real humdingers in 12 gauge, and 20-gauge loads as heavy and effective as the maximum 12s in 1913. Also, it is important to note that with our current plastic-protected shot charge and gas-sealing wads, we get better patterns than ever before, with some 20-gauge spreads much better than the best 12 gauges of years gone by.

The 28-gauge shell was loaded with ⅝ ounce of shot sixty years ago, while today it is loaded, in 2¾-inch length, with ¾ and ⅞ ounce of shot. In recommended upland-game loads (1913), nothing was listed smaller than the 16 gauge. Today, recommendations are made by degree of choke and shot size, rather than by gauge and shot size.

Don't get the idea that I am pushing magnum and long-range loads for upland-game hunting. As a matter of fact, in the 12-, 16- and 20-gauge guns, and for the hunter who wants everything uncomplicated, it is not a bad idea to settle on a 1-ounce load of shot, which experience indicates is adequate for most upland hunting. For all-around upland loads, I prefer No. 8 or 7½ shot in an open-choked gun. It is on the light side only for big fat pheasant in a wide cornfield, where shots should be passed up.

However, there is more than one side to any question, and many hunters of experience maintain that heavy loads—more shot in the air—result in fewer wounded and lost birds. On the other hand, heavier shot charges may result in mangled, no-pot game at near ranges, or in the hunter's trying to reach out too far and thus defeating the conservation purpose.

Now that we know that we have an edge when using modern shotshells, how about shotguns?

Brother, are we in luck in that department, too! We have shotguns to meet the demands, desires and whims of practically every shooter. Repeating shotguns, pump-type and autoloader, as well as the bolt-action, are American developments, which sometimes

are frowned on by our British friends. I have been a guest at upland shoots in several places around the world, and here is a point
made by an English chap I met while hunting in northern Italy:

"In England we prefer the double gun. However, if a sportsman shoots for pleasure, and shoots alone or with others who have
similar ideas, the best gun for him is the one that pleases him best,
be it a repeater, an over/under or a side-by-side double. If he
shoots away from home and with others who have different ideas,
and perhaps by their favor, then he owes consideration to their
views and prejudices."

Seems reasonable.

Up until around the turn of the century, the single-barrel,
single-shot gun and the double shotgun (side-by-side barrels)
were paramount in the United States. With the development of
reliable repeaters, single-shots and doubles almost disappeared
from the American scene. But since World War II, both side-by-
side and over/under guns have made great inroads in overall
popularity in the United States and Canada.

It seems to me that many upland hunters are overgunned. I
honestly believe that many people now using 12-gauge guns
would be better off with a 20- or 16-gauge. And from observation, I know that many guns used in the uplands are overchoked.
In the Northeast, too many hunters traipse around carrying 12-
gauge guns having 30-inch full-choke barrels while looking for
ruffed grouse or pheasant, maybe kick-up or maybe with a bird
dog. In this part of the country, the cover is brushy, brambly and
thick. Shots, more often than not, have to be taken at very close
range, especially with grouse—say at around 15 to 20 yards—or
not at all. The fellow with the full-choke barrel is very poorly
equipped.

This, in fact, is the one area in which upland gunners most
consistently go astray—the selection of their choke. Years ago, the
vast majority of scatterguns had long (30-inch or so) barrels and
were choked to throw full-choke patterns. That is, they would put
70-plus per cent of their shot inside a 30-inch circle at 40 yards.
Because many of the shot pellets would be deformed on their
trip up the bore and stray from the pattern, this tight choking
was desirable to maintain a dense pattern that birds could not fly
through.

However, with the advent of the plastic shot collar and over-powder wad, which drastically reduces pellet deformation and makes patterns far denser than they used to be with the same amount of barrel constriction, upland gunners who use guns choked full are kidding themselves if they hope for hunting success. The point is those short ranges at which the birds are shot. With the full-choke's tight pattern—about 23 inches at 30 yards and about 15 inches at 20 yards—they will either miss the bird entirely or mangle it into uselessness if they connect.

What you want is a gun that's choked improved-cylinder (if you have a single-barrel gun) or improved-cylinder and modified if it's a double. An improved pattern will run from 45 to 55 per cent, while modified will go from about 55 to 65.

If you shoot skeet, you know how a clay target is smoked if taken from Station 1 at about two-thirds the distance to the mid-field stake (the high-house-low-house target crossing point), per-haps at 15 or 16 yards away, or even at the stake, which is at 21

When walking up on a bird, keep the muzzle of the gun pointed away from the dog, and concentrate on the spot that you think the bird will emerge from. (Photo courtesy of Winchester News Bureau)

yards. This is most frequently done with a skeet barrel (about .004-inch constriction, or slightly less than improved-cylinder choke), which puts its shot charge into about 30 inches at 20 yards. It will do the same on grouse or pheasant. A gun choked skeet and skeet thus is also a good choice for the uplands.

The hunter who wants one gun for all kinds of shooting can have an adjustable, or variable, choke device fitted to the muzzle. Some such devices offer a complete range of chokes by the turning of a collar; others have interchangeable tubes. With either type, the hunter can change the amount of choke or constriction to meet conditions. And I might add, a number of American shotguns are available with factory-fitted variable choke devices.

However, even if you buy the right choke, you must still pattern it with the shotshells you'll be using to make sure of two things: first, that your gun is shooting "where you look"—not high, low, left or right—and second, that you are indeed getting the desired percentage in your pattern. Many foreign-made shotguns shoot much tighter than they are marked, so you can easily find yourself with a modified barrel that shoots full-choke patterns. Shooting at game with a shotgun that hasn't been patterned is like going deer hunting with a rifle that hasn't been sighted in.

The problem in every shooting instance is putting the shot pattern on the target. Proficiency in shotgun pointing is learned only by experience and practice. Shooting skeet, in which targets are taken at various angles, and trapshooting can be excellent for learning lead and follow-through.

Most crossing or sharply angling targets are missed by the gunner's shooting behind them, either because of not enough lead or by stopping the gun and not following through with the swing. Elements involved in leading a target can be divided into three groups:

First, there are those having to do with the gun and shotshell load—lock time, or the interval between the pull of the trigger and ignition, including hammer or striker fall; ignition time; and time of travel of the shot charge from the gun to the target. Second, there is the personal reaction time of the individual—the time interval between his mentally willing the shot and his actual release of the trigger. Third, there are the distance to the target, its angle and its speed of flight.

Even though this shooter has a considerable forward lean, his feet are solidly planted and his balance is good. Note that his head is firmly on the stock. (Photo courtesy of Winchester News Bureau)

The only elements that are constant are lock time, ignition time and the velocity of the shot column. How the hell we ever hit anything I'll never know!

Actually, there are a couple of ways of obtaining lead and hitting flying targets. One is sustained lead, in which the target is tracked with the gun moving ahead of it at the same relative speed as the target. You maintain the proper lead until after the gun is fired. The amount of lead here depends on the speed of the target, its direction and its distance from the gun—a lot of variables and quite a chore, mastered by few.

The swing-through method of obtaining lead is probably the most used and easiest to learn. The shooter moves the gun from behind the target, passes it and pulls the trigger when the space between the target and sights looks correct. He continues the follow-through as in swinging a golf club. Here too, the distance to the target, its speed and its direction have to be considered.

The late Norman Clarke of the Holland & Holland shooting school of England—who was a really great shotgun handler—once said something that I will always remember. Several of us were engaged in a shooting game on the school grounds. One fellow asked Norman how much lead was necessary on a certain angling, almost crossing, target.

The master looked at him in amazement and said, "No lead."

The guy asked him, then how the hell could he hit the target?

Then came the explanation, which was a revelation to me. I hope that he wasn't kidding, because that is the way I shoot in the upland fields.

He said that on incoming and crossing targets, you swing on them fast, pull the trigger as the shotgun bead is on the target and continue the fast swing. The faster the target, the faster the swing, and the reaction time in willing the shot and pulling the trigger takes care of any gun advancement necessary in making the hit. So, you see, no lead.

Actually, he was advocating a kind of follow-through. It made sense for the targets we were shooting at, with the incoming ones like exaggerated Station 8 skeet shots and the crossing ones about like exaggerated Station 3, 4 and 5 shots. As a matter of fact, this way of shooting can work well at skeet with some shooters who call for targets with the gun unmounted.

One element in shotgun shooting that gets very little attention is trigger control, or trigger timing. This is something that every great trap and skeet shooter and every accomplished game hunter knows about but says very little of. It can eventually be of utmost importance to every gunner.

Trigger control, or trigger timing, is elemental. It is releasing the trigger at exactly the right time—that is, when every other element in making the shot successful is exactly right.

You and I have seen misses on comparatively easy targets, whereupon the shooter let out a few vehement words and maintained that everything had been in perfect order. How come the shot was missed? Probably trigger timing. At the instant the mind willed the shot, something went wrong with the shooter's normal reaction time. Perhaps he hadn't slept well the night before, maybe he had a slight hangover or there might have been any other of a number of reasons. Regardless, the trigger timing was off—too quick or too slow—and the shot pattern missed the target.

A fault that can lead to poor trigger timing is improper contact between the trigger and trigger finger. This may seem like a lot of gibberish to fellows who slap the trigger, but it is a fact. Shooters with long arms and large hands shooting guns with short buttstocks have a tendency to wrap the index finger around the trigger, making the mistake of contacting the trigger with the insensitive crease at the first or second joint. The proper contact point is near the tip of the finger, the most sensitive portion.

Many shooters maintain, however, that the proper placement of the finger on the trigger *is* at the crease of the first joint because there is less meat at that point and the gun goes off immediately when pressure is applied. It is probably a good idea for you to try both ways and use the one that is more successful.

Get a shotgun "that likes you," ammo suitable for the game—and head for the uplands. And remember, 40 to 45 yards is maximum range in upland hunting (or any other kind of shotgun game), regardless of gun make, gauge and barrel choke! Remember!

12

WATERFOWL HUNTING

BY ERWIN A. BAUER

WATERFOWLING has been a traditional rite of every autumn since the first Europeans waded ashore onto North American soil, and there is evidence that duck hunting was practiced by Indians in California at least five hundred years before that. Interest in both the birds and the gunning has never been greater than it is today —and no wonder. There is no more fascinating or exciting way to spend a cold and windy day in fall than in hunting waterfowl.

Altogether, 247 kinds of ducks, geese and swans inhabit the face of the earth; and of these, 44 live permanently on this continent or at least visit here occasionally. That means there is waterfowl hunting in every state from Alaska to Florida, although it is far more productive in some places than in others. And, of course, the methods of hunting also vary greatly from one region to another.

America's waterfowl can be divided into three categories: puddle ducks, diving ducks and geese. In addition, there are three species of swans (trumpeters, whistlers and mutes·), but only whistlers are hunted, and on such a restricted basis that they will not be considered here.

The puddle ducks, or puddlers, are typically birds of shallow fresh-water marshes and rivers rather than of large lakes and bays. Some can dive, but ordinarily they tip up or dabble rather than submerge completely when feeding. Puddlers are also much more at home on dry land than are divers. The category includes the mallard, black, pintail, widgeon, gadwall, shoveler and wood duck and all of the teals.

Diving ducks tend to frequent larger, deeper lakes and rivers, coastal bays and inlets, but are not at all restricted to these locales. Divers are grouped together because they usually feed by submerging, often to considerable depth. And when flushed or taking flight, they taxi along the surface until airborne, while puddlers flush straight upward, almost as if catapulted. A list of diving ducks includes the following: canvasback, redhead, greater and lesser scaups, ringneck, goldeneye, bufflehead, old squaw and the eiders and scoters.

Ten kinds of goose or brant may end up in hunters' bags, and these are normally distinguished from ducks by their larger size and longer necks. They more closely resemble puddle ducks in their feeding habits (which may be more terrestrial) and diving ducks in their manner of take-off.

No matter what type of duck hunting an outdoorsman prefers, it is most important nowadays to be able to identify ducks quickly and accurately, even under the poor light conditions that often prevail during "good" waterfowling weather. There are a number of reasons for this. First, the season is not always open on *all* ducks; and second, the limits are lower on certain species than on others. Therefore, a hunter can be in violation of Federal regulations by shooting the wrong kind of duck or taking too many of another kind. In addition, not all ducks are of equal edibility; there is no sensible reason to shoot mergansers, for one example, because they usually taste strongly of fish.

The best way to begin identification is to obtain a good waterfowl guide and to watch for color and pattern of plumage, both of birds in flight and of birds on the water. Try to get as close a look as possible. But knowing plumage alone isn't enough; the complete duck hunter also checks the habitat (shallow or deep water), the action or behavior (noisy or quiet), the shape and silhouette (large duck or small), the pattern of flight (rapid wing beat or slow) and even the voice of the bird. Consider a few typical examples:

Mallards, pintails and widgeon form loose groups as they ma-

neuver above a pond or near a blind prior to landing. Sometimes
the individual ducks in one of these flocks are so scattered that
they seem to be going in all directions at once, although aimed
toward the same place. By contrast, teal and shovelers flash past
in small, beautifully coordinated groups. When fired upon, the
groups seem to explode, but quickly regroup to fly in unison
again.

Redheads tend to boil up in short flights all across a lake, and
the careful observer gets the impression that the species is always
nervous. Approaching canvasbacks undulate from irregular wavy
lines into loose Vs and back again. Mergansers normally fly in
single file. Often, wood ducks can be immediately identified by
the repeated cries of *whoo-eeek* during flight. Even the sounds
of wings can be telltale. Canvasbacks zoom past with a steady
rush of wings, while the pinions of goldeneyes whistle at high
speed. The very best way to become acquainted with these characteristics is to study the field guides beforehand and to go out as
much as possible. Visit zoos, refuges and other wildfowl sanctu-
aries whenever there is an opportunity and observe the birds
close up. By doing this, it is even possible to learn their calls and
to duplicate this calling when you're hunting later on.

As in every other type of hunting, success depends greatly on
knowing the species you are after—where it lives, how it travels
and reacts, where you are most likely to find it. Although it is
possible now and then to find a few ducks almost wherever there
is pure water, they are normally concentrated where the environment best suits them—where there is sufficient food plus open
water. The waterfowl of North America (with scattered exceptions) mostly breed in the northern United States and Canada.
All species winter farther south, the largest number in the southern United States and some even as far as South America.

When traveling between breeding and wintering areas the
birds follow four major flyways: Atlantic; Mississippi; Central, or
Plains; and Pacific. Birds of the Atlantic and Pacific flyways tend
to parallel the coasts. Mississippi birds tend to funnel down the
Missouri-Mississippi drainage area toward the Gulf of Mexico.
The path of Central Flyway ducks and geese is less clearly defin-
able, because they travel in a wide band over all of the Plains
States. Hunting seasons everywhere are set to coincide with the
fall flights southward.

Contrary to common belief, it is instinct (or some other, un-known, factor) rather than changing weather that moves ducks southward. The movement or migrations occur at nearly the same time every year. A serious waterfowler can eventually, by keeping notes, estimate the arrival of birds at certain places at certain times. Of course, such knowledge is common and may even be reported in outdoor newspaper columns in important duck-hunt-ing areas. Local fish-and-game departments also may dispense the information in news releases.

The best shooting generally occurs after a fresh flight of birds arrives from the North, and fresh birds or not, the best times are very early and late in the day—as early and late as the law allows. Every season has notable exceptions, such as when noontime shooting is unaccountably fast, but days when the weather is terrible average much better than good ones. Cold and advancing storm fronts or very windy weather apparently make waterfowl nervous or restless, and they trade about more freely. Of course, that gives any gunner more opportunities to shoot.

There are two basic ways to hunt waterfowl: to play the wait-ing game, and to actually go afield looking for birds. There are many, many variations of both techniques and even combinations of the two. But let's consider them one at a time.

The traditional way to hunt has been to build a blind in a suitable waterfowl area, to pitch out decoys and then to sit down and wait for action. The hunter may or may not use a call to fur-ther entice any passing birds. The method may appear simple and uncomplicated, but it really isn't.

It should be noted here that most of the best waterfowl areas —the productive marshes, sloughs, swamps and grainfields—are already owned outright or leased for duck and goose hunting, mostly on a club basis. They are private and not available to free public hunting. If you are a member or somehow have access to one of these clubs, your problems are solved. The blinds, boats, decoys, dogs and, hopefully, the ducks are waiting. But if you are a nonmember and therefore in the majority, your duck hunt-ing should begin before opening day.

This is not a suggestion to break the law. Rather, it's advice to get out and locate the ducks on unposted land—and the sooner the better. By personal reconnaissance of all local waters, deter-mine where birds are feeding, their paths of travel between feed-

Scouting before the season opens pays off. Look for ducks, such as these mallards, on remote ponds.

ing and resting areas and where the greatest number of birds are spending their days. When you know all this, you're ready to build a blind to take advantage of their habits and possibly to intercept them somewhere between feeding and resting areas.

In some states there are public areas where gunners are free to hunt in whatever manner they choose. Check with the state fish-and-game department about these. There are other areas where a blind maintained by the state can be rented by the day for a nominal fee.

A good part of the success in blind shooting comes from the hunter's ability to conceal himself. All waterfowl have extraordinary vision, and they seldom pass within shotgun range unless the hunter is completely hidden. Therefore, much depends on the quality as well as the location of the blind.

A blind can be either a permanent or only a temporary structure. The framing should be sturdy enough to resist high winds, and rough-cut or used (weather-beaten, if possible) lumber is good enough for this. Keep in mind how many hunters will occupy the blind at one time (more than two is impractical and unsafe) and allow sufficient space for that many to be comfortable. It is better if the hunters can sit down, rather than stand. And plan some extra space for a retrieving dog or two.

Ordinarily there is enough natural material on hand to cover or camouflage an aboveground or above-water blind. Among the best materials are marsh grasses, bullrushes, cattails, willow, alder and cornstalks. All of these can be woven into "blankets" and wrapped around a framework to provide perfect camouflage. Lacking natural material, old burlap, netting and weathered camouflage cloth will do the job.

Above-surface blinds come in more different designs than it is possible to describe in one volume. Most common is the rectangular shape meant for two shooters; it is 6 to 8 feet long by 4 four feet wide and 5 or 6 feet high. With these dimensions, two gunners can sit down, completely hidden, but easily rise up to shoot. However, there are also circular blinds, tree blinds, rock blinds, portable (either by boat, on skids by Jeep or carried afoot) blinds

This is a typical blind, camouflaged with cornstalks, on the shore of a small lake.

This duck is about to be collected from a rock blind on a lake shore.

and collapsible models. The difference is all in the builder's own ingenuity.

Some other factors beside permanence and camouflage must be considered in the building of a blind. Will it be left high and dry or washed away by fluctuating tides? Can a hunter reach it on foot (possibly in early-morning darkness), or is a boat necessary? Is it too close for safety to other blinds?

In some situations a floating blind may be more suitable. This is a boat or pontoons to which sufficient camouflage material has been added to make it resemble a floating island. Elsewhere, sunken or pit blinds may be much more effective, especially where ducks or geese are feeding in grainfields on land. But no matter where the pit is dug, the same camouflage and placement factors are important. It should be made deep enough to accommodate the hunters in comfort and still keep them hidden from approaching birds. The most ardent waterfowlers may choose to add sliding or pop-open tops on pit blinds for the greatest effectiveness.

A bewildering selection of decoys is available on sporting-goods shelves today, a good many of them being at least fair replicas of live wild waterfowl. Keep in mind three factors—durability, drab finish and weight—when buying them. There isn't much use in buying dekes that will not last long under the punishment of normal duck hunting. Plastic is the best material available today, but not necessarily the most artistic. If anything at all can spook ducks before they are in range, it is a decoy with too bright and shiny a finish. Many veteran wildfowlers use only dull, drab dark gray blocks no matter what the plumage color of the ducks they are hunting. The anchor lines should be stout, of dark (never white) twine, with a very secure anchor weight on the business end.

The heavier the decoys, the more difficult it is to carry them very far, and that is an especially critical factor with goose dekes. For geese, silhouettes or nesting sets of hollow plastic birds may prove out as well as large full-bodied blocks. Incidentally, everything from baby diapers and white laundry cardboards to chunks of muskeg and dead geese propped up has been used successfully as goose decoys.

Not many waterfowlers agree on where and how best to place the decoys—the "stool." Wind is always the biggest factor, and the blocks should be so located that as birds drop into them

This is a cornfield pit blind, with goose decoys in the background.

Snow geese can be decoyed by folded pieces of white cardboard. This is a rice field in Texas.

(normally landing *into* the wind) they will be in convenient shooting range of the hunters. Decoys farther than 30 yards from a blind are seldom effective, except to encourage the crippling (but not killing) of birds.

Most of the time, the more dekes in a stool the better, and that is doubly true when the birds are diving ducks. Of course, it is hard to put out and collect blocks from icy-cold water, but in the case of divers it is well worth the effort. Diver dekes can be scattered out over a wider area than those for puddlers, which should not be set in a regular pattern. Teal blocks should be bunched very close together and only in very shallow water.. Often it is worthwhile to add a few "confidence" decoys such as coot, gull and goose blocks to a duck stool. If a blind is located on open water, it is good tactics to completely encircle the structure with dekes, but to place most of them on the downwind side.

In no phase of waterfowling is there more disagreement than over the value of calling; and after a great deal of duck-hunting experience completely across the land, I find that easy to understand. At times the most skilled callers seem to drive birds away, while in other situations certain strange sounds that resemble nothing in nature—even remotely—seem to entice both ducks and geese. Witness the Eskimos and Indians of the Far North who call honkers only by growling deep in their throats. What is best, probably, is for every hunter to be guided by his own experience —and to keep calling if he enjoys it.

Many excellent calls are on the market, and there are instructional records as well on how to blow them. Perhaps the consensus of the most successful waterfowl guides is that too much calling when birds are approaching is a mistake, and that poor calling is much worse than none at all. On the whole, geese respond to calling better than ducks, particularly in areas where the hunting pressure is heaviest.

Although, as I've already pointed out, most wildfowling areas on major flyways are already in private ownership, there is still considerable opportunity for any enterprising scattergunner. The alternative isn't as easy as sitting and waiting in a blind. But it can be very productive and very exciting—maybe even more exciting than hunting the traditional way. Call this "free lancing," for want of a better term.

Free lancing is a combination of sneaking and crawling with upland or jump shooting. Instead of waiting for birds, you locate them and go after them, getting into shooting range before they spot you. Obviously, it can be hard and dirty work slogging through and over freezing mud. But the rewards can be worth it.

The first step is to get out and scout all the un-preempted waters you can reach. Concentrate on farm and ranch ponds (there are more than a million of these in the United States today) and the rivers, especially the smaller ones. Some places can be reconnoitered by car; elsewhere it is necessary to go afoot. But carry binoculars, maybe a spotting scope, and look most carefully at all waters that are not easy to see or easy of access.

Assume you locate a raft of ducks on a small farm pond. The first step is to get the landowner's permission to hunt there. Then you go alone, or with a buddy, and attempt to infiltrate close enough to shoot. That means approaching entirely unseen, either behind the best available screen of cover or from behind the dam. Two can approach from opposite directions, attempting to sandwich the flushing birds in between.

Virtually the same tactics can be used anywhere that ducks are spotted on smaller bodies of water. The secret of bagging birds is all in the crawling, which is a talent in itself. Here's how to do it: In a prone position, place your gun across the crooks in your elbows. Carry it right there. While keeping head and buttocks down, move forward by advancing the left elbow and left knee at the same time, then the right elbow and knee. It's slow and tedious, but the hunter will be hard to spot by even the wariest birds at water level.

Floating for ducks is another technique in the category of free lancing. It is usually the best bet when ducks are known to be on small, flowing waterways. For this, a shallow-draft boat or canoe is necessary. The craft is camouflaged as well as possible with streamside vegetation or burlap to resemble a pile of floating trash. The hunters then drift downstream, hopefully to get into range of ducks before they flush. If the floaters do not make any undue noise or commotion, they have a 50-50 chance of scoring.

Paddling should be done only when necessary and by the boat-man in the rear. The forward hunter is the gunner. When round-ing bends, keep on the inside of the curve and watch for ducks hidden in sloughs, deadfalls or oxbows along the way. Occasion-ally, birds will be spotted far ahead on the river, and that is a good chance to pull directly into the nearest bank. Then while one hunter circles around—out of sight and on foot—to a point downstream from the ducks, the man in the boat resumes the drift. The goal is to sandwich the ducks in between so that one or both shooters get action.

Two other duck-hunting techniques are designed for shooting on large open bodies of water. These are called layout boating and sneak shooting. In the first, the hunter lies supine in an an-chored specially designed craft with a low silhouette and is sur-rounded by a spread of decoys. He gets shooting—often sudden, fast shooting—when rafts of divers swing in close to inspect the stool. In sneak shooting, a similar craft is used and the boat is left free to drift with the wind, hopefully within range of rafted div-ing ducks. This is a very cold, damp business reserved for out-doorsmen who really relish duck hunting under any conditions.

Countrywide, most geese of all species are bagged by gunners staked out (most often in pit blinds) in the grainfields in which the big birds feed. It is necessary first to observe the flight pattern of geese and then (say, late in the evening) to watch from a dis-tance where they feed. If they are undisturbed during the evening

Canada geese come in over a gunner in a pit blind.

flight, the odds are fair that the geese will return the next morning or next evening to exactly the same site. The idea is to dig a pit in that spot, put out decoys and be waiting underground when they arrive.

In every good goose-hunting section of America, the sport has gone commercial. Local landowners in whose fields the geese are feeding prepare blinds, furnish decoys and lease or rent out both to sportsmen. Depending on the location, goose blinds rent for $10 to $25 per person per day, or until a limit is bagged.

In recent years a shocking statistic concerning waterfowl hunters has come to light, and for the good of all it should be mentioned here. It is simply that the nationwide loss of ducks and geese by crippling (wounding birds and not recovering them) exceeds 25 per cent of the total kill. This is no guess or estimate, but rather the result of scientific examination by X ray and autopsy in many places. It is much too high to tolerate.

But how do we reduce that loss? Simply by retrieving more ducks that are hit and downed—and the best way so far discovered to do that is with well-trained retrieving dogs. It is almost impossible to overestimate the value of a good dog in any kind of waterfowling. He is a pleasure to watch, a welcome companion in a lonely marsh and a valuable ally. No really dedicated waterfowler should be without a dog, both for his own sake and for the future of waterfowling.

Dogs of many different kinds, from mongrels and assorted cross-breds to purebreds, have been used as waterfowl retrievers. But only a few are totally qualified to do the job. Since nearly all retrieving must be done from water, which is usually icy or extremely cold, dogs must be adapted physically to this unpleasant work. An average house dog might not be able to survive a day of duck hunting, but a good retriever can plunge into icy water time and again.

The breeds of dog most frequently used today in waterfowling are the Chesapeake Bay retrievers, the American water spaniel, the Labrador retriever, the Irish water spaniel, the golden retriever, the springer spaniel, the curly-coated retriever and the flat-coated retriever. But by far the most popular of all, and deservedly so, is the Labrador. The dogs of this handsome breed have great noses, are strong, are adapted to general gun work, are superior in water and persevere in finding any downed birds. The Lab's coat is short and dense, and beneath it the animal is all muscle and heart.

Besides its excellence as a water dog, the Lab's great popularity can be attributed to other qualities. It is always a willing worker, eager to please, a fine family dog and watchdog, good for upland gunning and very easy to train. That last factor is extremely important, because training a young retriever and watching it de-

A good retriever like this one can cut duck losses in half—and add pleasure to the sport.

velop has added a new dimension to waterfowling for many out-doorsmen. It takes hunters afield before and after the season and provides good physical conditioning for both dog and master.

The other great retrieving breed for waterfowl is the Chesa-peake. Dogs of this breed have suffered a marked decline in pop-ularity during this century because, along with their considerable virtues, they incorporate some serious faults. In terms of sheer cold-blooded efficiency, the Chesapeake has no competition. Water and weather conditions that would send a Lab into shock will not faze the Chessy. The breed has tremendous stamina and strength, and a no-fooling-around approach to life in general.

On the other side of the coin, the Chesapeake is hardheaded, willful and difficult to keep in line. It is not noted as a good family dog and does not get along well with other breeds. These tend-encies are so marked that few wildfowlers have the patience to cope with such dogs. But in terms of bringing in ducks, they have no equal.

The most crucial point in retriever training is basic instruction in obedience, and this can begin early. Most retrievers of good background will willingly—eagerly—fetch downed birds from water or land without any coaxing or training. But the dog (of course, it should come immediately when called) must be taught to follow at heel, to lie down quietly and to stay down until com-manded to do otherwise. A restless or obstreperous retriever in a small blind can become a huge nuisance.

Probably more has been written about guns for duck hunters than about any other phase of the sport. But from this writer's standpoint, it's the subject that rates the least attention. The best gun for *any* duck hunter is simply the one in which he has the most confidence—the one with which he can make clean kills the most consistently. It doesn't matter if the gun is a pump or a double, old or new, with a long or a short barrel.

For the record, however, America's favorite waterfowl gun is the 12-gauge pump with a 28- or 30-inch full-choke barrel. Sur-veys in a number of midwestern and eastern states have found that at least half the gunners use this. Next in popularity is the 12-gauge autoloader, which is used by 25 per cent of all waterfowlers. But keep in mind that by Federal regulation only three shells may be loaded in a pump or auto.

There is considerable evidence that a hunter should be more discriminating about the load he chooses than about his gun. Studies have revealed that an average of five No. 4 pellets are needed to kill a mallard duck. If struck with fewer than five, it will probably become a cripple. No. 4 shot is probably best for ducks and either No. 4 or No. 2 for geese, but no matter which, it is the hunter's moral responsibility to fire only at targets less than 40 yards away, and the closer the better. We often hear hunters brag about shots up to 70 and 80 yards, but these are only cheap stunts for which they should be condemned.

Too many uninformed shooters are lulled by the claims that

A hunter aims at a duck flushed from a small pond. The retriever has already hit the water.

modern magnums double their range and double their killing power. This is completely false. A magnum shotshell is more effective at normal or sensible shooting ranges only because it offers greater pattern density—in other words, more pellets (253 No. 4s in a 3-inch 12-gauge Magnum shell as compared with 169 No. 4 pellets in a standard load). The magnum load does not shoot farther than the regular load.

Any waterfowler can increase the odds for his own success before the season opens by becoming a better shot. A series of rounds at skeet or trap can help tremendously. With a hand trap and plenty of clay targets, another hunter can simulate all of the angles and shots a duck hunter is likely to face when out on the water.

Proper warm clothing is vital in most sections of the country. Standard equipment today are feather-light quilted down or Dacron undergarments worn beneath camouflaged and water-repellent outerwear. For most duck hunting, either hip boots or waders are essential, and these should be of the insulated variety. On bitter days hand warmers can be worth their weight in gold nuggets, and so can fur-lined mittens and ear muffs. Especially in coastal situations, or on any large or deep body of water, he is a very wise waterfowler who either wears flotation garments or carries some kind of Coast Guard-approved life preserver.

Of all forms of hunting, perhaps none demands so much of a man's patience and ability to endure discomfort as bagging waterfowl. No matter how warmly you dress, the bitter, relentless cold and wet always penetrate, so that by the end of the day you gather up your decoys in a kind of shivering stupor. And sometimes you will have nothing at all to show for your stoicism.

But perhaps no other sport offers so many moments that live in your mind forever. The first pale rays of dawn break across the horizon and the cackling of a flight is heard from the semi-darkness. Then there is light enough to shoot by, and a pink-orange flame leaps from the muzzle of your shotgun. A bird smacks into the water—and at that moment, the discomforts of the coming day seem very, very small indeed.

13

HUNTING LAND GAME
WITH A SHOTGUN

BY JIM CARMICHEL

THE LIGHT was not good, and the leopard had crouched on the thick limb in a position that largely obscured his vitals. As a result, the rifle slug raked in too low and too far back. The cat was hurt, judging from the blood spot where he hit the ground, but there was no doubt that he had enough life left to keep him in a murderous rage for the next day or so.

"Well," said the white hunter, gazing intently into the heavy bush where the cat had disappeared, "here's where I start earning my wages." Then, taking a bearer aside, he gave orders betraying the grimness of the situation:

"Take our client back to camp and fix 'im a spot of tea. If I'm not back in three hours, call headquarters and tell them what happened."

Then, taking the short-barreled 12-gauge Holland from the rack, he slipped in two shotshells. "Come on," he said to another bearer, "let's see what old Chui's up to."

"You can't be serious!" protested the client. "Going into the thicket with nothing but a shotgun? Here, take my magnum rifle!"

"Thanks, but it might get a bit sticky in there, what with the leopard and God-knows-what-all else. Might not be time to aim a rifle; but this double full of buckshot gives some comfort. And *do* keep the tea hot, will you?"

The lines are familiar enough. They might be from any of a dozen or so novels of life and love on safari.

The point here, however, is that a load of buckshot, combined with the fast-handling, quick-pointing characteristics of a shotgun, is one of the most potent close-in game stoppers available to the modern sportsman.

There has been much discussion about the worth of buckshot for deer-size game, but unfortunately, much of the talk has been so colored by opinion that it presents few facts. Some sportsmen feel that a shotgun loaded with buckshot has no place in the American hunting scene. Others feel that under certain conditions, no other type of sporting arm or load is nearly so suitable for the purpose.

To properly evaluate the worth of such claims, let's begin with a ballistic analysis of the popular 12-gauge oo buckshot load and then apply our information to actual hunting conditions.

The 12-gauge oo buck shotshell is loaded with nine pellets of .33-inch diameter and 54-grain weight which have a muzzle velocity of 1,325 fps. This combination of weight and velocity gives an energy level of 210 foot-pounds per pellet at the muzzle, or a combined energy level of 1,890 foot-pounds for the load. This muzzle energy is close, but not quite equal, to that of the .30/30 rifle cartridge, which, with the 150-grain bullet, delivers 1,930 foot-pounds.

It would seem easy enough to explain that the oo buck load is approximately equal to the .30/30, at least at ranges up to several feet. This does not mean, however, that the oo buck load and the .30/30 are equals in killing effectiveness. The buckshot load, because of its unique size and shape, has considerably greater wounding efficiency. Also, and this is one of the paradoxes of ballistic science, the wounding or killing efficiency of the buckshot load *increases* over the first several yards; this is because the expanding pattern increases the size of the wound delivered and results in a large area of shock-torn tissue. This wounding efficiency reaches its peak when the pattern is about the size of a widespread hand. Beyond this point, the aggregate effect disappears as each pellet creates an individual, nonoverlapping wound pocket. This, as we shall see, does not mean that the buckshot load ceases to be an efficient killer. It has in its favor other factors.

It has been suggested, possibly with good reason, that some deer hunters prefer buckshot simply because they have no faith in their ability to hit anything with a rifle and thus prefer to trust their luck to the random scatter of buckshot, hoping that at least one of the shot will hit the target. If this were true, it would place buckshot hunting in general and buckshot hunters in particular below the lowest echelon of sportsmen.

Before passing judgment, however, let's compare field reports with actual test data and see how things stack up.

I have heard and read of deer being killed with standard 12-gauge nine-pellet loads of oo buck at ranges of 60 yards—and even beyond with the new sleeved and cushioned buckshot loads. In an effort to determine whether these reports were only isolated instances or fair examples of the killing effectiveness of modern buckshot loads, I spent two days patterning various buckshot loads with six different shotguns of various chokes.

At extremely close ranges such as this, either buckshot or a slug would be effective.

In the two days of testing, *there was not a single 60-yard pattern that I would consider a sure kill.* My minimum criterion for a sure kill for testing purposes was three or more shot near enough to the point of aim to be considered within the vital zone of the chest area. To be sure, there were individual patterns that grouped three or four pellets quite close; but these were all accidental, and not once did the groups come within 10 inches of the point of aim. On the other hand, there were several instances in which one or two pellets were quite close to the point of aim. But would this be enough for a telling wound on a deer-size animal? Let's look at the figures: At 60 yards, a single oo pellet has a remaining velocity of 930 fps and a remaining energy level of 105 foot-pounds. This is only slightly more than the energy (97 foot-pounds) delivered by a .22 Long Rifle bullet at *100* yards! And what sportsman would consider shooting a deer at 100 yards with a .22 rimfire? Clearly, this is an inadequate energy level, and even if one or two pellets (which statistically is the best you can hope for) are well placed, the chances are heavily in favor of the wounded animal's being lost. It must be added here that the greater part of my 60-yard testing was done with the 2¾-inch magnum load, which carries twelve pellets rather than the standard load's nine. The standard load was completely hopeless.

At 50 yards, the pattern became distinctly more promising, with better than half of the 2¾-inch magnum loads printing three or more pellets within the "vital area." Still, this "better than half" does not favor the hunter and certainly not the deer. However, the 3-inch magnum loads with fifteen oo buck consistently placed what I would consider a killing pattern within the vital zone at this range.

At 40 yards, we reach what I consider the *practical maximum* range for the oo buck load in standard or 2¾-inch magnum loading. Without exception, most or all of the pellets printed close enough to the point of aim to result in a massive wounding effect in a vital area.

By and large, the foregoing information is incomplete until we define it in regard to effective choking. It is indeed possible that results at 50 and 60 yards might have been better if the test shotguns had been more suitably choked. There are individual shotguns which seem to have an affinity for certain loads, and

resulting patterns with these loads are unusually close and uniform. However, the six shotguns employed in the test represent a
fair cross section of what might be used by the average hunter,
and thus the results must be regarded as typical.

Interesting examples of "unusual patterning characteristics"
are the extremely rare cylinder-bored shotguns I've heard of that
produced "hand-sized" patterns with oo buckshot at 40 and even
50 yards. Throughout my tests, however, tightness of pattern con-
formed strictly to degree of choke, with the cylinder-bored shotguns giving the most open patterns and the full-choke guns giving the tightest. Thus, all of the pattern testing at 50 and 60 yards
was done with a Winchester Model 12 pump chambered for the
3-inch magnum shell; this gun was found to give the tightest pattern at 40 yards. From this it may be assumed that the other five
guns of my test battery would have given even poorer patterns
at the longer ranges.

At 40 yards, however, even the cylinder choke would, on the
average, cluster six pellets fairly close to the point of aim.

Anyone planning to use buckshot for hunting should pattern his
shotgun and learn firsthand exactly what-size groups he can expect at various yardages. It could be that he has one of those
"one in a thousand" guns that will keep the whole pattern in a
tight wad, in which case 50- or even 60-yard kills will be distinctly possible. On the other hand, it could be that patterns will
be such that shots over 30 yards will not be sporting.

Another good reason for checking out a shotgun before the
hunt is to see where the center of the pattern strikes in respect to
point of aim. In that shotgun shooting is a matter of pointing
rather than aiming, the problem of getting the buckshot pellets to
cluster around the "point of aim" can be cause for more than a
little consternation. Some shotguns tend to center their patterns
well away from the natural point of aim, and as a result the main
charge from a seemingly well-aimed or -pointed shot can go wide
of the intended mark. At 40 yards, this can amount to 2 feet or
more.

With single-barreled shotguns such as pumps, autoloaders or
single-shots, the tendency of misalignment is usually high or low
in direction. With doubles, especially side-by-side models, the
deviation can be in almost any direction, with the two barrels,

likely as not, printing in two different areas. In this case, the best move is simply to get another gun.

It is important to bear in mind that there is likely to be a difference in point of impact according to whether the shotgun is *aimed* or *pointed*. When he's testing a pattern or shooting at a stationary target, there is a tendency on the part of the shooter to "aim" the shotgun by aligning the front bead low over the center of the receiver or, in the case of a ribbed barrel with two beads, by aligning the beads one behind the other. When he's shooting at a swiftly moving target, however, the tendency is to look over the barrel without paying too much attention to bead alignment. Thus, even with the same gun, the difference between "aimed" and "pointed" shots can be considerable.

In areas where the use of buckshot is required, and within practical buckshot ranges, the likelihood of a shot at a standing deer is remote. Thus it is wise to practice pointing rather than trying to learn how to aim the shotgun. Try snap shots at the pattern board by quickly raising the gun from waist level and firing just when your cheek meets the comb.

For some really effective practice, try shooting at an old tire as it rolls and bounces down the side of a hill. You can cut some pasteboard sheets to fill the center of the tire and thus be able to tell exactly how close you're coming to the center. This practice gives you good experience in fast gun handling and learning to lead a running target. When you can get six or more buckshot into the center at 40 yards, you can judge yourself competent—and then some.

With this in mind, let's consider the use of buckshot loads in the field.

As a rule, buckshot is used only in areas where, for safety reasons, rifles or rifled-slug shotshell loads are prohibited by law or where nothing else is quite so suitable for the purpose. Among the latter are dense, swampy areas such as those in some parts of southeastern states. I've hunted in coastal North and South Carolina where the combination of marsh grass and the Spanish moss-laden trees reduced visibility to 25 yards at best. In such cover, deer appear and disappear like ghosts. Here, one needs a fast-handling gun and the reflexes of a quail hunter. An aimed shot is usually out of the question, as there is barely time to point and fire at the fleeting game. In situations like this, nothing is quite so effective as a load of buckshot; and at such reduced ranges, a load of buckshot performs with devastating effectiveness.

In this country, "walking up" the game is out of the question. Instead, the wise hunter takes a stand in a tree or on an elevated platform, if possible, near a game trail and waits for the deer to come to him. A little preliminary scouting can pay big dividends. Look for a stand that will give good visibility of the game trail with as few obstructions as possible. While it is a good idea to get pretty close to the trail, don't get close if it means that you will have only a fleeting glance at the passing deer. It is better to have more of the trail in view even if it means standing somewhat farther back.

The soft, moist earth in swampy areas muffles the sound of approaching game, and even in autumn, dry, crackly leaves and brittle underbrush are the exception rather than the rule, so there is little or no warning of the approach of the "swamp ghost" deer. Dogs are frequently used to jump and run deer, bears and boars in the South, so the baying of the hounds may alert the hunter to approaching game. This also means that the game will be going flat out as it passes the stand, so have your gun up and ready.

When you get a shot in dense terrain, don't follow the "old hunter's advice" and wait for the deer, bear, boar or whatever to "bleed out" before going after it. Where a deer-size animal can completely disappear in one step, you want to be on the scene as fast as possible, with your gun ready for a follow-up shot if necessary. This is especially true if the game is being pursued by dogs. Its adrenaline is already flowing at top level, thus making it even harder to keep down.

All the foregoing information, as you've noticed, has dealt only with 12-gauge shotguns and oo buckshot. This is purely intentional. Though smaller-size buck is frequently used for deer and other medium-size land animals, I have never been able to observe any fair reason for doing so. During the five years in which I served as a field agent for the game-and-fish commission of a southeastern state, I had numerous opportunities to observe the effect of buckshot on deer, bears and wild boars and study the reports of other professional wildlife-management personnel on the subject. The overwhelming evidence from these observations is that shot pellets smaller than oo buck must be regarded only as cripplers of game. Likewise, gauges smaller than 12 don't come in oo loading. So the best advice for buckshot hunting boils down to a few essentials.

Use 12-gauge 2¾-inch magnum oo buck loads—or better yet, if your gun has a long chamber, 3-inch shells—and keep your shots at game to 50 yards or less.

Every turkey hunter has a hard-luck tale to tell. My personal catalogue would make *Webster's Unabridged Dictionary* look like a dime novel. Like the time in northern Florida when I made my way into a swampy thicket by flashlight so I'd have a good stand by first light. When the dawn broke, I couldn't believe my eyes. Every tree around me seemed completely filled with roosting turkeys. It was like a scene from some sort of weird movie, with the mist rising from the ground, spooky-looking snags festooned with Spanish moss and everywhere, silhouettes in the gray light, the statuelike hulks of dozens of turkeys. All I had to do was take my pick and give him a load of No. 2s and I'd be back at the lodge in time for bacon and eggs.

So what happened? I tried climbing up on a slippery log for a better position and wound up heels over head in the muck below. By the time I cleared the ooze out of my eyes and located the shotgun, there wasn't a turkey in sight. But what a wonderful sound they made taking off!

The story ends on a happy note, however. Next morning I was back at the same spot, armed with BB shot loads, and this time I got my turkey.

The reason I switched from No. 2s to BBs was simply a matter of tactics. The first morning I wasn't at all sure what I might encounter. There was the possibility that I might have brought a tom to call and thus gotten a set shot, or I might have had to shoot at a flying bird. Thus the load of 2s was a compromise between the No. 4s I prefer for flushing or flying turkeys and the BBs I like for turkeys on the ground.

The reasoning for these selections is simple. The wild turkey is a tough, heavily muscled and densely feathered bird that can make a speedy getaway by air *or* ground. A turkey on the ground has the additional protection of his wings folded about him, and even if his wings are disabled, he can still run like a spook. For this reason, I prefer larger, heavier shot for nonflying turkeys, the idea being to achieve sufficient penetration and bone damage to ensure complete immobilization. Of course, a shot or two in the head is best, but there's no way to depend on hitting the head unless you're mighty close. For shots at flushing or flying turkeys, a magnum load of No. 4s gives a denser pattern and is quite effective, since a turkey is more vulnerable when on the wing.

A full-choke 12-gauge shotgun is the rule, preferably a magnum, and the shorter the range, the better. A wild turkey is a magnificent bird, fully deserving his big-game status, and he cer-

This is the author's idea of what "taking them up close" means. A load of BB shot is ideal for such a situation.

tainly deserves better than to be shot at too long range, hit by too few pellets and caught by foxes while in a weakened condition. The late Nash Buckingham once made a statement about shooting waterfowl that certainly reflects my feeling about turkey hunting and loads for turkey. "I prefer to take them close and hit them hard, very hard."

In short, you'll never hear a true sportsman brag about how far away he dropped a turkey with a shotgun.

Ask five hunters for their thoughts on rifled slugs and chances are you'll get five firm opinions ranging from utter disgust to total devotion—all with personal experience to back up the opinions.

For the most part, the use of rifled slugs is limited to some states in the East, Midwest and South where the use of high-powered rifles is prohibited by law. The reason for these regulations is that rifles are supposedly unsafe in regions of high population, where there are large numbers of hunters in a relatively small area or in flat terrain where a rifle bullet may carry a considerable distance.

From the ballistic standpoint, there is little quarrel with the *short-range* efficiency of the 12-gauge rifled slug. The muzzle energy of nearly 2,500 foot-pounds (based on a 1-ounce slug fired at 1,600-fps velocity) is approximately midway between those of the .30/30 and the .30/06 rifle cartridges. At 50 yards, the rapidly decelerating slug still has 1,340 foot-pounds of energy, but at the 100-yard mark, the energy and velocity levels have dropped to 875 foot-pounds and 950 fps. By comparison, the .30/30 has 1,360 foot-pounds of energy at 100 yards. These figures, however, don't tell the whole story. They don't take into account the potency of the thumb-sized slug in terms of actual wounding effectiveness.

In practical terms, the big slug has been used effectively even on dangerous game up to and including Cape buffalo. At ranges up to 75 yards, the massive slug combines awesome knockdown power with massive tissue destruction. When it comes to slaying deer-, bear- and boar-sized game, few animals take more than a couple of steps after receiving a well-placed slug. Yet highly critical rumors, some of them apparently well founded, persist.

One criticism of rifled slugs is that they will "shoot out" the choke in a shotgun barrel. This is simply not so. In fact, the hollow, thin-walled slug actually puts less pressure on the constricted or choked area of a barrel than does a normal wad of shot, which is, in effect, a solid mass of lead. It all boils down to a simple question: Which is tougher, lead or steel?

A better-founded criticism is that of inaccuracy, with more than a few irate hunters charging that the rifled slug is so inaccurate that deer are missed altogether or that the errant slug hits a nonvital area, allowing the wounded deer to escape and perhaps to die later.

Quite frankly, this supposed inaccuracy of rifled slugs is not so much a matter of the slugs as of the guns in which they are used, and the underlying reason never ceases to amaze me. No hunter with an atom of wits would consider using a rifle without both front and rear sights. Yet literally thousands of deer hunters go afield each season with a shotgun equipped with nothing more than a bead at the end of the barrel and expect to hit the vital area of a deer, some 15 to 20 inches square, at ranges up to 100 yards! The wonder is not that so many are missed but, rather, that so many are killed.

The first common form of one-piece projectile for shotguns was the now obsolete "pumpkin ball," a solid lead sphere which was used in either single or multiple loading. Without any sort of spin to stabilize their flight, the solid balls were notoriously inaccurate; about 50 yards was their outside accuracy range (even though they were deadly at much greater distances). With the advent of the rifled slug during the 1930s, the *accurate* range of shotgun projectiles was virtually doubled.

The distinctive "rifling" on a rifled slug has been the cause of much discussion and speculation. Among the most often voiced questions are: Does the slug begin to spin in the barrel? Only after it leaves the barrel? Or does it spin at all? Then, if it does spin, is this what makes it more accurate than the old-fashioned pumpkin ball?

The slug does not begin to spin while it is traveling through the barrel. This is simply because there is nothing within the slick tube to gain purchase on the slug's angular ridges. It is conceivable that if a shotgun bore were rough enough the slug might grab or gain purchase and begin to spin—but that would serve no purpose.

This is a typical slug load in cross section.

Once free of the bore, however, the "rifling" on the slug serves as a fin as it passes through the air and causes the slug to spin. The speed of rotation is directly proportional to the velocity, and as the slug slows, the rotational speed falls off.

The inherent accuracy of a rifled slug has virtually nothing to do with the rifling. Instead, the slug is held in relatively stable flight by its weight-forward design. The best illustration of this is the badminton shuttlecock, which flies nose-forward simply because that's where the greater part of its weight is. Even if a rifled slug were to be loaded nose-down in its case, I suspect it would turn around and fly nose-first within a few yards.

Accuracy tests performed by myself as well as other experimenters indicate that there is no significant difference in accuracy between rifled slugs and slugs of the same design and cross section but without the rifling. Why, then, bother with the rifling at all? From the manufacturer's standpoint, the rifling is necessary mainly because the consumer expects it. If it has any value, it may be that the rifling reduces the surface area and thus reduces friction within the barrel.

Two significant departures from the standard "American" rifled slug are the German-made Brenneke slug and the French Blondeau slug. The Brenneke slug gets its flight from the shuttlecock effect, but rather than having a heavy nose with thin skirt, as do the American types, the Brenneke simply takes its light felt shot-

From left to right are: an unrifled slug cast in a Lyman mold, a rifled American slug and the Blondeau slug.

shell wadding along on the trip. The column of felt wadding, attached to the lead slug by a screw, serves as a very effective stabilizing device.

Far more radical in design is the Blondeau. The blunt-nosed and blunt-rumped all-steel French product (with lead bands around the edges to protect the barrel) does not depend on the shuttlecock principle for stability; in fact, the slug is actually heavier toward the rear. In-flight stability is accomplished by the action of air pressure on a conical tail area. If the slug begins to topple in flight, the tail section becomes exposed to the slipstream and is forced back into an in-line position.

The Blondeau weighs 500 grains, as compared with the 1-ounce (437-grain) standard American lead slug (the Brenneke weighs 471 grains), and is said to create a tremendous wound pocket. Though I have never tried it on game, I did give it a test on a stack of catalogues each of which was about 1 inch thick. The Blondeau penetrated five of the catalogues and caused large radial rupture lines in the sixth and seventh. The hole through the first two catalogues was as clean and sharp-edged as if it had been made by a giant paper punch. The third, fourth and fifth catalogues suffered a greatly expanded hole caused by the paper's being accumulated in front of the slug and shoved forward. The effect on tissue is said to be the same, and I don't doubt it a bit.

So, how accurate is the shotgun slug? My personal tests—using

Here, the author is testing the accuracy of rifled slugs. The gun is a High Standard slug/buckshot model with a ramp front sight and peep rear.

a 12-gauge High Standard cylinder-bored 24-inch-barrel shotgun equipped with ramp front sight with ivory bead and Williams 5-D receiver sight, and firing from a rest—gave consistently good accuracy at 50 yards, with some three-shot groups running as small as 1½ inches. In no instance did groups go over 6 inches for five shots. These tests included both domestic and foreign makes of slug loads as well as a variety of handloads.

This degree of accuracy is certainly good enough to place a slug in a deer's boiler room at 50 to 75 yards, and it dispels any misconceptions about slugs being inaccurate. Was I just having exceptional luck? Not at all. The good results occurred because of the inherent accuracy of the slug combined with a *properly sighted and zeroed* gun.

Realizing this, every major U.S. manufacturer of sporting arms and some foreign firms are now marketing one or more shotguns in a short-barrel, open-choke version complete with rifle-type sights. Most of these models also come complete with sling swivels. A sling, by the way, is mighty handy for carrying a shotgun, and it can become almost a necessity, as anyone who has tried to carry a gun with one hand and drag a deer with the other will tell you.

Still, there are those who look upon the rifled slug as some sort of economy measure which allows them to use their shotguns for a once-a-year deer hunt. If such is the case, then they at least owe it to themselves—and to the game animals—to have some sort of removable rear sight attached for occasions when they plan to shoot rifled slugs from their gun. Of course, even this will be useless unless some preliminary shooting and adjusting is done.

Speaking of sights, why not a telescope? If you are accustomed to telescopic sights and have come to appreciate their advantages, there's no reason why you shouldn't put a scope on your shotgun. For years Weaver has made a one-power (1X) telescope for rifles and shotguns which is ideal for slug use—where the range should never be greater than 75 yards anyway. At this distance, you'll never need more than 2½X magnification. Also for the scope fancier is Weaver's Qwik-Point scope which superimposes a bright red "aiming dot" on the target. There is no magnification with the Qwik-Point, the eye relief is unlimited and a model for shotguns is available.

When using the rifled slug, we come to the matter of proper "zeroing" of the sights in respect to the slug's trajectory. If the shotgun is sighted to strike about 1½ inches high at 50 yards, it will be no more than a couple of inches low at 100 yards. This, for all practical purposes, allows a dead-on hold at all ranges within the limits of the slug.

Pump, autoloading, bolt-action and single-shot shotguns are fine for shooting slugs—but not side-by-sides or over/unders. The reason is that the barrels will not deliver two slugs to the same place.

Barrel length does not influence the flight of a slug, though choke does have a slightly adverse effect on accuracy in that it tends to somewhat deform the projectile. Thus, the best selection is a cylinder-bored (no-choke) shotgun with a short barrel. The reason for the short barrel is simply to reduce weight and make the gun more manageable in heavy brush. Naturally, this is exactly how slug shotguns of the various manufacturers are designed.

Regarding gauge, the 12 has a clear-cut advantage, with the 16 being acceptable within 60 yards. The 20-gauge and the .410 just don't have enough energy to be seriously considered.

So, for success with rifled slugs, use a 12-gauge gun, preferably with short barrel and cylinder bore, definitely with front and rear sights, properly zeroed. *And by all means, take time out to do a bit of practicing before the hunt!*

Helpful Hints
and Interesting
Miscellany

14

THE OUTDOORSMAN'S OPTICS

BY PETE BROWN

EXPLORING the science of optics will soon have one soaring into the upper strata of higher mathematics. But there is really nothing complicated about basic optical concepts, and some understanding of them is all a sportsman needs in order to choose and use his equipment. I'll venture a guess that the average American shooter goes equipped with at least *one* of the most common optical instruments. I know outdoorsmen who have the works—telescopic sight, optical bore sighter, spotting scope, binocular and camera. In fact, some have more than one of each to take care of specific needs.

Optical equipment is designed to form an image of a subject. Generally, the apparent size of the image is enlarged for better viewing, and this is referred to as magnification, or power. The symbol "X" is used with a figure to indicate the number of times a subject is enlarged. For example, 2X designates a magnification of two times (twice the size that we see with the naked eye). Where the camera is concerned, it is a matter of focusing the image on film for the purpose of recording the image.

The image we view is formed by an optical element, or a combination of optical elements. One of the most common optical elements is the mirror. As anyone can plainly see when looking at himself in a mirror, the image appears to be formed behind the mirror. Images apparently formed behind the optical element are called *virtual* images. In most of our sporting optical equipment we are dealing with *real* images. A real image may be projected onto a screen.

The most important thing about the image is its clarity or sharpness of detail. This is referred to as *definition* or *resolving power*. The fineness of definition and the freedom from aberrations (distortion) are the quality criteria for the optics in an optical element or system. Of course, there are also the matters of the ruggedness of the system, mechanics, finish and convenience. All these properties, considered altogether, determine the quality of the instrument as a whole.

A process for lens coating, developed during World War II, was a great step forward in the quality of optical instruments. It permits the passage of about 3 per cent more light at each air-to-glass surface. When light strikes a glass surface, it is bent, and most of it passes through, but a part of the light is reflected. This is lost and also may cause ghost images. For example, a scope with uncoated lenses passes only about 65 per cent of the available light.

A thin, transparent magnesium fluoride coating, which is only one-fourth of a wave length (between five and six millionths of an inch) in thickness, will minimize reflection. Coating can readily be detected by a straw to light purple color on the lens surface. If an instrument has as many as ten coated air-to-glass surfaces, the increase in light transmission will be improved by about 30 per cent. This benefit, together with a better image contrast, provides the remarkable improvement in performance over optics of pre-World War II days. Optical coating is applied to prisms as well as lenses. All air-to-glass surfaces must be coated for the process to deliver its full benefit.

There are basically three kinds of lenses—convex (positive), concave (negative) and a combination, with one side concave and the other convex. The convex lens bends rays of light toward the image point on a line through the center of the lens (axis). The greater the curvature of the lens, the closer the focal point where the image will be formed. The image formed is a "real" one.

The concave lens bends the light rays away from the central axis of the lens. With the divergent rays projected backward through the lens, the image forms on the same side of the lens as the subject. The point where these backward-projected rays meet is referred to as a negative focal point. The image thus formed is a "virtual" one.

The lens with a convex curvature on one side and concave curvature on the other will act as a positive or negative lens according to which surface—convex or concave—has the greater curvature. In our sporting optics, we will be primarily concerned with convex (positive) lenses.

Every lens has an optical center (which may not coincide with the geometric center). Assume that a line is run through the geometric (measured) center of the lens. The optical center may be on a line apart. In an optical instrument this may result in a displacement of the image. This will cause no great problem in a fixed-power telescope, because once the rifle is sighted in, the relationship between the aiming reticle and the bore of the gun remains fixed. Nevertheless, the elements of a good scope should have optical and geometric centers that are very nearly the same.

No lens is free of all the six aberrations that are damaging to optical performance. These are known as chromatic aberration, distortion, spherical aberration, coma, astigmatism and curvature.

Chromatic aberration is present when the light rays of the different colors, on striking a glass surface, do not bend to the same degree. Thus, the rays are separated, in the same manner in which a rainbow is formed. The condition is corrected by the use of two different kinds of glass, cemented together, to form one lens. The two kinds of glass bend the light at slightly different angles, and the net result is the focusing back to one point of the colors separated out of the white rays. A lens so corrected is called an *achromatic* lens. All lenses must be corrected to free an optical system of this aberration, and all good optical instruments make use of achromatic lenses.

Distortion occurs in an optical instrument when the magnification is not the same throughout the entire field of view. "Pincushion" distortion is apparent when the magnification is greatest toward the edges. It is "barrel" distortion when the magnification is greatest toward the center. When selecting a binocular, for example, look at a building, a flagpole or anything else with straight lines to see if they are bent as you view them at the edge of the field. A well-designed instrument should be free of distortion.

Spherical aberration results when a lens does not have the same focal length at its center position as at its outer zones. Naturally, this makes it quite impossible to obtain a sharp focus. The instrument with this fault lacks definition—something to watch for when you're checking out a scope or binocular.

Coma is a form of spherical aberration. The term "coma" comes from the "comet" shape of a distant point viewed through an improperly made lens.

Astigmatism is another form of lens defect, and you can detect it by viewing a set of parallel lines placed vertically and then placing the set horizontally or at various angles. Through an optical instrument characterized by astigmatism, the lines may be sharply defined when they are placed at one angle, but it may be impossible to get sharp definition when the lines are rotated 90 degrees. If you are viewing a subject across the street and you can't rotate the parallel lines (bricks, perhaps), rotate the instrument to detect the astigmatism.

Curvature concerns what is known as "flatness of the field." When evaluating a telescope or binocular, focus on a large flat surface such as the face of a building. If you find it impossible to bring the center of the field into focus at the same time the outer part of the field is in focus, or vice versa, you have observed curvature.

Chromatic and spherical aberrations influence the definition at the center of the field of view. Astigmatism, coma, curvature and distortion are apparent toward the edge of the field. In careful viewing, a binocular or telescope may prove to have a minor degree of one of the aberrations, such as distortion. If the price of the instrument is attractive enough, you might decide that you can live with the defect. If you are going to be extremely critical of optical performance, you must generally be willing to pay the price. Optical perfection is achieved by design and extreme care in manufacture. It rarely happens by coincidence.

If light strikes a glass surface at an angle greater than the "critical angle," it will be reflected rather than bent and will not pass beyond the surface. (The critical angle depends on the type of glass.) A ray of light directed into a piece of glass with angular surfaces will strike one of those surfaces at more than the critical angle. It will not emerge from the glass at that surface, but will be reflected.

A simple reflecting prism can be used to turn light 90 degrees, or the light can be directed to bounce off two surfaces and be turned around. Two reflecting prisms can be arranged to bounce the light off four surfaces and send it off in the same direction in which it entered. Such a prism is called a *Porro system* and is used in many binoculars and spotting scopes. It accomplishes one very necessary function in these instruments: it erects the image, so that it does not appear upside down, and it makes it possible to design a shorter instrument.

If we had only an objective lens and an eyepiece in a telescope or binocular, the image we would see would be inverted (upside down). The instrument could be used this way, but it would be hard to get accustomed to it. Consequently, it is necessary to use an intermediate, or erector, lens which serves to turn the image upright. It has already been shown how Porro prisms are used in some instruments to turn the image to an erect position for viewing.

The reticle, or cross hair, comes in a truly wondrous assortment of shapes and sizes. There are dots, posts, cross hair-post combinations, tapered cross hairs, cross hairs and dots and even range-finder reticles that measure distance by subtending (covering) a target of known size at a given range.

To the neophyte, this assortment can be bewildering, and many people make the mistake of investing in a scope with a reticle that would confuse a computer. The choice is this simple: most target shooters are happy with fine cross hairs, a half-minute dot (a dot that covers ½ inch at 100 yards) or a cross hair-dot combination. Hunters are best off with a medium cross hair or a tapered cross hair that's thick at its edges and thinner toward its center. Experienced hunters like simple reticles. The more complicated ones sound fine on paper, but in actual practice they're not what they're cracked up to be.

Of course, a "cross hair" is not a hair at all. It may be a spider web, it may be a very fine wire or it may be lines etched on a plain lens.

Here is a diagram of a modern variable-power hunting scope. (Diagram courtesy of Leupold-Stevens Instruments) 1. Objective-lens element. 2. Objective-lens mount. 3. Objective-lens bell. 4. Elevation adjustment. 5. Erecting lenses. 6. Power-selection ring. 7. Reticle. 8. Ocular lens elements.

The etched reticle has one advantage in that almost any form of it—a circle, a square, etc.—can be used. It has two disadvantages. One is that a spot of dust, lint, etc., on a reticle lens shows up as part of the image. The second is that it adds two more lens surfaces in the instrument, and this diminishes the light coming through the scope.

The reticle may be placed at the focal point of the objective (front) lens or at the focal point of the eyepiece, as an image is formed at each location. Most hunting scopes·used to be made with the reticle at the focal point of the objective lens because that was where the adjustments could be most conveniently placed, and sight adjustment was made by moving of the reticle. However, it has been common practice to locate the reticle of target scopes, using external windage and elevation adjustments, at the focal point of the eyepiece.

The first variable-power scopes had the reticle at the focal point of the objective lens, because that way any play in the moving elements for changing power (magnification) would not affect the sight setting. There was one great disadvantage in this placement: as the power was adjusted upward, the reticle would also be magnified, often blotting out the target.

The latest variable-powers have the reticle at the focal point of the eyepiece, and it remains the same size irrespective of power adjustment. Scope manufacturers must hold to close tolerances in the movement of the power-change mechanism. A tolerance of ½ minute of angle in the shift of impact resulting from a power change seems to be typical. If the variable is to be used at long range, the thing to do is sight in with maximum power at long range and accept the insignificant error at short range. This is fine for a game scope, but even a half-minute error at short range would not be acceptable in a target scope.

The entrance pupil is the unobstructed objective lens, and the exit pupil is the bright spot of light in the center of the eyepiece. This exit pupil is an image of the objective lens. The diameter of the exit pupil is the diameter of the entrance pupil divided by the true magnification. This formula will work unless there are diaphragms in the instrument which blank out the outer edge of the objective lens.

The relative brightness of an optical instrument is frequently misunderstood. It has nothing to do with optical quality. It is merely the square of the exit-pupil diameter in millimeters. Assume that a 6X scope has an objective-lens diameter of 30 mm. The exit pupil should be $30 \div 6 = 5$ mm. The relative brightness is 5 squared, or 25. The square of the exit pupil is used because it is related to area, and where the comparative light is concerned, we are dealing with an area.

As you no doubt know, the iris of the eye opens or constricts to admit a comfortable amount of light. During the darkest hunting conditions, it is little more than about 5 mm in diameter. During bright light, the iris of the eye will close down to possibly 2 mm. If an optical instrument has an exit pupil of 5 mm and the entrance pupil of the eye is opened to a 3-mm diameter, obviously the whole exit pupil of the instrument is not being used. Consequently, where light is concerned, there is no need for it to have an exit pupil larger than the maximum opening of the eye, which is about 5 mm.

The area seen through a scope or binocular is the field of view. Generally it is a round field, and its measure is given in diameter (feet) at 100 yards. At 200 yards, the field would be twice the 100-yard figure; at 300 yards, three times, and so on.

The size of the objective lens has no bearing on the field of view, but the eyepiece *does* affect the field. Provided there are no obstructing diaphragms, the larger the eyepiece aperture, the wider the field of view. There is an inverse relationship between magnification and field of view: as magnification is increased, the field of view decreases.

Here the author sights in a big-game rifle. A spotting scope, right, is a necessity for this kind of work.

The eye relief, or eye distance, is the optimum distance that a viewer's eye must be from the eyepiece of the instrument. The normal eye relief for a big-game scope on a high-powered rifle varies from about 2½ to 5 inches. However, there have been some low-powered scopes (2X or less) made with an eye relief of 8 to 18 inches for mounting on the rifle barrel forward of the receiver. There have also been some low-powered scopes with long eye relief for use on handguns.

Eye relief can easily be measured. Aim the objective end of a scope at the sky or some other light source. With your eye perhaps 20 inches from the eyepiece, you will see a bright spot of light in the center. This is the exit pupil. Move your eye toward the eyepiece until you see the full field of view in the scope. At this point your eye is at optimum eye relief.

The exit pupil can also be projected onto a piece of paper.

Move the paper away from the scope to the point where the clear bright spot on the paper is largest. This is at the proper eye relief. Measure it. Don't confuse the dim, extra large circle of light from marginal rays with the exit pupil. This may be detected beyond the proper eye relief.

A means of focusing is essential in scopes, binoculars and cameras. First, there are differences in people's eyes. Therefore, the eyepiece of a scope should slide or screw in and out so that it is possible to bring the focal point of the eyepiece exactly onto the image formed at the focal point of the objective lens or the image formed by the erecting lens. Second, the image formed in the scope, binocular or camera by the objective lens varies in distance from that lens. The image of a distant subject will be closer to the objective, while the image of a close object will be farther away. This is why it is necessary to focus a camera lens to place the image sharply on the film.

It is possible in a binocular or spotting scope to adjust for both the eye and the distance with the eyepiece alone. There's a good reason why one focus does the job. No reticle on which the objective image must be sharply focused is involved. This also applies to hunting scopes up to 6X.

To check for parallax, a shooter should move his head from side to side to sweep his eye across the exit pupil. If there is movement of the reticle relative to the target, he is observing parallax.

In the lower-powered hunting scopes, the objective lens is in a fixed relationship to the reticle. The parallax is therefore eliminated at one given range only. Many manufacturers settle on 200 yards as the parallax-free range. Parallax at longer range is then minimal, and in big-game shooting, parallax at short range is of little consequence. Even if parallax is present, it is not a source of sighting error if the eye is always centered in the exit pupil. It is worth noting that the larger the exit pupil, the greater the possibility of parallax error.

To demonstrate parallax, let's assume it is eliminated in a scope at a range of 200 yards. In sighting at 100 yards, the objective image will fall beyond the reticle. At 500 yards, the image will fall short of reaching the reticle. If the reticle and image are not in the same vertical plane, there will naturally be relative movement when the eye is shifted from side to side.

The variable-power Weaver V12 is an internally adjusted scope that ranges from 4X to 12X. It has an adjustable objective lens to permit removal of parallax at various ranges.

The movable (focusing) objective lens must be moved outward or inward to bring the reticle and objective image together. Here is a good parallax rule to remember: If the aiming reticle appears to shift in the opposite direction from the eye movement, the objective should be moved inward. If the reticle appears to shift in the same direction as the eye movement, the objective should be adjusted outward. Some scopes provide a means other than moving the objective to bring the reticle and objective image together at different ranges.

There is a way you can measure magnification. Pick out a number of uniform, evenly spaced lines such as are found in the louvers in a neighbor's garage, brickwork, a picket fence, a wrought-iron fence, etc. Let's assume there is a wrought-iron fence about 75 yards away and the vertical bars are about 6 inches apart. The range and spacing are really not important factors, however.

Rest the scope on something steady and look at that iron fence with both eyes open, one eye looking through the scope. You should see the magnified bars with one eye at the same time you see the nonmagnified bars with the naked eye. Now see how many of the nonmagnified spaces between bars you can fit into one magnified space. If four spaces fit in neatly, you have a 4X scope. If the scope is supposed to be a 4X but only 3½ spaces fit, it is apparent that the scope doesn't come up to specification.

Since World War II there has been a continuing improvement in hunting scopes. The most significant scientific breakthrough was lens coating, which has already been mentioned. This increased the light transmission in the average optical instrument from about 65 to about 90 per cent. That's something to crow about.

Scopes have been made virtually waterproof, there have been great improvements in finish, the internal adjustments have been made more positive, the instruments are generally more attractive and variable power was introduced and has become popular with many hunters.

A constant-center reticle has been welcome. In the old scopes, internal windage and elevation adjustments moved the reticle, and naturally, the center of the reticle didn't always end up in the center of the field of view. Now, instead of the reticle, the erector lens is moved to effect corrections; the reticle stays fixed in the center of the field.

At the present time there is a trend toward more compact scopes, and this is welcomed by the hunters. You can now get a 6X that is about as short as most 4X scopes.

Over the years the 4X scope has proved to be by far the most popular. It makes a good choice, but when a scope is chosen strictly for big game, the 2½X or 3X, without the flared objective, is lighter, provides a large field of view and is less bulky. It is not necessary to magnify big game to shoot it—even at long range a low-power scope is adequate. There are low-power variables (1X to 4X or 1½X to 4½X) for big game. These have been popular and have merit. The lowest power is fine for hunting in tight cover, and 4 or 4½ is adequate for plains shooting.

When you're hunting in tight cover, there are definite advantages in a 1X or 1½X scope. Without magnification, or with scarcely any, it may seem as though the purchaser is getting little for his money. But the advantages of scope sighting—one focal plane (that is, your eyes having to focus at only one depth rather

than at two or three, as with iron sights) and focus adjustment
for eyes that require it—are there in the low-power as well as in
higher-power scopes. These are points worth taking into consideration when you're selecting a big-game scope.

There are many forms of varmint shooting, including close-
range shooting at animals called in. But when we talk about varmint rifles and varmint scopes, we generally think in terms of precision shooting at long range. The prime varmint targets have
been woodchucks, prairie dogs and crows. All of these are pretty
small targets at 250 yards, and certainly at 500 yards. Some varmint shooters in the West have even specialized in shooting chucks
at ranges up to 1,000 yards.

Scopes designated as varmint scopes used to generally be 8X
target-type instruments with external dovetail mounts. Long-
range and varmint shooters moving into bench-rest competition
often used regular target scopes from 10X to 30X.

In recent years 8X, 10X and 12X scopes with internal adjustments and rigid mounts have also become very popular for varmint shooting. These scopes are in a power range in which a focusing objective lens is called for to remove parallax and obtain a
clear image at various distances. Scopes in this range are so
equipped, and they generally have a range scale (a calibrated
lens ring or dial) so that adjustments can be made quickly in the
field.

For the usual run of varmint shooting, a 6X scope serves beautifully. Scopes of this power offer no objective focus, but if they
are parallax-free at long range, the short-range parallax isn't any
problem.

Then, of course, there are the variable-powers in 2X-to-7X,
3X-to-9X and 4X-to-12X ranges of adjustment. The shooter who
wants a scope for both big game and varmint hunting must decide
on the basis of the type of shooting he does, bearing in mind that
the higher the power range, the heavier and bulkier the scope
will be.

Target scopes must be near perfection mechanically as well as
optically. It must be possible to remove the scope from the rifle
and return it without changing the sight setting. The windage and
elevation adjustments must be positive without any slop in the
system.

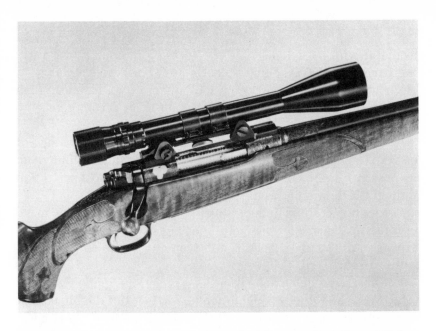

For many years, Bausch & Lomb has offered externally adjusted Balvar scopes, which employ windage and elevation adjustments in the mount. The model shown here is the Balvar 8, a 2½X to 8X variable.

Target scopes have, as a rule, been made with external adjustments with ¼-minute or ⅛-minute micrometer-click adjustments for windage and elevation.

Tests have shown that aiming precision increases with magnification up to about 10X. Beyond this there is very little gain in precision with added power. In fact, it is too slight to be of any practical value. However, there are other advantages in magnification above 10X, such as making it possible to see the bullet hole in a small-bore target at 100 yards.

The sportsman has at least three good uses for a spotting scope. One is for competitive target shooting, another is for sighting in a rifle and the third is for observing game animals at long range to evaluate them as trophies.

The highly competitive target shooter (or the man who sights in a rifle at long range) needs a scope that will give him absolute top performance. This means a prismatic telescope with an objective lens about 60 mm in diameter. Telescopes giving the performance expected cost about $100 or more. They are usually

available with interchangeable eyepieces of different power varying from 15X to 60X. Some shooters prefer 20X and others 30X.
Higher powers under most conditions are more of a handicap than
they are an advantage. With some scopes, there is compromise in
a 25X eyepiece.

There are zoom spotting scopes that cover the usable range of
power. They are convenient and have their advantages, but zoom
scopes can't be expected to have quite the same optical perfection
throughout their range as the fixed-power models.

Pistol shooters and indoor small-bore-rifle shooters can make
best use of the smaller prismatic spotting scopes or the even less
expensive draw-tube scopes. A 20X scope with a 40-mm objective
will serve very well.

For observing game animals at long range, the guide or hunter
sometimes needs the best definition he can get, but the big 60-mm
scopes are a burden to carry. They weigh from 2 to 2½ pounds,
while 40-mm scopes are available that weigh 20 to 25 ounces and
are not nearly so bulky as the larger scopes. The big 60-mm zoom
scopes, if carried in a vehicle or on a horse or mule, can be ideal
for observing game animals.

The prospective binocular buyer should understand the relationship between objective size, exit-pupil size, magnification and
eye entrance pupil. He will be sorry if he buys more power and
more objective lens than he really needs. Anything above 8
power is difficult to hold steady for good viewing. A large objective lens adds weight to the binocular, and if it is carried around
the neck, every little bit of weight reduction helps.

A 7-power binocular is what the average user will find most
satisfactory. There is the 7x50 (7X and 50-mm objective), which
weighs about 35 to 40 ounces, and that is pretty heavy. It has an
exit pupil of about 7 mm, and that is more than anyone will ever
need for daytime, dusk or dawn viewing. The 7x35 is the most
satisfactory all-purpose binocular. There are wide-angle binoculars which may be fine for watching or reporting a football game,
but the wide-angle feature makes them much heavier. A 7x35
wide-angle will weigh almost as much as a 7x50.

Then there are the little lightweight binoculars that can be carried in the breast pocket and weigh about 7 ounces. They have a
small exit pupil of about 2.5 mm, but that's not too bad; in ordi-

The dotted line in this diagram represents the path of the light rays as they pass through the objective lens, the prism and the ocular lens.

nary daylight the entrance pupil of the eye will be no wider than 2.5 mm. They will not give the performance of a 7x35 under all conditions, but they are sure handy to carry, and they have their uses.

Cheap cameras use a single meniscus (quarter-moon) lens. It is made from one piece of glass. Such lenses are slow, because a small aperture must be used, and they do not produce a very sharp image because of uncorrected aberrations.

By cementing of another lens, thinner at the center, to the meniscus lens, some of the aberrations are corrected, but this is not the final answer for the best cameras.

To make more corrections, two lenses are used. This makes for a faster lens system. Some of the best short-to-medium-focal-length lenses have six or seven lens elements, and in a 1,000-mm lens there may be as many as twenty-five elements involved.

Camera lenses are designated by the focal length and the maximum f-stop opening. For example, take one of the most universal lenses in a 35-mm camera, the 50-mm f/2.0. A 25-mm lens is considered a wide-angle, and a 35-mm would be a compromise.

A short-focal-length lens is not used only for wide angles; it is possible with a good short-focal-length lens to focus down to within a few inches of a subject.

There are many fine combinations of cameras and lenses. Here is an example of one combination that has worked well for taking pictures of action in the outdoors: a well-made 35-mm single-lens reflex camera with built-in meter, automatic lenses, bayonet type of lens attachment and detachable motor drive. Two lenses seem to fill the needs; one is a 35-mm f/2.8, and the other is a zoom 80-to-250-mm f/3.8.

The internal meter permits the photographer to read light and adjust the f stop without taking his eye from the subject, which may be a wild animal running or one about to bolt. With an automatic, there is the advantage of focusing with the lens wide open for maximum light. The lens automatically closes down to the set f stop as the picture is taken. The bayonet mount is for ease in changing lenses. All of these features speed up the process of taking a picture—sometimes making the difference between getting a picture and not getting it where wildlife is concerned.

When you're photographing action in the outdoors, it is seldom possible to stage or pose what you want, and if you have to crank the film forward, there may be a chance for only one shot. By letting the motor drive take over, you can make a series of shots. One of these during the course of action could prove to be exactly what is desired. The motor drive greatly improves the chances for a sensational picture.

My parting thoughts are these: First, remember that cheap optical equipment of any kind offers no saving. It is always inferior to good merchandise, and you'll end up being disappointed in it. Second, don't assume that the more powerful the hunting scope is the better it is. Stick to the lower powers—say, 4X at most.

I hope I've shed some light on the subject of optics for you.

15

CUSTOM GUNS

BY JOHN AMBER

I UNDERTOOK to write this chapter reluctantly, for I felt—and feel —that I may not be the best man for the job. The reason is that I have a lot of fixed ideas—prejudices, if you like—about custom guns and what actually makes for one. If you're at all familiar with the subject, this will become readily apparent before you have read very far; and if you are a complete tyro, remember that these are the words of a man who has pretty well made up his mind. If what I write here seems arrogant, I can only explain that my arrogance stems from forty years' experience with all types of firearms. I've seen fads come and go, and I have a pretty fair idea of what endures and what is forgotten—and best forgotten!

Few terms in the shooter's lexicon are as abused as the phrase "custom gun." It has been applied to the grotesque and the beautiful; to guns that did not deserve the classification by any stretch of the imagination, and to those that warranted it richly. For our purposes here, a true custom gun is "a completely unique expression of a shooter's ideas, largely handmade by one or more gunsmiths who specialize in custom work." A true custom firearm is unlike—except in broad terms—any other gun that came before it and any other that will follow. A barreled action, straight from the

267

factory, fitted with a "custom" stock shaped almost entirely on a duplicating lathe does not rate the title. We will now see what does.

Since the vast majority of made-to-order arms in the United States are rifles, we'll deal primarily with them, starting with a brief description of their background.

The custom rifle as we know it today got its real start shortly after World War I. During that conflict, the 1903 Springfield established an enviable reputation for accuracy, long-range effectiveness and dependability, and shooters wanted a sporting version of the '03. The idea of customizing a military rifle for sporting purposes had actually gotten its start as early as 1912, when gunsmith Louis Wundhammer built Springfield sporters for E. C. Crossman and novelist and African hunter Stewart Edward White. After the war, however, the practice gained its real impetus, and gun writers such as Colonel Townsend Whelen and Ned Crossman spread the gospel of the custom rifle.

The years between 1918 and the outbreak of World War II saw the creation of some magnificent examples of the gunsmith's trade. Craftsmen/artists such as Alvin Linden, Bob Owen, Adolph Minar, Thomas Shelhamer and the gunsmiths at Griffin & Howe turned out rifles that were things of beauty. As testimony to their value, a rifle made by any of these men is worth far more today than it was when new—to the person who is lucky enough to find one for sale.

After World War II, the country was flooded with military rifles, many of less than admirable quality. Simultaneously, there was a great clamor for sporting arms, which had not been made in five years. The result was the creation of the "instant gunsmith," often a guy who repaired lawn mowers for a living and butchered actions, barrels and stocks in his spare time. During this period, the unwary buyer of a "custom rifle" all too often found himself owning a monstrosity far inferior to a factory rifle.

In time, however, most of the quacks and fakes went back to their lawn mowers, and the custom-gun trade has flourished. If anything, the level of workmanship demanded by customers is higher now than ever before. One gunsmith I know, who got his start in 1950, says that he would go broke today with the skills he had then, simply because the average seeker of custom work is far more knowledgeable than he once was.

gunsmiths appreciate the most. The sight of his face lighting up when he takes delivery of a finished rifle constitutes a large part of their wages.

Now the question arises, how do you go about picking a man to work for you? Well, that depends both on what you want and on the fields in which various gunsmiths work. Some will build you a complete rifle, working over the action, chambering a barrel, polishing, bluing, making a stock, even engraving. Many, on the other hand, do only stockwork or metalwork. Your first step should be to visit the gunsmiths near you and look at their work. If they are any good at all, they'll be happy to show what you can get for your money, and if you should buy a rifle, they will back it up with no equivocation.

As an illustration, an acquaintance of mine recently took delivery of a rifle from a well-known custom-gunsmithing firm. All told, it cost in excess of $1,000. As he was looking it over, the manager of the firm spotted two minute scratches near the safety, hardly noticeable to the naked eye. Outraged, the manager sent the gun back to the shop—over the customer's protests—and had it completely reblued before he would let the client take it home. His explanation was "You paid a lot of money for us to do the job right, and that's the way we'll do it." This sort of attitude prevails among the sort of men you want to deal with.

What do you get for your money? First, you will almost surely get a rifle that is a good cut more accurate than all but the best tuned-up factory jobs. (If it's not accurate, a good gunsmith will take it back and work on it until it is.) Second, you'll have the pleasure of owning something that is unique—a rifle made according to your ideas of what it should be, and one that fits you like a glove. Finally, you have an investment. If you had bought a rifle from Adolph Minar in the 1930s, you could practically name your own price for it today. But now we come to the matter of taste.

In order to illustrate the point I wish to make about guns, let me use the automobile as an example. Some years back, tail fins were the rage, and a Detroit maker of luxury cars endowed his autos with a pair that would have done a shark proud. That year, it was proclaimed to one and all that whoever had a pair following

Really fine wood is scarce, and a good blank is extremely expensive. This fabulous French walnut stock was made by Keith Stegall.

So let's take a look at what's involved in buying a custom rifle. First, you had better be prepared to spend money. As this is written, about the least you can pay for a first-class job, a complete rifle, is $850. In all likelihood, the cost will come to over $1,000. There are several reasons for these seemingly high rates. First, you are paying for hand labor, which, in the United States, does not come cheap. Second, you are paying for the services of a man who not only is highly skilled in a mechanical sense, but is an artist in the truest meaning of the word—a very rare combination of talents. Lastly, good stock wood is growing scarce—a good blank of French walnut will cost $150 to $200 before the gunsmith puts a file to it.

Actually, when you consider the hours they put in, most of the best gunsmiths are grossly underpaid. They could make far more in other lines of work, but stick at their trade because they derive a sense of satisfaction from it that would be lacking in any other walk of life.

It is also a fact that the average buyer of a custom rifle is not a rich (or even a well-to-do) man. In almost all cases, he is a fellow of average means who loves fine rifles, is determined to have the best and has saved until he can afford it. This is the customer

Most fine custom rifles are relatively unadorned. This superb Mauser-actioned sporter was made by Richard Hodgson.

him around had the money to buy a brand-new C------c. The next year, the fins simply looked foolish and grotesque, which they were.

Therefore, don't invest your money in something that is gaudy, flashy and extreme. Ivory inlays, silver and gold plating, dazzling blond stocks are all eye-catching; but, apart from their making the rifle impractical for hunting (you might as well carry a neon sign), in time they will only be regarded as odd, faintly amusing, but what the hell good are they? Without exception, the gunsmiths who are regarded as "greats" and the rifles that have turned into treasures over the years are all conservative.

A fine, conservative rifle is not eye-catching, except to someone who knows firearms. Most gunsmiths prefer to work in French walnut, which is basically brown, with dark streaks and swirls. The finish is soft, not bright or flashy. It gleams rather than shines.

The checkering is plentiful, on both the forearm and the pistol grip. It will run anywhere from 22 to 26 lines to the inch. There will be no border around it, for a border is a crutch to cover sloppy work. Each diamond will be like every other diamond—perfectly shaped, and sharp. There will be no runovers, gouges or signs of imperfection.

The forearm tip, if the gun has one, will be of horn, ebony or bakelite plastic, black, with no white-line spacer. Blued, checkered

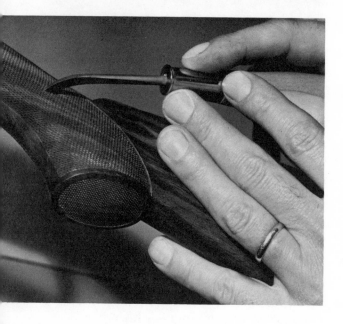

One of the things you pay for in a custom gun is fine hand checkering. The checkering on the pistol grip (shown here in the process of "pointing up," or final sharpening) runs 26 lines to the inch. The checkering on the bottom of the grip is 32 lines to the inch.

steel is used for the grip cap and the butt plate. Or, if a recoil pad is fitted, it will be dark red or brown, with no colored spacers.

For an action, a gunsmith is likely to use a pre-1964 Winchester Model 70, a good 1898 or commercial FN Mauser, a Sako, a Champlin, a Weatherby or, more rarely nowadays, a Springfield. He will checker the bolt knob, hone the action so that it works more smoothly, tune the trigger, make sure the safety works silently and jewel or damascene the bolt and raceways. He may fit a tang safety or a hinged floor plate. If necessary, he can also lighten the action by drilling out metal from the magazine box, hollowing out the bolt knob and slimming down the trigger guard or fitting a new guard of his own design. If you're not happy with the issue trigger, he will fit a custom one like a Canjar or Timney.

If you have given him a barreled action to work with, that's fine, as most factory barrels are of excellent quality. Assuming you don't, he will fit and chamber a custom one from a maker such as Hobaugh, Shilen, A&M, Douglas or Hart, making the chamber to wildcat, or special, dimensions, if you wish. He will install any kind of iron sights that you want, and will even make them up from scratch if necessary. Griffin & Howe, for example, makes its own front sight, a band-type ramp, from bar stock. It costs $65, it is both screwed and sweated onto the barrel, and you couldn't loosen it in several centuries of shooting. G&H or Champlin will also make you a three-leaf English express sight—for $200 or so. Expensive? Yes, but it's all done by one patient, highly skilled man working hour after hour with a file.

You can have any kind of scope mount you want (within reason), and some shooters like to have the bases sweated onto the receiver, so that they will never shoot loose. A few gunsmiths will even make a custom mount of their own design (or yours, if it looks workable).

When the metalwork is all done and the stock is completely shaped and fitted to the barreled action, the gun is blued. Good, conservative bluing, like a good stock finish, does not dazzle. The metal shows no polishing marks, and the color is a deep, dull blue-black.

If you have not yet run out of money, and would really like something special, you can have your gun engraved. A few very rare individuals can do magnificent engraving as well as build a complete gun. Or a firm such as Griffin & Howe can engrave the rifles that it builds. But as a rule, engraving is a specialty, and you must choose a man on your own.

How much you spend on this aspect of the work depends on how elaborate a job you want. A top engraver will give you a goodly amount of beautiful scrollwork and perhaps an animal figure or two for about $300. If you want something extremely special, you can have a gun profusely inlaid with gold and exten-

One of the few companies that build entire custom rifles, Champlin produces first-rate arms around its own actions, made in both right-handed and southpaw versions.

sively engraved—but don't overdo it! A luxurious job, tastefully done, from a first-rate man will likely set you back $2,000-plus, but will enhance the value of the rifle enormously. Engraving of the very first rank, like a great painting, increases in value over the years.

On more than one occasion, I have seen fine guns ruined by engraving that was simple butchery—and the owner of the defaced firearm was blissfully certain that he owned a thing of beauty. The ability to recognize good, or great, work of this type is a skill that must be cultivated, but here is a brief guide as to what to look for. First, look for realism and accuracy of detail in all inlays and engravings. A pheasant should look exactly like a pheasant—feathers and all—and not like a lump of gold or the last of the dodos. Perspective and anatomical detail must be perfect. Scrollwork should be neatly done, with no slips or gouges. Straight lines should be straight, and curves should curve with grace and symmetry.

Probably the best way to study engraving is to examine the works of established masters, and then compare the work of other men with them. Here are some of the very best in the United States at this time: John Warren, Alvin White, Josef Fugger, Lynton McKenzie, Rudy Marek, Frank E. Hendricks and Robert Swartley. When you gaze upon the work of these men, you are looking at the best.

If you haven't already gone through the mill in the custom-

Only a small number of top gunsmiths do both wood and metal work. Al Biesen, who is one, made this .270 on a Winchester Model 70 action.

This beautiful single-shot is based on a British Farquharson action re-barreled to .243 Krag and stocked by the late Tom Shelhamer.

rifle field, all of this must sound very complex (maybe it is). Therefore, I'll use myself as an example and describe how I came by one of my own custom rifles. As you'll discover, you need not only money and knowledge in large amounts, but patience as well. Gunsmiths will not be rushed.

Early in 1965, I found myself with a pre-'64 Model 70 barreled action in a caliber that I was less than enthusiastic over. I sent the metalwork to Fred Huntington of RCBS, asking him to fit a 7-mm Magnum barrel by Hobaugh into the action. Earlier, I had seen some fine-looking walnut blanks at Pachmayr's in Los Angeles, and one of these, along with the barreled action, went to gunmaker Al Biesen. I gave Al complete details on all the metalwork I wanted done. This included checkering of the bolt knob, damascening of the bolt body and raceway, fitting of a special Conetrol mount and installation of a front sight. I gave Al the stock dimensions I wanted along with special instructions to make the cheekpiece full, especially toward the comb nose (I have high cheekbones), and asked that the pistol grip be oval in cross section and 4½ inches in circumference. Butt plate and grip cap were to be of checkered, blued steel (with a trap door in the butt plate), and a floor-plate release was to be installed inside the trigger guard to replace the original Model 70 one.

The promised delivery time was six months from Biesen to me. But it didn't work out that way. Almost five years after I gave Biesen the components and specifications, I received the finished rifle. It is a thing of beauty, well worth waiting for. But what a wait! Some gunsmiths actually can deliver an entire job in six months (Griffin & Howe can, at present), but you'll be more realistic if you resign yourself to a wait of one or even two years. You can encourage your gunsmith gently from time to time, but don't push. At best he'll ignore you, and the more independent kind will tell you to go to hell on a rail.

I firmly believe that the money you invest in a top-quality custom rifle is cash well spent. The $1,000 or so you pay now will almost certainly grow into a far larger return should you want to sell the rifle in the future. A lot of people seem to agree with my way of thinking, as most of the top gunsmiths have long waiting lists, year after year.

Shotguns are seldom built from the ground up in the way rifles are. With a few notable exceptions, most field shooters are content to leave their pieces as they bought them. Competitive scattergunners, on the other hand—especially trapshooters—are forever tinkering, modifying and trading in hopes of adding a few birds to their score.

Using our already stated definition of a custom arm, let's take a look at shotguns and see what can be had. First, he who would invest in a genuine custom scattergun had better be prepared to lay out far more money than he would for a rifle. The reason for this is simple: almost all custom shotguns are side-by-side doubles or over/unders, and it costs far more to make an action of this type than it does a bolt action for a rifle.

I would guess that a rock-bottom figure for a first-rate custom shotgun would be about $1,250, and if your taste runs to the English-made Purdey, Boss or Holland & Holland, then you can *start* in the neighborhood of $4,000 to $5,000. At present, there are only three American firms building complete shotguns to order. These are Champlin, Winchester and Ithaca. Winchester's pride and joy is the Model 21 side-by-side, the cheapest version of which runs $1,750. It is a plain gun, with no decoration, but it is built almost entirely by hand, to your dimensions and specifications as to stock, barrel length and choke. From a strictly functional standpoint, the 21 is probably the finest double in the world.

If you'd like a fancier 21, you can lay out $3,350 for the Pigeon grade, with fancier wood and checkering, plus engraving. The top of the line, the $4,350 Grand American, is an eye-popper, profusely gold-inlaid, boasting the fanciest walnut and elaborate checkering—and a presentation carrying trunk is included in the price.

For many years, Ithaca has enraptured trapshooters with its single-barrel trap gun, again an entirely handmade proposition.

The Winchester Model 21 is one of the world's finest shotguns. This beautifully stocked and lavishly engraved specimen is the Grand American grade. All Model 21s are built to order, and delivery time is about a year.

The basic grade is the 4E, which costs $1,500; above it is the 5E at $2,000, and the top of the line is the $4,500 Ejector grade. These are beautiful arms, well worth their price and the wait of two years for their manufacture.

Champlin's excellent shotguns, made to your measure and to your specifications as to barrel length, chokes and the like, are built on handsomely engraved, first-quality actions made in Italy. These are usually over/under guns on which Champlin puts superb walnut stocks and forearms, and all is done as you like it.

The most prestigious guns in the world are undoubtedly those very few turned out by the best British firms. Many of the fine old English companies have gone under, while others have been brought under the wings of extant concerns. As matters stand today, the three names to conjure with are Boss, Purdey and Holland & Holland. There are two ways to order one of their guns. You can visit the companies' showrooms in London, or you can make an appointment with a representative who visits American stores such as Abercrombie & Fitch once or twice a year.

Most likely, the best place an American can turn for a high-grade shotgun at a price within sane limits is to one of the better Belgian, Italian or Spanish imports. For many years, Browning has brought in its Superposed shotgun in various grades. The Midas, at the top of the line, is mechanically splendid and gold-inlaid and offers fine wood and profuse checkering. It is a lot of gun for $1,300 or so.

Garcia offers several grades of the Italian Beretta in a series of sidelocks, the SO models. The SO2 costs $1,000 and is the least expensive of the series. Above it are the SO3 at $1,200, the $1,400 SO4 and the $1,900 SO5. This last and a companion side-by-side, the SO7 (same price), are paragons of the gunmaker's art and are worth far more than their prices represent, simply because so much hand labor can be obtained so cheaply in Italy.

Two other Italian firms rate mention. One is Perazzi, which specializes in very-high-grade, no-nonsense competition guns, but also produces some knockouts, such as the Lusso grade, which is a fancy piece of work indeed and is very expensive.

Another firm worth considering is Armi Fabbri of Italy, which builds double guns entirely to order for prices starting at $2,000 and ascending to $8,000. The company employs only fifteen men and makes shotguns that are things of magnificence.

Spain produces a great many shotguns, and there are a profusion of firearms manufacturers, both large and small, that call the country home. Some Spanish guns, like the top-grade AYA (which is a copy of the Purdey but costs far less), are fine in most respects, offering wood as beautiful as you'll see anywhere and, quite often, very good engraving. However, Spanish shotguns have a not entirely undeserved reputation for temperamental performance, and the Spanish gunsmiths seem to have a good deal of trouble with such things as ejectors, selectors and triggers. You may get a jewel, but you may also get stuck.

Among handguns, the most popular candidates for customizing are probably the .45 Colt automatics. These guns, especially the military-surplus ones, are subjected to a dizzying number of alterations, which include custom sights, refinishing, custom grips, custom slide, barrel and bushing, safety modifications and so on. Some of these autos are brought so far from the originals that they really qualify as custom. However, for the most part, aside from custom grips, shooters are content to leave their side arms alone.

Some factory guns will not be improved by modification. Colt's .357 Python and Smith & Wesson's Model 29 .44 Magnum revolver, for instance, are splendid pieces of machinery, and all you can do with them is have them engraved. Smith & Wesson, as a matter of fact, has a long list of optional features that can be incorporated into your gun at the factory, while Colt will cheerfully sell you an engraved handgun if you wish.

On the other side of the coin, there are a great many revolvers and automatics that will benefit from a little extra work. Nonadjustable sights are an abomination and should be replaced with the target type if you hope to hit anything. Many double-action revolver triggers can be vastly improved with some adjusting by a competent gunsmith. If you wish to spend the money, you will not regret having a set of grips carved to fit *your* hand, particularly if you own a hard-kicking revolver.

I think that the best advice I can give you is to look at the work of several men, and spend lots of time and thought before you spend your money. And listen to your gunsmith. I can vividly recall Henry Vogt, a top-level stockmaker and a fine gunsmith, telling a customer with whom he disagreed, "I make the shtock the vay it should look und fit, gottammit." Henry was a gentleman who had certain very strong ideas about the way a gun should be made—and far more often than not, he was absolutely right.

16

CARE,
CLEANING AND REPAIR

BY DAVID E. PETZAL

ONE OF MY more vivid memories of Army basic training concerns the night before we were to hand in our M-14 rifles. Having fired them for the final time, we were told that they must be immaculate before they would be accepted by the company armorer. So we worked from seven at night till three in the morning disassembling, scrubbing, brushing, polishing, dusting, scraping and buffing. Several weapons were taken into the showers by zealous troops and given steam cleaning.

Eventually, all the M-14s were returned to storage, where they would sit for a week. They would then be issued for another eight weeks to the next cycle of trainees—and given another scouring at the end. As a result of this treatment, most of the M-14s I saw that had been in service for a year or so looked as if they had fought several wars. The wear and tear came not from actual use, but from the cleaning they had had to undergo.

The moral of this tale is that you can wreck a gun through too much—and improper—care just as easily as you can by neglect. There is no formula for maintaining firearms; the amount of attention you pay them depends on what kind of gun is involved, how you use it and how much you use it. Also, bear in mind that like so many other aspects of the shooting sports, this is an area in which two people seldom agree. So, ultimately, the best guide is your own experience and good judgment.

Therefore, let's break down the various types of firearms and see how to maintain each one, starting with the simplest, the .22 rimfire rifle.

The best advice I can give you concerning the care of a .22 is to leave it alone as much as possible. About the only maintenance that a .22 really needs is regular removal of grit, carbon and unburned powder from the action, and an occasional wipe with an oily rag to keep its exterior parts from rusting. The barrel should be left largely alone.

One of the reasons that a .22 is less expensive than a centerfire rifle is that the barrel is machined from mild, or soft, steel. There is so little friction from the passage of a bullet up its bore and so little heat erosion from the tiny powder charge of a rimfire cartridge that this softer metal, which is less expensive to work with, can be used without detriment to the quality of the finished rifle.

It also means that a .22 bore is more easily worn by a cleaning rod, which can scratch and abrade its delicate finish. However, this is not a problem because, unless you live in a rain forest, there is no real need to clean a .22 barrel very often. In years past, corrosive priming and bullets that turned rifling into a lead mine made the life of a .22 owner a lot less pleasant than it is now. Today's ammunition, however, not only does not harm the bore, but actually protects it. Plated bullets do not leave lead deposits, and the dry lubricant that they carry has a rust-proofing effect on the barrel.

Among my rifles is a Browning T-bolt .22 that has had a lot of customizing performed on it. Its total worth is in excess of $200. As you can see, this is a valuable firearm, yet I clean the barrel only every 1,000 rounds, and use only two or three wet patches. The only other care the gun receives is removal of residue from the action and a wipe with an oil-saturated chamois cloth after use. If it is suffering under this regimen, I cannot detect it.

Naturally, a gun that has been rain-soaked or used in a snowstorm should be disassembled as far as possible and wiped down with an oily rag, but that is the only concession you need to make.

Proper equipment for cleaning a big-bore rifle includes a solid support, such as a vise, and a good rod, like the Parker-Hale used here.

Rimfire target rifles have been fired 500,000 rounds with no appreciable accuracy loss, so, treated intelligently, a good .22 should last much longer than you figure to.

The lives of centerfire rifles are not nearly so carefree as those of the rimfires. It is a hard fact of life that in order to maintain its accuracy, a centerfire *must* have its bore cleaned out every 50 rounds or so. This is a rule of thumb only. A medium-bore rifle (a .338, for example) can fire strings of 80 or 100 shots with no detectable accuracy loss from fouling. A .222, however, will begin to suffer after only 20 shots or so.

The fouling from a centerfire cartridge consists of copper deposit from the bullet jackets and powder residue. The first shows up as copper-colored streaks in the bore. The amount left there will vary with the hardness and composition of the bullet jacket, the speed at which the bullet is fired and the smoothness of the bore itself. It does not pose a problem unless it builds up to the point at which lumps of jacket metal are plainly visible.

Powder fouling is a hard, greasy film that can build up fairly rapidly. If present in sufficient quantity, it can reduce a rifle's

If you have to clean a rifle from the muzzle, guide the rod with your fingers to avoid wearing down the rifling.

accuracy; and there is reason to believe that it retains moisture, which in a damp climate can cause rusting.

Happily, neither of these types of fouling presents much of a problem, since they can almost always be removed with little trouble.

Your first requirement for cleaning a centerfire rifle is a stiff rod that will not bend in the bore and has a ball-bearing device either in its handle or at its tip so that the patch or brush can rotate through the rifling. I have found that the best rod is the one made by the English firm of Parker-Hale. It is an excellent design in every respect. You will also need a brass-bristle brush, solvent and oil or rust preventive. Your rod should be of the proper caliber for the gun you're cleaning.

First, soak a patch in powder solvent and pass it through the bore from breech to muzzle. If your rifle is a semiauto, lever or pump, you'll have to work from muzzle to breech, so be careful to keep the rod from scraping the rifling near the muzzle. This first patch will remove a good deal of the fouling. Now let the rifle rest horizontally, slightly muzzle-down (so that the solvent does not run back into the action), and leave it alone for a half-hour. In this time, the solvent will loosen a lot of the fouling, making your job easier.

Now, soak a brass brush in solvent (never use a dry brush in the bore) and make about ten passes through the barrel. Remove the brush and shove a couple of solvent-soaked patches through. If the second one comes out almost clean, your job is nearly over. If it comes out stained dark gray, bordering on black, or bright, rich blue-green, you have some work left to do.

In the latter case, leave the bore wet with solvent and let it sit for another half-hour. Then take a few more swipes with the wet brush. Follow with a couple of dry patches. At this point, they should have only faint stains on them. If so, that's all the scrubbing required. Wet a patch with oil, run it through the bore a few times, then stand the gun muzzle-down in a corner for a half-hour to let the excess run out the barrel.

Do not try to clean the barrel to the point at which the patches come out spotless. Before that happens, your gun will be a smoothbore.

Now, wipe off the metal surfaces of the rifle with an oily chamois and you're through.

Two words about oiling while we're on the subject: Go easy! The crankcase of an automobile engine holds quarts of oil, but the film of lubricant that actually does the work is only a few molecules thick—and that's all you need in the action of most centerfire rifles. Too much oil will freeze in cold weather and can render your gun unserviceable. It will also soak into the wood of your stock, making it soft and punky. Perhaps worst of all, oil collects dirt, and dirty oil can cause wear in your rifle just as it does in a car engine.

If you anticipate hunting in cold weather, it's wise to remove *all* the oil from your gun and replace it with powdered white graphite, which is dry and will not freeze up when the mercury drops. In any event, when it comes to oil, the less the better—by a long shot.

In the field, your rifle also needs some attention. I always carry a small repair kit that consists of screwdrivers to fit the screws in the rifle and scope mount, a chamois wiping cloth, a takedown cleaning rod, patches and a small can of WD-40, an aerosol rust preventive that I've found to be very effective. When you stagger

A wood cleaning rod is excellent for shotguns, since it can't mar the chambers.

back to camp at night, give your gun a once-over with the wiping rag and, if it's been raining and water went down the barrel, get out the cleaning rod and the patches.

Shotgunners have had a much easier time of it since the introduction of plastic shot collars which keep the lead pellets from contacting the bore on their trip to the bird. In years past, you could expect to look up a scattergun tube, find great gouts of lead clinging to its walls and know that you were in for some heavy work with the brass brush. Nowadays, scattergun cleaning is not nearly the chore it once was.

Wearing out the barrel is not a problem with shotguns, since there is no rifling, so cleaning them is not a delicate operation. You can use an aluminum or a wooden rod, and a takedown model is fine. I start on the bore by cutting out a big patch of white flannel, soaking it in powder solvent and shoving it through a couple of times. This will bring out a lot of the fouling. Then, as with a rifle, let the gun sit for a while. Now take the brass-bristle brush and have at it, making sure to wet the brush with solvent beforehand.

The brush breaks up the powder residue in the barrel and

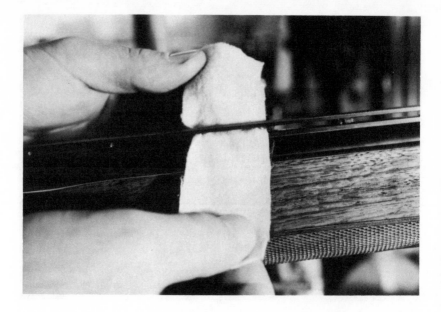

If your scattergun has been exposed to wet weather, run an oily rag under and around the vent rib to keep rust from forming.

leaves a greasy mess. To get rid of this, I wad up a piece of paper towel so that it fits the bore tightly, shove it an inch into the barrel and push it through with the rod. I then repeat the wet-brush-paper-towel treatment until the wad comes out clean. Then oil the bore lightly and it's done.

There are, however, qualifiers. If you own an automatic shotgun of the gas-operated type, it behooves you to periodically clean off the gas piston and the bleed hole leading from the barrel into the piston chamber. If carbon builds up on either of these, your faithful firearm will someday answer you with silence instead of spitting out the empty and chambering a fresh shell.

I doubt if the average duck hunter or upland enthusiast fires four boxes of shells a year. However, the average trap or skeet buff will consume that many hulls in half a day of shooting. I am a trap addict of the most depraved sort, and have gone through 300 shotshells in a day's competition. This adds up to much dirt, much heat and much wear on the gun. Therefore, my previous words of wisdom about the less oil in a gun, the better do not necessarily apply here.

If you use a single-barrel or over/under, a little grease—not oil —judiciously applied will do much good. The metal-to-metal tolerances are much less in these guns than in other types of firearms. Add to this the fact that when guns are hot from firing, they swell, reducing those tolerances even further. The result is much friction, and much wear. If enough wear takes place, the gun will shoot loose, and you will have a big repair bill facing you.

The way to prevent this is lubrication—in moderation, of course. I have used a good many different oils, and I take a dim view of them. They are all right on a gun that does not heat up much, but for a trap gun that's fired so fast you can't touch the barrel without burning yourself, they don't hack it. The best lubricant I have found is a grease called Lubriplate, which comes in a tube and is sold at hardware stores. It's cheap, doesn't make a mess and stays where you put it, even under extreme heat. A dab or two spread on the barrel flats and hinge pin of your gun will work wonders.

Handgun owners fall into two categories—those who own automatics and those who don't. Most autos are easy to field-strip and clean, while most wheel guns are complicated devices whose disassembly is best left to a gunsmith. In the case of a .22 auto, the treatment is largely the same as for a .22 rifle. Leave the bore alone except for an occasional cleaning, keep the mechanism free of carbon deposits and wipe off the fingerprints. Once every couple of thousand rounds, it's not a bad idea to tear the gun down and clean it completely, using a stiff-bristled brush and solvent to remove the accumulated gunk. Ditto for centerfire autos, except that it pays to watch for lead and metal fouling in the bore, and remove it as you would from a rifle.

A short time ago I was lounging in my favorite gun store, balancing my greed against my checkbook, when in walked an officer of the law. He complained to the owner of the place that his service revolver didn't work. He and his partner had just been called in on a bank robbery that was in progress, and when he tried to pull the trigger of his trusty .38, nothing happened. Luckily, nothing happened to *him*; but sure enough, that gun was froze up good.

It seems that enough soot and gummed-up oil had accumulated

The cylinders of a revolver should be cleaned as well as the barrel. Note that the gun is supported in a vise.

to keep the cylinder from turning and the loading crane from being swung out. When the cylinder finally was freed, it was discovered that the cartridges were corroded firmly in the chambers, so that if the officer had wanted to eject the empties from his gun, he'd have needed a mallet.

The moral is plain: Neglect a revolver and it will sooner or later fail you. Most cylinder guns are fairly delicate creatures compared with automatics, with many very tightly fitted parts that have to be adjusted—and kept adjusted. If they are awash in dirt or gummed-up oil, they will jam. So do not blithely squirt oil into the guts of your six-gun. Keep it free of dirt and go easy on the slippery stuff—a drop on either side of the hammer now and then is all that's needed. It will work down into the mechanism and make things work smoothly. Flood the action and you'll end up paying a gunsmith. The bore should be given the same care as that of a centerfire rifle.

I suspect that, deep down inside, every shooter believes himself to be an amateur (or professional) gunsmith. Unless you have real mechanical aptitude, this is a snare and a pitfall, and will cost you dearly in both grief and money. Some jobs are within your competence; others are most definitely not. Firearms and their component parts vary greatly in their complexity, and you will have to be the judge of what lies within your capability. For instance, I can easily take apart the bolt of a Savage 110 rifle, as can anyone with an IQ of 70 and a quarter for a screwdriver. However, I still bear three magnificent scars across the fingers of one hand from a losing battle with a Weatherby Mark V bolt. Almost anyone can take down a Ruger Security Six double-action revolver. Yet he who tampers with the Colt Python double-action has rocks in his head. The best rule of thumb is, if you have doubts, don't try it.

The list goes on. It is easy to adjust the triggers on many rifles, for they have adjustments incorporated into their design. Shotgun and handgun triggers, however, can be altered only by careful honing with a sharpening stone, and this is skilled work, for the expert only. You can clean the lenses of your scope with a soft cloth and a little household dishwashing detergent mixed in water, but don't try to take the thing apart. (I recall a sentence from a piece I read long ago that went "There are two kinds of people that take telescopic sights apart—those who know how and damn fools.")

There is, however, one job that most of us can take on successfully. That is refinishing a stock. The factory finish on many rifle and shotgun stocks is excellent, but on many it's atrocious, and will crack, chip and peel with a minimum of wear. If you want to refinish a shoulder arm's wood, here's how to go about it.

First, remove all the metal from the wood, and mask off the recoil pad and checkering with tape. If the original finish is varnish or lacquer, you can get it off with paint remover. This is a messy job, best done outdoors or in the garage. Slather on the paint remover, give it a few minutes to work, then scrape off the resulting mess, using a butter knife or some other dull instrument that won't mar the wood. Repeat this treatment until the original finish is entirely gone; then wash the stock with alcohol.

If the finish won't dissolve, you will have to remove it by sanding, using o or oo steel wool. Be very careful here not to alter the shape of the wood or round off sharp edges. Work slowly and carefully. When the finish is off, wipe the wood with a damp sponge and then hold it over a flame. This will raise whiskers on the stock. Sand them off with 600-grit wet or dry paper, and repeat the process until no more whiskers arise.

For the new finish, I suggest the oil type. It isn't the most waterproof, but it's easily applied, tough and a cinch to keep looking like new. The two most popular oil finishes are George Brothers' Lin-Speed and Casey's Tru-Oil. Bearing in mind that there are as many ways to finish a stock as there are people who try the job, here's mine.

First, apply a coat of spar varnish to the wood and let it dry— thoroughly. Now sand it down to the bare wood. This will leave the pores filled and prevent the stock from soaking up oil until it is punky. (Use a fine grade of sandpaper for this last job.) Now, wipe on a thin coat of oil, going slowly, taking pains to make the finish as even and as thin as possible. Beware of runs, drips and blobs. When the stock is completely coated, wipe off as much oil as you can with a lint-free cloth. Stand it in a dry, dust-free place and leave it alone until it is completely dry. This state is not achieved until the oily smell has gone, regardless of how the finish feels to the touch.

Now apply a second coat of oil. Wipe it off, let it dry and finish again. Repeat this process until you have about fifteen coats built up. You'll notice the finish developing bit by bit, so be patient and be meticulous. When the finish looks rich and even, complete the job with a coat of hand-rubbed floor wax. I have finished a number of stocks quite successfully using this formula, and if I can do it, you certainly can.

Sooner or later, all guns get put away, but how they emerge from storage depends on you.

First, before you retire a gun for the season, clean it thoroughly. It used to be an article of faith that a gun going into storage had to be greased to the gills, and I used to follow this practice. However, I have strayed from this ritual, which is a pain in the neck, and simply wipe off the guns with that faithful chamois, saturated in WD-40. Although I live in a damp climate, I have yet to see a fleck of rust, even on guns that have lain around for two or three years.

It should be added that if your gun needs repair work, the sooner you get it done, the better off you'll be. The tale about the hunter racing to the gunsmith the day before the season opens is an old one, but very true.

Most people store their guns in a rack or in a closet—neither of which is especially good, particularly if you have kids. Firearms lying about in plain sight are an invitation to mischief, sometimes of the tragic variety, or theft. If you store your artillery upright in a closet, you will sooner or later be treated to that sickening crash of toppling smokepoles that means dented stocks, busted sights and other calamities. The best way to store your guns is to lock them in a luggage-type case and put the case somewhere out of the way, such as in the attic or (if it's dry) the cellar. That way, your guns will be safe and your mind will be at ease. Do not rely on a soft case for any real protection. One that's lined with sheepskin will rust metal, and none is any protection at all against a good hard knock. Spend the $40 or so on a foam-lined hard-plastic case. You'll never wear it out, and in the end, it will save you money.

In twenty years of shooting, I have developed an overall philosophy of gun care that resembles the old hoss-cavalry proverb that went something like "First you bed down your mount, then you take care of yourself." The same goes for guns. Before you get out of your hunting clothes, go over your deer-dumper or goose-getter. It really isn't that much work, and the few minutes that you spend each time will pay off handsomely in the appearance and performance of your firearms.

JOHN AMBER has, for 26 years, been the Editor of *Gun Digest*. He is one of America's foremost authorities on all aspects of firearms, a hunter of worldwide experience and a collector of fine custom arms.

GARY ANDERSON is the finest competitive rifleman America has produced in modern times. He has twice—in 1964 and 1968—won Olympic gold medals. He is a specialist in the 300-meter centerfire free-rifle event, and is barely 30 years old.

DICK BALDWIN has won so many honors on the trap field that only the highlights can be mentioned here. He was selected as a member of the *Sports Afield* All-America Professional team seven years in a row, from 1962 through 1968. In 1965, he won the Professional High Over All Championship. Dick joined Remington Arms as a professional shooter at the age of 20, which gives some indication of his ability.

ERWIN A. BAUER has long been a familiar name to anyone who enjoys reading about the outdoors. He has written well and widely about almost every aspect of hunting, fishing and camping. However, he has a special fondness for waterfowl hunting and is the author of many articles on the subject.

HOWARD BRANT begin his career as a competitive skeet shooter 26 years ago, and has since won 150 championships, including 11 New Jersey state titles. In 1952, competing in the New Jersey championships, he took first place in every gauge, won the High Over All and was a member of the winning two- and five-man squads. He is Outdoor Editor of the Newark, N.J., *Star-Ledger*.

PETE BROWN has been Shooting Editor of *Sports Afield* magazine for two decades. He is an expert with rifle, pistol and shotgun and has a special expertise in the technical aspects of shooting.

JIM CARMICHEL has, in a relatively few years, become one of our most widely read writers on firearms. He is expert in all phases of shooting and is an excellent (and self-taught) gunsmith. Jim is a Shooting Editor of *Outdoor Life* magazine.

JEFF COOPER is Handguns Editor of *Guns & Ammo* magazine. He is one of our leading authorities on handgun hunting and has written widely on other firearms subjects as well.

STEVE FERBER has been a competitive handgunner since 1963. He has held 12 national records in reserve, open and team categories in both conventional and international-style competition. Steve has taken six state and regional championships, holds the Distinguished Pistol Shooter's Badge and was All-Reserve National Pistol Champion in 1966. He is now Field Editor of *Argosy* magazine.

JIM GILMORE has competed in bench-rest meets for six years and reports on this phase of shooting for *The Rifle* magazine and *Gun Week*. In addition to his shooting, he is a skillful amateur gunsmith and makes much of his own equipment.

BOB HAGEL has excellent credentials to write about big-game hunting. He has taken major trophies throughout the western states and Alaska, both as a hunter and as a guide. Bob contributes frequently to the major outdoor magazines on hunting and shooting subjects.

PETE KUHLHOFF was, until his death early in 1972, Arms Editor for *Argosy* magazine. He was expert in all phases of shooting and had hunted widely over North America and Africa.

JOHN LACHUK is one of our foremost experts on varmint hunting. He contributes regularly to *Guns & Ammo* magazine and is a Technical Editor of *Gun Digest*.

WARREN PAGE,   for almost 25 years Shooting Editor of *Field & Stream* magazine, is now Executive Vice President of the National Shooting Sports Foundation. One of the world's outstanding big-game hunters, Page is the holder of several Boone & Crockett records and was awarded the Weatherby Trophy in 1958, the third man to be so honored.

DAVID E. PETZAL   is Managing Editor of *Field & Stream* magazine and has written widely on both hunting and shooting. He knows whereof he speaks in his chapter on care and repair of firearms, having faced more dirty guns in 20 years of shooting than he cares to remember.

CHARLES F. WATERMAN   is one of our best-known outdoor writers and has hunted widely for all types of game, both large and small. He has written articles for all the major outdoor magazines and is the author of several books on hunting.

Handload ammunition (*cont.*)
 for handgun
  deer hunting, 161
  target shooting, 138
 rifle target shooting and, 36, 39, 43
 for varmint hunting, 94-95
Hardball bullet
 hunting with, 149, 156
 trajectory of, 153
Harrington & Richardson Ultra Automatic rifle, 98
Hart, Clyde, custom barrel of, 49-50,
  272
Heavy Varmint rifle, 45-46
 accuracy of, 56
 cartridge for, 51
 scopes for, 50
 types of, 48-50
Heikes, Rolla "Pop," 173-74
Henderson, Woolfolk, 174
Hendricks, Frank E., 174
Herrett handgun grip, 149
Hiestand, Joe, 174
High-house target, of skeet field, 190
 leads for, 199-205
High-Power Long-Range rifle event, 36
 ammunition for, 43
 target for, 22
High-Power-Match-Rifle event, 36, 43
High-power rifle
 handloads for, 39
 military target shooting with, 37
 sitting position and, 23, 27
 spotting scope for, 38
High-power scopes, 261-63
 focus of, 259
High Standard pistol
 Superautomatic Citation, 136
 target shooting with, 136-37
High Standard shotgun, 246
Hirsch (red deer) hunting, 127
Hobaugh custom barrel, 272, 275
Hodgson, Richard, 271
Holland & Holland custom shotgun,
  233, 276-77
Holland & Holland shooting school, 215
Hollow-point bullet
 bench-rest shooting with, 59
 handgun hunting with, 153, 155
 varmint hunting with, 92, 94, 96
 woodchuck hunting with, 78

Holster for handgun, 148
 Berns-Martin, 159
 sight and, 151
Hook butt plate, of target rifle, 34, 36,
  42
Hornady bullet, 118
 bench-rest shooting and, 59
 spire-point, 125
 target rifle and, 43
Hornet cartridge, 92-93
Hunting scope
 for big game, 261-62
 lens coating of, 261
 parallax of, 259-60
 power for, 266
 reticle of, 255-57, 261
 for varmints, 262
Huntington, Fred, 275
Hurlbutt, Mrs. Gertrude, 190

Ignition time of shotgun, 213-14
Image of optical instrument
 aberration of camera, 265
 definition of, 252
 displacement of, 253
 inversion of, 255, 261
 magnification of, 251
 of objective lens, 259-260
Improved-cylinder-choked shotgun
 rabbit hunting and, 73
 skeet shooting and, 198
 squirrel hunting and, 64
 upland-bird hunting and, 209, 212-13
Internal meter of camera, 266
International Army Winchester M70
  rifle, 42
International Division of National Skeet
  Shooting Association, 193
International handgun target shooting,
  132
 air-pistol event, 145-46
 centerfire event, 144-45
 free-pistol 50-meter event, 143-44
 rapid-fire event, 144
International rifle target shooting
 ammunition for, 43
 events of, 33-35
 gun for, 42-43
 spotting scope for, 38
 targets of, 22
 training for, 40-41

Target (*cont.*)
  of handgun competition
    conventional, 132-35, 138
    international, 143-44, 146
  of rifle events
    air rifle, 22
    high-power, 22
    international, 34-35
    national/recreational, 35-36
  of skeet shooting, 189-90
    lead for, 196, 198-205
    speed of, 193
  Stoeger deer, 162
  for trapshooting
    original, 170-73
    lead for, 185-87
    speed of, 174, 177
Target air rifle, 21, 42
  ammunition for, 43
  squirrel hunting with, 63
Target ammunition
  for handgun, 137-38, 155
  for rifle, 43
Target rifle, 37, 42-43
Target scope, 36, 262-64
  deer hunting with, 122
  Redfield, 50-51, 98
  reticle of, 255-57
Target shooting, *see* Handgun target
    shooting; Rifle target shooting
Telescope
  erector lens of, 255
  lens aberrations of, 253-54
  Weaver, 247
Telescopic sight, 251
  of handgun, 150-51
  repair of, 289
  for shotgun, 247
  of rifle
    sight alignment, 31
    target shooting, 34-36
  See also Scope
Thumbhole stock of target rifle, 34, 42
Timed-fire handgun shooting, 132-34,
    137, 138, 142
Timney custom trigger, 272
Tombstone (Arizona), pig hunting in,
    160-61
Topperwein, Mrs. Ad "Plinky," 174
Training
  of retrievers, 229-30

Training (*cont.*)
  of squirrel dogs, 65
  for target shooting, 40-41, 138
  military, 19-20, 113, 191
Trajectory
  close-range deer hunting and, 100
  handgun hunting and, 153
  long-range rifle hunting and, 114-16
    range finding, 122-25, 127
  mountain shooting and, 79
  of shotgun slug, 247
  varmint hunting and, 92, 94, 96-97
Trap, 174-75
Trap gun
  aiming points for, 185-87
  ammunition for, 188
  placement for, 181-84
  trigger of, 184
  types of, 178-80
  stock of, 177-78
  swing technique for, 181, 183-86
Trap house of skeet field, 190, 195-96
Trapshooting, 11
  ammunition for, 188
  gun for, 176-80
    cleaning of, 386-87
    Ithaca custom, 276-77
  history of
    clay targets, 171-73
    glass-ball era, 170-71
    "Old Hats," 169-70
  hunting and, 213, 215, 232
  leads for, 185-87
  matches of, 175
    women and, 173-74
  positions for, 181-84
  swing technique and, 181, 183-86
Trigger
  adjustment of, 279, 289
  of bench-rest rifles, 49
  Canjar custom, 49, 272
  of custom rifles, 42, 273
Trigger-control technique
  handgun hunting and, 149, 162-63
  handgun target shooting and, 138-39,
    141-43
  rifle and, 32
  trapshooting and, 184
  upland-bird hunting and, 213, 215-16
Trigger/sear mechanism, 141
Troeh, Frank, 174